My Mother Who Fathered Me

A STUDY OF THE FAMILY IN THREE
SELECTED COMMUNITIES IN JAMAICA

EDITH CLARKE, O.B.E.
Dip. in Anthropology, London

new edition

WITH A PREFACE BY
SIR HUGH FOOT
K.C.M.G., K.C.V.O.
Sometime Governor of Jamaica

AND INTRODUCTION BY
M. G. SMITH
*Professor of Anthropology
in the University of California
at Los Angeles*

LONDON
GEORGE ALLEN & UNWIN LTD
RUSKIN HOUSE MUSEUM STREET

FIRST PUBLISHED IN 1957
SECOND EDITION 1966
SECOND IMPRESSION 1970
THIRD IMPRESSION (PAPERBACK) 1972
FOURTH IMPRESSION 1974
FIFTH IMPRESSION 1975

ISBN 0 04 573010 5 *paperback*

Printed in Great Britain by
Unwin Brothers Limited
The Gresham Press, Old Woking, Surrey, England
A member of the Staples Printing Group

MY MOTHER WHO FATHERED ME

In accordance with your wishes the most scrupulous care has been taken to preserve your anonymity. Where personal names are used in quoting from Family Records these are not the names of the actual parties concerned. If the names given refer to any living person this is accidental and no reference is intended.

The same applies to all place names. There are Orange Groves in Jamaica but none is the original of our farming centre, while Sugartown and Mocca are both fictitious names.

E. C.

PREFACE

BY

SIR HUGH FOOT

Sometime Governor of Jamaica

I first met Edith Clarke when I came to Jamaica in 1945. She was then Administrative Secretary of the Board of Supervision which has control of poor relief throughout the Island, and when I had official dealings with her I soon discovered that she was a most unusual official. To tease her I once told her that as a Government official she was a very good anthropologist. I really meant that as a compliment. I meant that she is not so much concerned with the routine of an official—which she coped with admirably—as she is with studying the lives of the people. She is intensely interested in the people of Jamaica not only as social problems but as human beings. I discovered that she is the most unusual combination of an able administrator and a skilled anthropologist, without the narrowness and lack of sympathy which we often find amongst officials and without the superior detachment and the obscure jargon to which lesser anthropologists resort.

Then I began to know her better and to discover something about her remarkable family. I learnt that after she had taken her diploma in anthropology she had intended to pursue anthropological research in Africa and elsewhere. But when she came back to Jamaica from her studies in England she had been caught up in a whole network of emerging social welfare activities here in Jamaica and then in hard Government work amongst the poorest people of all.

I learnt about the contribution and the character of the Clarke family. I learnt about her famous grandfather, Henry Clarke, preacher and politician, whom Lord Olivier once described as 'one of the most sincere, courageous and hard-working men I have ever known'. Henry Clarke worked and fought throughout his long life to serve the ordinary people of Jamaica. He had a fierce faith in their qualities. He was utterly fearless, almost reckless, in fighting as a champion of their cause which he represented in the old Legislative Council.

Hugh Clarke, her father, was not a fanatic but he was a strong and vigorous character—devout, determined and devoted—who gave his whole life not to a political cause but to the Parish of Westmorland, working to get better housing and water and light for the common people.

In these days there are many Clarkes of Edith's generation making their contribution in Jamaican agriculture and in public affairs. None of them has gone as deep as she has in knowledge of the people of Jamaica.

I have worked for eight years or so in the central Government of Jamaica, concerned with the whole range of Government business. I have presided over the Executive Council and I have had to know something of the working of every Department of the Government. I have had to consider every aspect of Government policy, and I have constantly been brought up against one basic difficulty. It is the difficulty which arises from the fact that so many of us at the centre know so little about the lives and the homes and the families of the great bulk of the Jamaican population. I myself have travelled through Jamaica more than most people in the past decade, but it is not surprising that someone like myself who was not brought up in Jamaica—and who still has a good deal of difficulty in understanding the lovely dialect of the Jamaican people—should not know a great deal about their home and family lives. What has astonished me has been to discover that even in a comparatively small island with a population of about a million and a half people there is such ignorance amongst Jamaicans themselves—such ignorance amongst some sections of the community about the lives of the others. How few people there are amongst the upper or middle classes of Jamaica who really understand how the other people live. There are many people who spend their lives in Kingston and St Andrew who, if they found themselves living amongst the cultivators of remote Jamaican hillsides, would feel that they were in a foreign country. All the time we are coming up against this ignorance.

When, for instance, we are establishing a new land authority or seeking to carry out some agricultural improvement or development, we are constantly reminded how little we know of the attitudes and suspicions and weaknesses and aspirations and all the fine qualities of the country people. In housing when we came to carry out the big programme of reconstruction following the 1951 hurricane, again we discovered how little we knew about the way the ordinary Jamaican families live. It has been the same in carrying out all branches of Government policy—in our health services, in our education and in industry. We build the superstructure without a real knowledge of the foundations.

In every aspect of national life, and specially in the fields of labour and land tenure, Edith Clarke has shown us how important and urgent it is to base policy on knowledge acquired and recorded without bias and without sentimentality.

Of course Jamaican Ministers and officials know much more about basic social conditions in Jamaica than I can, but even they, in planning and carrying out Government policy, have had to depend largely on the necessarily limited range of their own personal experience. There has been precious little skilled and penetrating research into the social questions that matter most of all. I am quite sure that such research can best—I almost said can only—be carried out by Jamaicans, and I know of no one in training and experience and sympathy better qualified for work of this kind than Edith Clarke.

With all our preoccupations with questions of policy and administration, the most important problems of all are, I believe, the problems which arise from the family life of the people. We can have the best constitution in the world and the most efficient administration and the wisest government policy, but they will all be of no avail if most or many of the children of Jamaica are brought up in conditions of neglect. We could even have a prosperous island and still fail if the children growing up to share that prosperity were brought up without the security and confidence of homes in which they can enjoy the care and guidance and love of both mothers and fathers.

For these reasons the book which Edith Clarke has written is of first importance to Jamaica. I am glad that she has brought to it the results of her experience and her research, and brought to it too the devotion of Jamaican patriotism.

The book will certainly be important to Jamaica. It will also be valuable to those who are concerned with the problems arising from the thousands of Jamaican workers in the United States and the tens of thousands now in Great Britain. Indeed it will be valuable to all who are genuinely interested in Jamaica, including the people of other West Indian territories, and including our other neighbours in the Caribbean and in North and South America who are now taking ever-closer notice of Jamaican advance.

For all of us concerned in Jamaican public affairs and indeed for everyone concerned about the future of the Island this book must be an asset and a challenge.

HUGH FOOT

King's House
Jamaica
1957

FOREWORD

The research on which this study of family life in Jamaica is based was sponsored by the Colonial Social Science Research Council and financed by the Colonial Office from funds provided for research under the Colonial Development and Welfare Act. The field-work was supervised by an advisory committee of the London School of Economics, consisting of Professor Raymond Firth, Professor Glass, and Professor Schapera. I cannot too deeply express my gratitude to all these, both for giving me the opportunity to do the work, for the invaluable help during the preliminary stages of planning the programme, for guidance during the field-work and for reading and criticizing the report. I am particularly grateful to Professor Firth, Professor Schapera and Dr Audrey Richards, also a member of the Research Council, all of whom, in spite of their own heavy academic programmes, gave me generously of their time and experience. In the preparation of the book for publication I am deeply indebted to Dr Lucy Mair for invaluable criticism and advice.

While in the field I derived much stimulus and encouragement from visits from Professor Arthur Lewis, Dr Audrey Richards and Professor Franklin Frazier. Among the many who read and criticized my manuscript in draft I should like particularly to mention the late Sir Thomas Taylor, first Principal of the University College of the West Indies, Miss Dora Ibberson, C.B.E., Social Welfare Adviser to Colonial Development and Welfare, Dr Kenneth Little, Mr Dossie Carberry and Dr M. G. Smith of the Research Institute of the University College of the West Indies. The wording of my title is derived from the passage in Mr George Lamming's book *In the Castle of My Skin* which I quote on page 161.

My thanks are due to the Government of Jamaica for releasing me to do the research, and to the many Government Departments, particularly those of Health, Education, Labour and Statistics which accorded me access to material; and to the Secretary and field officers of the Jamaica Agricultural Society, members of the Sugar Manufacturers and All Island Jamaica Cane Farmers' Associations for help in the selection of the Centres.

This account of the family in rural Jamaica consists of a comparative study of three communities which reflect the different ways in which the rural population is organized, and attempts to show how these different ways of life affect patterns of family life, the relationship between the members of the family, and the composition of the household.

The people engaged in agriculture comprise the bulk of the population in Jamaica and may broadly be classified as wage-labourers working on properties devoted to large-scale production of such crops as cane, bananas, citrus and cattle; owners and operators of mixed farms, using only a minimum of paid labour; and smallholders renting plots ('grounds') and growing subsistence crops for home use, selling any small surplus in the local markets. The invariable factor in wage labour is its dependence on seasonal work and a very small proportion of the labouring population are employed all the year round. Many wage-labourers also rent 'grounds' and the majority would like to do so to carry them over the periods of unemployment. Conversely, the smallholder needs to earn money in the out-of-crop seasons. These categories therefore are not mutually exclusive. In the second category, owner-farmers, there is considerable difference in the way of life and in the family organization (particularly in regard to housing), the conditions of soil, climate and accessibility to markets and the degree to which the size of the holding is adequate to the needs of the family.

The Reports of the 1943 Census of Jamaica and its Dependencies provided invaluable data for the preliminary work of deciding the areas from which we should select our communities. Tables 186 and 199 show that the rural population in Jamaica in 1943 was 1,013,000 out of a total population of 1,237,000. The total numbers of farms, ranging from 1 to 1,000 acres and over, was 66,173.

1 to under		2 acres	7,722
2 „	„	3 „	10,267
3 „	„	4 „	8,347
4 „	„	6 „	11,561
6 „	„	10 „	11,304
10 „	„	25 „	11,509
25 „	„	50 „	2,969
50 „	„	100 „	1,076
100 „	„	200 „	497
200 „	„	500 „	381
500 „	„	1,000 „	207
1,000 acres and over			333

Over 97 per cent of them were thus under 50 acres, the largest number being between 4 and 10 acres. In addition there were 146,515 'holdings' of under one acre. Since the large plantations were devoted to production of such crops as cane, bananas, cattle and citrus using wage-labour to a greater or lesser extent, it was on the smaller holdings that the bulk of the farming population was to be found. We therefore decided to work in two farming centres, one with holdings between 4 or 5 and under 50 acres, and the other with less than 5, which would include an example of people living on the smallest units, the one acre farms and the 'holding' of less than an acre, which might either be 'owned' or rented. For our third centre we needed an area where the population was primarily dependent on wage-labour.

We were concerned that our centres should illustrate other particulars. We were aware that there existed a theory of what was called 'family land' which affected both the use of this land and the organization of the group associated with it. We also wished to study any other forms of organization, social or economic, which might exist.

In regard to the wage-earner, the sugar industry employs the largest quantity of labour, had an active trade-union organization, and presented us with the best picture of a proletariat imposed seasonally on a local community. Sugartown was selected because it also included all categories of cane-farmers large and small; had average social amenities; and because production was under the control of a company in what is becoming the normal pattern. Mocca illustrates the way of life of the small cultivator and his method of disposing of surplus crops locally, and also, to a high degree, the system of inheritance and transmission of family land. Orange Grove was chosen from the group owning holdings from 5 to under 50 acres, owned, operated and occupied by the farmer and his family with a minimum of hired help and highly organized for the practice of mixed farming. In their case the staple crop was citrus for export which requires regular and skilled care.

The field research covered a period of two years, nine months of which was spent in Sugartown which allowed us to observe the different pattern of life in the *tempo moto* as compared with the working season when 'crop' was on. A similar period in Orange Grove covered the seasonal variations and allowed us to observe the full cycle of agricultural activities. Mocca, small, compact and with less complicated problems and structure, was completed in approximately two months.

Living as we did in the midst of our communities for a continuous period we were able to establish the intimacy necessary for the participant-observer technique. In 'free' interviews we encouraged people to talk on any subjects that interested them, while setting ourselves the task of obtaining, when the time was propitious, 'basic' information in regard to family and household. These data, shown in Appendix 1, were later tabulated on cards and incorporated into a number of Appendices, some of which are included below.

My gratitude and thanks are due to my colleagues, Dr Madeline Kerr, her assistant Miss Vera Dantra, Miss Daphne Hall and to the following members of my Jamaican field-staff for their wholehearted co-operation during long periods of strenuous and exacting work: Frank du Cille, Wilfred Forrest, Ivy Dale, Daisy Barrett, Ruby Palmer, Marie Brown and Winston Fisher.

E. C.

CONTENTS

PREFACE   *page* 7

FOREWORD   *page* 11

INTRODUCTION   *page* i

1. THE BACKGROUND   *page* 17

    i The historical background to social organization
    ii Comparative description of Centres studied
    iii Definition of terms

2. LAND TENURE   *page* 33

    i Historical background of settlement
    ii Establishment of 'ownership'; customary theory of inheritance by 'all the children'
    iii Definition of family land; principle of inalienability; anomalies and conflicts
    iv Inheritance 'through the blood' and 'by the name'; social and legal legitimacy in inheritance; rights of wife or concubine; of individual members of the relevant kin; importance of land and value set on freehold
    v Inheritance of houses; effect on household structure and family life
    vi Summary of conclusions in regard to inheritance and use. Acceptance of and opposition to the customary system; weaknesses and value in conserving family solidarity; the external pressures

3 MARRIAGE   *page* 73

    i Legal requirements, civil and religious rites
    ii The extent to which the legal requirements are properly understood
    iii The conditions in which marriage may properly be entered into; economic pre-requisites; trial period and birth of children; religious sanction; association with class and status; comparison between the Centres
    iv Summary; examples of marriage ceremony

4 SEX, PROCREATION AND THE INSTITUTIONS OF CONCUBINAGE   *page* 90

    i Comparison between the Centres of patterns of behaviour in regard to sex, procreation, marriage and concubinage; illegitimacy
    ii Sex training for girls and boys; behaviour of mother at daughter's first pregnancy; relationship with lover; casual or housekeeper unions
    iii 'Matrilocal' unions in relation to family land
    iv 'Purposive' concubinage; courtship; role of kin; expectation of fidelity; economic partnership; responsibility for children; causes of separation; effect on children of insecurity of union
    v Legal aspect of concubinage; paternal responsibility; procedure for Court Order for maintenance; Poor Relief

5 THE ORGANIZATION OF THE HOUSEHOLDS   *page* 113

    I Distribution of population by size Centre, sex, age-group, conjugal status; period at which marriage occurs; number of children born by age and conjugal status mother; distribution of population in different types household; children in family homes by parentage and total number born; presence of 'outside' children according to basis of union in marriage or concubinage; childless couples; simple and extended type households in relation to marriage or concubinage

   II Special features of extended family households; the four main types; range of kin included; relative size family households in relation to marriage or concubinage

  III Denuded family type households; distribution and characteristics in Centres; simple and extended types; proportion of children present compared with number born; according to presence of mother or father; whereabouts of children not in home; single-person and sibling households

  IV Grandmother and great-grandmother households; distribution; extended, denuded and conjugal-sibling types; grandchildren in relation to number lines of descent, descent through son or daughter and presence or absence of one or both parents; conjugal status of grandmother; number and relationship of adult males in household; association of these households with family land

6 THE DEVELOPMENT OF KINSHIP ROLES   *page* 141

    I Different family situations in which parental roles may develop; examples of family life in the three Centres

   II Description of denuded family households and ways of living of 'single' women; distribution of single-person households

  III Training of children in home; precepts and discipline; role of parents; the paternal relationship; mother-son inter-dependence

  IV Going to school; the break with the home; the private school; discipline in the schools

   V Adolescence; the problem of earning a living; the role of the kin; the relevant kin

  VI The step-parent relationship; homes in which step-children present; 'adopted children'; types of 'adoption'

 VII The role of the grandmother; the development of the relationship according to age grandmother, presence or absence of own mother; the mother's sister; the step-grandfather; the 'single' grandmother

VIII The role of the family in the Centres compared; other organizations and forms of association, economic, social and religious

APPENDICES   *page* 191

The Death and Burial of Mrs Malcolm   *page* 217

INDEX   *page* 216

INTRODUCTION

This book is one of the fundamental studies of West Indian
family and social organization; and it is therefore appropriate
on this occasion of its re-issue to review the earlier and recent
development of these studies and to assess our present knowledge
of West Indian family structure. Perhaps in this way we can best
appreciate the significance of this book as a contribution to our
knowledge of West Indian society and to the general study of
mating and family.

I

The family life of West Indian 'lower class' Negroes or
folk presents a number of equally important academic
and practical problems. In this region family life is highly
unstable, marriage rates are low, especially during the earlier
phases of adult life, and illegitimacy rates have always been
high. Many households contain single individuals, while others
with female heads consist of women, their children, and/or their
grandchildren. The picture is further complicated by variations
in the type and local distribution of alternative conjugal forms;
and, characteristically, differing communities, social classes and
ethnic groups institutionalize differing combinations of them.
Excluding legal marriage, mating is brittle, diverse in form and
consensual in base among these Creole or Negroid populations.
The implications of this mating structure for the composition
and stability of familial groups is perhaps most easily appreciated
by comparing these Creole patterns with others current among
East Indians of comparable socio-economic position in British
Guiana and Trinidad.

Among these local East Indians, men settled in differing
villages arrange the first unions of their children during early

adolescence and celebrate these marriages by traditional Hindu or Muslim rites. The girl then leaves her natal village to join her husband in his father's community. Between one-fifth and one-quarter of these arranged marriages recurrently dissolve, usually not long after their celebration and before children are born to the couple. Following this the girl almost always resumes cohabitation with another partner, often after returning briefly to her parental home. If the earlier marriage had not been registered as legal, this second union may be legalized by such registration. Otherwise, although non-legal, it is usually life-long. (1)

Creole 'lower class' mating patterns differ from those of the local East Indians in two important ways. Firstly, all Creole systems for which we have adequate data institutionalize extra-residential, non-domiciliary, or visiting relations as one of several alternative conjugal patterns. In this conjugal form the partners live apart with their separate kin while the man visits his mate and contributes to the support of herself and their children. According to Stycos and Back, this extra-residential pattern is the most common form of mating among 'lower class' Jamaicans, especially during the earlier adult years. (2) It is also the most diverse in its content and social contexts, the most brittle and formally unstable type of union; and, given the partners' domestic dispersion, the most vulnerable to disruptive influences of various sorts. For this reason among others, durable visiting relations are generally converted into cohabitation, whether legal or consensual by their principals. When these unions break down, the children usually remain with the unmarried mother or her kin.

Among East Indians in Trinidad and British Guiana this pattern of extra-residential mating is either absent or extremely rare; (3) and in consequence the great majority of East Indian children usually grow up in their father's home and under his care. Among West Indian Creoles, given their predilection for unstable extra-residential unions, the reverse is more nearly the case. For example, of children living in the Creole households studied in Carriacou, Latante and Grenville in Grenada, and in Kingston and rural Jamaica, only 37.6 per cent, 52.6 per cent, 35.7 per cent, 34.7 per cent, and 49.3 per cent were found in homes containing their fathers; (4) and as Edith Clarke shows in this volume, the pattern of domestic dispersal by which children are separated from their fathers is heavily influenced by the character of their parents' conjugal union and by the children's birth status. (5) Clearly these differences in the mating organizations of the 'lower class' Creoles and East Indians correspond with parallel differences in their modes of institutionalizing paternal roles and in their emphases on nuclear families as the basis of domestic organization. Despite comparable 'denudation' of domestic nuclear families through widowhood, migrancy and other conditions, these ethnic differences in family patterns are striking. (6)

The second major difference between these Creole and East Indian family systems consists in the age and conditions under which cohabitation and marriage are institutionalized. In the Caribbean, as elsewhere, East Indians prescribe cohabitation by customary rites of marriage at an early age for both sexes. Among lower-class Creoles the ideal and modal ages of marriage are both much higher; and typically consensual cohabitation with the same or other partners precedes marriage by several years. Thus, whereas East Indians marry before having children, lower-class Creoles normally marry in middle or later age after the women have ceased to bear children or are already grandparents. (7)

These differences in the age and conditions of marriage among the East Indians and Creoles have obvious and important effects on the organization and stability of family life and on the average number of mating unions that characterize the two ethnic groups. Few East Indians engage in more than two conjugal unions and despite differences of ecological and social context, apparently at least three-quarters have only one. (8) *Per contra,* among 'lower class' Creoles few individuals have only one conjugal union, however this may be defined; and a substantial proportion engage in three or more. Thus whereas East Indian mating practice institutionalizes lifelong unions following early 'marriage', that of the Creole lower class encourages serial matings of varying form and conditional character, with legal marriage as the terminal type of union. In consequence, whereas East Indian families are nucleated in separate domestic groups, among the Creoles nuclear or elementary families are systematically fragmented and dispersed throughout two or more households as a direct effect of their mating organization; and whereas among East Indians paternity is relatively fixed and constant in its form, content and context, among the Creoles its modes and effectiveness vary as a function of differing conjugal forms and their combination. (9)

2

The numerous practical or social problems presented by the characteristic patterns of West Indian (Creole) mating and lower class family life have attracted continuous attention ever since 1938 when a Royal Commission appointed by the British Parliament to survey the social and economic conditions of this region and to recommend appropriate programmes for action, dwelt on the evident 'disorganization' of family life and on the apparent increase of 'promiscuity' as against faithful concubinage, the 'common law' or consensual cohabitation which had hitherto been accepted as the Negro peasant's equivalent of marriage, and the basis of his family life. To halt this presumed spread of 'promiscuity', in 1944-5 Lady Huggins, wife of the then Governor of Jamaica, launched an island-wide campaign to marry off consensually cohabiting couples and any others whose mating status and relations seemed to warrant this. This Mass Marriage Movement was initiated in response to the Royal Commission's demand for 'an organized campaign against the social, moral and economic evils of promiscuity'. (10) However, being based on ignorance of Jamaican folk society and family life, the movement was equally misconceived in its methods and goals, and proved unsuccessful. At its greatest impact the movement lifted the Jamaican marriage rate from 4.44 per thousand in 1943 to 5.82 in 1946. By 1951 the marriage rate and the correlated illegitimacy ratio among annual births had reverted to their earlier level. (11) By 1955 the Mass Marriage Movement had petered out.

Several conditions ensured the failure of this Mass Marriage Movement, despite the energy and skill with which its director, Lady Huggins, marshalled the churches, schools, press, radio, welfare agencies and 'national' associations behind it. Above all, the campaign was based on the erroneous notion that because the élite and lower class employed a single word, marriage, to denote a particular conjugal institution, this had identical or very similar meanings, value and significance among these social strata. We now know that this view is only superficially correct, for reasons indicated below. Being thus conceived in error, the Mass Marriage Movement could hardly succeed; and its early signs of failure indicated the need for systematic sociological studies of those unfamiliar familial institutions with which the problems of 'promiscuity', marital instability, defective paternity and child socialization, high illegitimacy birth rates and low rates of marriage were all evidently linked, though in obscure and problematic ways. It was in this context that T. S. Simey visited the West Indies to survey its social conditions and to advise the recently constituted agency responsible for Colonial Development and Welfare. It was in these circumstances also that the Colonial Social Science Research Council in Britain asked Edith Clarke to undertake and direct a formal study of Jamaican family life. During the course of field-work she was joined by Madeline Kerr, a social psychologist from Bedford College, London. 'The object of the Survey was to obtain factual information on family and social life in a selected number of villages.' (12) While Edith Clarke studied the sociological contexts and features of the family organization, Dr Kerr concentrated on the social psychology of Jamaican class and community life, and on the distinctive features of socialization among its rural people. Together these two reports still represent the most comprehensive and detailed account of any West Indian family system yet published; and despite their different orientations, data and emphases, the two studies are remarkably congruent in their major conclusions and in the picture that they separately present.

Several of the most intractable social problems that confront West Indians centre on these conditions and patterns of mating and family life. The complexity of these problems is easily illustrated. For example, in its report the Royal Commission stressed that 'the policy of land settlement to which some West Indian governments are heavily committed depends for its success on the existence of a cohesive family unit'; (13) but, as Edith Clarke demonstrates, land ownership often promotes 'cohesive family units', sometimes to an excessive degree. Similar uncertainties apply to public programmes in the fields of health, housing and especially education. Grossly inadequate as are the local school systems in their physical and educational provisions, these deficiencies are magnified by the desultory attendance, and high drop-out rates associated with extensive child dispersal, weak family organization, defective paternity, and other social and economic conditions. (14) As regards the effects of such disturbing familial and educational contexts on the development of stable and well-adjusted adult personalities, Madeline Kerr concludes that the modal personality type of the Jamaican 'lower class' or folk is characterized by deep-set defensive mechanisms and tendencies to shift blame or responsibility for any lapse or misfortune to other persons or to external circumstances—an orientation which clearly minimizes adult learning capacities and reflects childhood experience. (15) In Kerr's view, two of the 'five major social situations giving rise to tension in Jamaica are: (1) dichotomy of concepts over parental roles: (2) lack of patterned learning in childhood'. (16) Both are directly connected with the modes of family organization and child rearing.

The material difficulties of West Indian economic and social development are thus compounded by instabilities and fluidities in the family organization on which the society depends both for the effective socialization of its young and for the adequate motivation of its adult members to participate vigorously in the social and economic life. These familial conditions affect labour productivity, absenteeism, occupational aspirations, training and performance, attitudes to saving, birth control, and farm development, and to programmes of individual and community self-help, housing, child care, education, and the like. (17) West Indian social and economic development accordingly presupposes adequate scientific study of these basic institutions, in order that programmes of public action to improve living standards, national integration, productivity and the quality of citizenship may be appropriately designed and effective. If the Mass Marriage Movement did little else, it should surely have served to demonstrate this vital need for adequate knowledge of West Indian social conditions in advance of the 'organized campaigns' mounted to remedy or reduce them. Intensive sociological research designed to elucidate the forms, 'causes' and implications of West Indian family organization should thus rank very high on the list of essential steps towards the reconstruction and development of local society; and the very limited and costly advances achieved by various schemes of social development launched during the past twenty years merely demonstrate the fundamental character of this need for scientific knowledge of these social conditions before proceeding with further schemes of this sort. (18) It is particularly in its contribution to the scientific study of West Indian (Creole) society, and especially to our knowledge of its family organization, that the present work is outstanding, both in regard to the quality, depth and range of its information, its conceptual clarity and precision, and its author's scrupulous exclusion of partisan bias, value judgments and over-simple theorizing. To appreciate the distinctive values of the present study, we must set it in the context of our advancing knowledge of Caribbean society.

Jamaican family life cannot be adequately understood in isolation. The Jamaican family is merely one of several similar systems which share many common properties of form and history, while differing in consequence of their particular social contexts and internal constitution. Most of these related systems are to be found in the Caribbean, especially among its Creole populations; but systems of similar character and historical derivation are current also among the Negroes of the United States, where they were first subject to careful study and controversial interpretation during the late 1930's and early 1940's. In that initial phase the late Franklin Frazier, who pioneered this enquiry, debated with Melville Herskovits the relative influences of African cultural persistence of New World slavery and *post bellum* socio-economic contexts on the determination and distribution of family forms, especially among the Negroes of the United States. (19)

This debate was essentially directed at problems of social causation and historical derivation. Both Herskovits and Frazier agreed that the Negro family in the U.S.A. and Caribbean was especially distinctive in its high rates of illegitimacy, marital instability and 'maternal' households consisting of a woman and her children, with or without her grandchildren. Herskovits argued that these organizational patterns were of African derivation; and that they were effects or correlates of practices through which Old World polygyny had been modified and reinterpreted by institutionalized serial matings. Frazier countered this argument by assembling voluminous data on the social history and situation of Negroes in the United States to demonstrate the influence of differing social and economic contexts on their mating and family patterns. For example, among Negro professionals and propertied families in Northern cities of the United States, marriage is the normal basis of family life and illegitimacy is very rare. Conversely, among southern rural immigrants in these cities, 'maternal families' and illegitimacy were common, while marriage rates were relatively low.

Although, like many other scientific controversies, this debate between Frazier and Herskovits was inconclusive, most subsequent students of Negro families in the New World have adopted Frazier's orientations and hypotheses rather than those of Herskovits. Thus, in discussing West Indian family organization, Simey and Fernando Henriques both accept Frazier's thesis that the social and economic conditions of slavery precluded development of stable nuclear families among New World Negroes; and both writers stress that the continuing 'disorganization' of West Indian family life expressed by the high incidence of conjugal turnover, illegitimacy and 'maternal' households, reflect the continuing situation of the West Indian Negroes as an economically and socially depressed class. (20) Both Simey and Henriques however emphasize that in Jamaica and other West Indian societies, 'illegitimacy', maternal families and concubinage or common-law marriage are socially accepted and statistically modal conditions of lower class life. (21) Henriques further distinguishes West Indian family structure from that of the Negroes in the U.S.A. as a natural development of local society and a system with its own distinctive properties. (22) Both Henriques and Simey emphasize the relations between differences of mating and family organization and differences of socioeconomic class; and both writers provide similar typologies of West Indian domestic families in this connection.

For Simey, the four principal 'family' types to be found in West Indian society were as follows: (1) 'Christian' families, defined as 'patriarchal' units based on legal marriage; (2) 'Faithful concubinage', also 'patriarchal' but without legal sanction; (3) 'Companionate' unions or consensual cohabitations of less than three years' duration; and (4) 'Disintegrate' families, consisting of women with their children or grandchildren. Henriques merely renamed the 'disintegrate' family as the 'maternal' or grandmother family and the 'companionate' as the 'keeper' family or union. (23)

Though suggestive, neither of these classifications was grounded on detailed study of the household or conjugal units to which they referred; and although both these familial typologies rested on distinctions of conjugal form and status, neither Henriques nor Simey gave explicit attention to extra-residential mating as a widespread institutional pattern. In brief, these early studies, however illuminating, lack the data essential for an adequate analysis of West Indian mating and family organization.

4

Only in 1956–7 were the first systematic studies of West Indian family systems published, by R. T. Smith on Guianese Negroes (24) and by Edith Clarke on Jamaica respectively. These two studies share numerous common features. Each reports and compares family organization in three selected communities by analyses of detailed censuses of household composition in these areas. Both studies emphasize the influence of current social and economic conditions on the organization and development of household groups; and both seek to 'explain' the observable variety of domestic groups by reference to current social and economic conditions and practices rather than by reference to the past. The two studies also differ in certain fundamental ways, notably in their analytic models and implied or expressed 'explanations', and since these differences have influenced subsequent work, they merit special attention.

R. T. Smith offers an analysis of family life among the Guianese and West Indian 'lower class' Negroes which rests on a series of interconnected propositions. These may be summarized briefly as follows: (1) the household is the natural unit of family organization and its sociological analysis. (25) (2) 'Common-law' unions and legal marriage are sociologically identical, at least in these lowly strata of West Indian society. It is neither necessary nor appropriate to distinguish between them. (26) (3) Children derive nothing of any importance from their fathers, who are marginal and ineffective members of their families of procreation, even when resident. It is indeed indifferent whether these husband-fathers live with their families or not, or even whether their children know them personally. (27) (4) Most or all Negro 'lower-class' households are 'matrifocal' and dominated by women in their combined roles of mother and wife; and this female dominance increases as children grow up and daughters bear other children whose fathers live elsewhere. (28) (5) Most or possibly all households begin as domestic nuclear families and all share a common cyclical pattern of growth, expansion and decay which varies in its phases within fixed limits, but which generally involves a period when its matrifocal character and organization is most pronounced and short matrilines of mother, daughter and daughter's children (Frazier's 'maternal' family) are usually present, with or without resident husbands and sons. (29) (6) Such matrifocality of household organization and the correlative marginality of men as husbands and fathers, is characteristic of low ranking sections in ascriptively stratified societies; these patterns are directly associated with ascriptive stratification, low rates of social mobility, restricted public roles for adult men, and an absence of 'managerial' functions, political responsibilities and status differentiation among them. (30) Thus wherever such rigid, typically racial, status ascription obtains, we should find similar conditions of male marginality in familial contexts and matrifocality in domestic organization, coupled with a single standardized developmental cycle for household groups based on the nuclear family in its initial phase. (7) Only those patterns of sexual association which involve co-residence of the partners merit classification as 'conjugal' unions or direct analysis in the study of family life. This is so because the family involves close and continuous association of its members; it is therefore inherently a domestic unit, and households and families are identical. Hence, men are truly marginal members of families begotten in extra-residential mating. (31)

Thus having eliminated several critical elements of the local family structure by denying their relevance, and having identified the nuclear family as the necessary basis for domestic organization, R. T. Smith has to seek the factors which determine the development and matrifocal qualities of these units in extrinsic conditions of social stratification. In his view the common distinctions between legal and consensual cohabitation, and between legitimate and illegitimate children are sociologically irrelevant. He likewise excludes extra-residential mating from the category of conjugal union relevant to analysis of these family systems; and finally he dismisses the internal differentiations among these villagers as irrelevant to his analysis, asserting that such differentiations are minimized because they are 'inconsistent with the criteria on which the colonial system of social stratification is based, and to which the inferior stratum *must* normatively subscribe.' (32) Why either of these two latter conclusions should hold is never revealed; and during Smith's field work in British Guiana, both the Negro and East Indian low status sections of the colonial society supported a political movement which he describes as 'truly revolutionary' since it sought to disrupt and discard 'the existing authority system' and explicitly rejected the European domination on which the ascriptive colonial stratification was based. (33)

Later, among the Guianese East Indians who rank beside or below the Negroes on ethnic and occupational grounds, R. T. Smith and his colleague Jayawardena found a distinctive 'Indian' system of status differentiation linked with prevailingly 'patrifocal' family organization, despite status deprivations imposed by the wider society quite as severe as any to which the Negroes were subject. (34) Smith accounts for the patriarchal character of family organization among these low-ranking East Indians by appealing to conditions of ethnicity, cultural autonomy and social separation; (35) but the Negro villages he first studied enjoy very similar conditions of isolation and ethnic homogeneity. It is also clear that these villagers are part of a culturally distinct section of Guianese society; and as such they possess some autonomy which, however limited, is imposed on them by their social situation. Under these conditions it would be remarkable if the villagers lacked their own internal system status differentiation. (36) Evidently Smith made little attempt to study this system in detail, or to appreciate its criteria and functions in sustaining the cohesion and solidarity of these 'black people's villages'. (37) Instead he dismisses the villagers' internal differentiations of age and sex as trivial, although his careful tabulations indicate that legal marriage is closely associated with increasing age in both sexes; (38) and it is also evident, despite his attempt to equate them, that marriage is regarded by these Negro villagers as having greater prestige than other forms of mating, and as the appropriate status for men and women of middle or senior age. If so, then marriages late in life can rarely fail to enhance the status and authority of men as 'husband-fathers' within and outside their homes, by simultaneously legitimating their unions and children and by conferring higher status on their wives while achieving corresponding increments themselves through their personal fulfilment of community norms.

Despite such data, R. T. Smith prefers to treat the people's community values and status structure as irrelevant or trivial and to analyse their familial institutions within a 'frame of reference' of the 'total social system' in which, by virtue of their low ascribed status, internal differentiations among these Negro villagers are indeed irrelevant, together with their institutional practice. Thus although 84 per cent of all domestic unions in the three villages studied were based on legal marriage, Guianese élite regard common-law unions as 'exclusively lower-class custom' and as 'part of the lower-class cultural tradition'. (39) From this vantage point, Smith ignored the distinction between common-law and legal marriage which his villagers' conduct show that they emphasize.

Such procedures represent a remarkable departure from the standard practice of social anthropologists, whose work repeatedly demonstrated that social analyses which are not based on a thorough and infinite appreciation of folk values, distinctions, conceptions and modes of thought can rarely if ever avoid serious error and misrepresentations of the people's way of life and social organization. Some illustrations of this truism in R. T. Smith's work have already been cited; for example, the arbitrary exclusion of extra-residential mating from the category of conjugal relations on which his analysis of nuclear family organization rests; the unsubstantiated assertion that resident husband-fathers are simultaneously marginal members of their own homes, and undifferentiated members of their local communities; the misleading equations of legal and common-law marriage, household and nuclear family; and the surprising assertions that differences in the closeness, continuity and quality of father-child relations are socially irrelevant, or that these Negro villagers fully accept the low social status ascribed to them and the criteria on which this ascription is based, although they supported a political movement expressly committed to overthrow the colonial social order.

In Grenada, Jamaica, Haiti, Trinidad and in other West Indian societies where ascriptive systems of stratification also employ racial criteria, distinctive status structures have been reported even among the lowliest people in all rural communities where they have been sought. (40) These community status systems do not always, or perhaps even usually, involve stratification by 'class', occupation, colour and other variables which are institutionalized in the societal stratification. For this reason, they are all the more distinctive, and repay careful study. Conversely, nowhere in this Caribbean region has any other student found men to be always 'marginal' as husbands and fathers. Nor has anyone observed the close association of nuclear families and household groupings on which the assumption of a uniform developmental cycle for domestic units is based. Instead several scholars have criticized these generalizations on theoretical and empirical grounds alike. (41) For decisive evidence on these topics, one needs look no further than the present text, which systematically demonstrates how differences in the forms of mating relation are associated with differences in men's roles as husbands and fathers, and with differences in their performance. Further, the present book shows how widely communities may

differ in the combinations of mating patterns that they institutionalize; and how such differences in community mating systems
determine parallel differences in their domestic organizations, as
shown by local differences in the incidence of household groups
of differing type, in their average size, stability, generation depth
and conjugal base.

By combining specialized definitions, value judgments,
exclusions of relevant data, and by assimilating dissimilar units
and relations, R. T. Smith seeks to generalize Frazier's theory
of the influence of the depressing social and economic conditions
on the family organization of American Negroes to all low-
ranking sections of ascriptively stratified societies. As hypothesis
or generalization, this formula is only meaningful on the following assumptions: (1) that the members of these disprivileged
strata accept the system of values with which the structure of
social inequality and their own deprivation is identified as
normatively valid; (2) that they lack distinctive status structures
for their own internal differentiation which are relevant to the
familial roles of men as husbands and fathers; (3) that alternative
patterns of mating, parenthood and nuclear family organization
current among such people are irrelevant to the constitution
and development of their family and household units alike.
Unless these three conditions are simultaneously present, the
generalization cited above cannot apply.

5

Like other social institutions, family systems have internal and
external aspects which are clearly related, though variably so in
differing cultures and societies. These family systems may thus
be analysed with primary reference to their internal constitution
and consistency, or with primary reference to their congruence
and articulation with the wider social system in which their adult
members participate. However, analyses of this second sort
presuppose prior detailed knowledge of the internal organization
of the family systems and societies concerned.

As social systems with clearly defined boundaries, family systems consist internally in a variable organization of several distinct modes of social relation, such as mating and affinity, filiation and parenthood, or descent and extended kinship, through which such units as nuclear or extended families, households and conjugal unions are established. Thus to analyse such systems we must examine closely their intrinsic components, that is, the elements and relations that give them their particular qualities and form; and in this task it is necessary to observe carefully all local distinctions between different types of relation whose mutual connections and relative weight constitute the system. In such analyses, mating forms and conditions clearly deserve most meticulous attention, since these relations are prerequisites of parenthood, and affinity and nuclear or extended families alike.

In this regard R. T. Smith's method of family analysis is most instructive. He begins by excluding extra-residential mating, with which the conditions of 'matrifocality' and 'male marginality' are closely linked, and by assimilating legal and 'common law' unions, although these are clearly distinguished by the community and society alike. In this way, Smith defines conjugal relations exclusively by the criterion of co-residence, though the villagers clearly do not; and on this ground he identifies the formation of household groups with the establishment of nuclear families consisting of couples and their children, whereas many nuclear families are never co-resident, and many households neither begin nor develop on this basis. (42) By the same token, since he denies the conjugal status of the widespread extra-residential form of mating, Smith denies the sociological relevance of paternity in such unions and accordingly interprets the presence of young women and children in their mothers' homes as evidence of familial matrifocality rather than as necessary and inevitable consequences of the mating pattern. Likewise, having identified the formation of household groups with the establishment of nuclear families by his exclusive definitions of conjugal and paternal relations, Smith concludes that a single model of their domestic form and development applies to virtually all these Negro families with limited variation. Indeed, having ignored locally significant differences between the roles of men as fathers and husbands in extra-residential, 'common law' and legal unions, all must be equally 'marginal' or central to family life; and since most children generally remain with their mothers during and after extra-residential or other types of union, male marginality is rather more evident than the alternative. Thus by eliminating these internal differences of mating form and parenthood, and by ignoring their implications for domestic grouping, Smith is free to seek the 'causes' or correlates of this male marginality in other spheres of the social system which, being non-familial, can only be either communal or societal. Here again, for reasons which are not quite clear, he elects to ignore the external social system of greatest immediacy and significance to the people concerned —their local community—and derives instead the predicated marginality of these Negro men from their uniformly low status in the colonial society. In short R. T. Smith combines a cavalier treatment of the features intrinsic to the family system with major emphases on the decisive influence of extrinsic societal conditions.

In his pioneer studies of American Negro family life, Frazier had tried to combine both planes of analysis, although he also over-emphasized the influence of external conditions and devoted little attention to its intrinsic elements. Since he was mainly concerned to contrast the family organization of plantation slaves and share-croppers in the Deep South with those of rural immigrants and 'black bourgeoisie' in the Northern cities, Frazier's failure to analyse the internal components of these differing structures, and particularly the relations between their patterns of mating and family form and development, escaped general notice; but it was precisely on these grounds that Herskovits challenged the general thesis of socio-economic determination of family form on which Frazier's analysis rested.

Following Frazier, and being unaware of the statistical and structural significance of the extra-residential mating pattern,

Simey first sought to interpret West Indian family patterns in terms of economic conditions, 'companionate' and 'faithful' concubinage being associated with low levels of income while 'Christian' marriage was linked with higher income levels, and the 'disintegrate' family was inferentially derived from the two preceding 'lower class' types. (43) In his turn Henriques, following Simey, noted differing social histories of West Indian and American Negroes and emphasized that West Indian family forms are *sui generis*, natural developments of local society, and not by-products of migration and urbanization such as Frazier had observed in Chicago and New York. However, like Simey, Henriques also failed to isolate the extra-residential mating pattern which Stycos and Back have recently shown to be the most common form of mating and the almost universal practice in early unions among 'lower class' Jamaicans. Accordingly, like Frazier and Simey, Henriques had to seek explanations for the prevalence of 'grandmother' or 'disintegrate' families in extra-familial social conditions. Like Simey too, he distinguished between stable and unstable consensual cohabitations on the one hand, and Christian marriage on the other, primarily by reference to differences of economic situation. (44) The 'grandmother' family was again derived from unstable 'keeper' unions, at least by inference. However, once we recognize the prevalence of extra-residential mating, especially during the early years of adult life, its pivotal significance for the organization and development of elementary and domestic families alike is immediately evident; and these earlier attempts to 'explain' West Indian family forms and their variations by reference to extrinsic economic and societal conditions lose their relevance and validity until the effects of these inner components have been clearly identified.

As an elementary rule of sociological method, it is always first essential to examine the interrelations, requisites and implications of elements intrinsic to any social system, family or other, in order to determine its structure and conditions of change or self-perpetuation, before seeking extrinsic determinants. By ignoring these intrinsic components and their integration within the family system, and seeking instead their determinants, requisites, or correlates in external social spheres, R. T. Smith combined an over-simple model of Guianese Negro family organization with a premature and misleading explanation which substitutes the societal stratification for earlier emphases on economic and social contexts of 'disorganization'. But this 'stratification' theory of the 'matrifocal' West Indian family organization which treats men as marginal husband-fathers, assumes that local differences of conjugal union and paternity are irrelevant, and also ignores local status structures which differentiate people by reference to sex, age, land ownership, conduct, marital and familial status and by locally relevant occupational and economic differences. Such an interpretation depends for its value on the demonstrable validity of the various assumptions, value-judgments and exclusions of data on which it rests. Instead of seeking 'explanations' of institutional systems in the remoter conditions of their social context, we must first attend meticulously to the specific distinctions, relations, and forms institutionalized within them, to determine the limits, degrees and conditions of their closure as self-perpetuating bodies of custom, and so to identify their extrinsic requisites and susceptibilities.

Indeed, by its careful analyses of household composition in relation to the mating status of household principals and the fragmentation of nuclear families within and beyond them, the present book conclusively indicates the deficiency of those attempts to 'explain' West Indian family patterns which assert the influence of extrinsic conditions on grossly oversimplified models of them. Whereas R. T. Smith chose to interpret West Indian family organization, kinship and mating from the perspective of the household group, and to interpret the community differentiation from the perspective of the colonial society, Edith Clarke shows how alternative types of mating relation influence the constitution and stability of household groups, and how differences in the organization and character of local communities are associated with significant differences in their patterns of family organization.

One of the major contributions of the present study is to demonstrate the influence that community organization and ethos have on local patterns of family life. Such community variations show how misleading it is to assume an undifferentiated and uniform pattern of family organization among the Creole 'lower class' which may be analysed without further qualification, as R. T. Smith, following Simey and Henriques, seeks to do. Careful comparisons of varying community patterns of family organization also show that simple economic differences are not themselves evident 'determinants'. Thus, despite its higher level of average income, Sugartown, for obvious reasons, has a lower ratio of domestic nuclear families and higher rates of individual isolation and marital instability than Mocca; and despite their differences of wealth and status, 'Mocca and Orange Grove, in their different ways, are integrated societies in which kinship plays an important role, whereas Sugartown is . . . a conglomerate of disparate sections, held together only by common involvement in a sugar estate'. (45) In Mocca, despite its 'extreme poverty' (46) 'where the conjugal pattern is concubinage for life, the family is all-important', (47) and 'the pattern of descent is predominantly patriarchal'. (48) In Orange Grove, marriage is 'part of the class structure and is reinforced with strong social sanctions'. (49) By contrast, 'there was no adult pattern of male conjugal or paternal responsibility' in Sugartown. 'It is to Orange Grove and Mocca that we have to turn to find examples of fathers lavishing care and affection on their children and carrying out conjugal and paternal duties.' (50)

The typical basis and form of cohabitation, the modal size, composition and stability of household groups, the differing modes of paternity and their statistical distribution, and the quality, range and density of family relations, all vary directly with differences in the composition, character and cohesion of the communities concerned. Clearly the 'integrated societies' of

Mocca and Orange Grove possess distinctive status structures which are normatively effective in regulating individual conduct at the familial and community levels. At Orange Grove this status system takes the familiar form of internal class divisions which, however insignificant at the national level, are locally influential and reinforce male responsibility and authority in conjugal and paternal roles. At Mocca, our data indicate that status allocations rest primarily on criteria of sex, age and familial position; thus while one-third of the Mocca girls aged between 15 and 19 marry—presumably for religious reasons and to men some years older than themselves—'concubinage increases rapidly in the next ten years until it reaches ... 61 per cent for the 25–29 age-group, marriages decrease in the same period, but climb again between 30 and 40, until at 35 the entire population is living in a conjugal union, fairly evenly balanced between marriage and concubinage'. (51) Such data indicate that while cohabitation in legal or common-law unions is prescribed for adults in their mid-thirties at Mocca, among younger people, mating is modally extra-residential. As age increases, so do the ratios of married and consensually cohabiting couples whose nubile daughters are beginning to bear children in their parents' homes through early extra-residential liaisons. Among Grenadian and Jamaican peasants this customary prescription of alternative conjugal forms as appropriate or inappropriate at successive phases of the adult life cycle has a similar character and supports very similar family structures at both the domestic and extra-domestic levels. By contrast, in the Grenadian and Jamaican towns of Kingston and Grenville, conditions very similar to those at Sugartown prevail, consequent on the disruption of this peasant mating sequence by proletarianization, migration and exposure to elite pressures and stimuli. (52) For Jamaica the independent enquiries of Stycos and Back have recently confirmed these general findings. (53) A careful reading will reveal that these recent advances in our knowledge have their foundation in the present book.

Briefly and schematically, among the West Indian Creole folk

or 'lower class', young people typically begin their mating career
with extra-residential relations of varying duration and publicity.
According to folk tradition these unions should receive the
consent of the girl's parents; (54) but often they are clandestine.
Particular unions may or may not lead to childbirth or to consensual or legal cohabitation; but when sanctioned by parental
approval and public recognition, these extra-residential relations
provide an adequate institutional context for the young couple's
mating. They also ensure in advance acknowledgment of
paternity for any children begotten in these relations. During
such mating the young girl normally remains in her parental
home until such time as she has achieved her 'womanship' by
bearing one or two children. Normally she will then be willing
to set up a joint household with her current mate; and if their
union later breaks down, she returns to her former home until
she finds another. Most successive matings begin as extra-residential liaisons, but in each later union the interval between the
initiation of mating and of cohabitation typically decreases; and by
their thirtieth year most women are living in conditional but often
stable consensual cohabitation (concubinage) with a man and
their common children. At this stage, unless their union is childless, the couple's children by previous matings are usually dispersed in other homes, typically with the children's maternal kin,
lineal or collateral.

Such consensual cohabitations face three possible courses of
development: disruption by desertion, conjugal disagreements or
widowhood; conversion into legal marriage; or persistence without formal change until widowhood occurs. At Mocca, and in
those communities which Stycos and Back designate as the
'Jamaican foothills', for example, in the parishes of St Catherine
and coastal St Thomas, consensual cohabitations are prevalent
and often lifelong, while marriage is statistically marginal. (55)
However, in most peasant communities of Jamaica, marriage is
prescribed as the appropriate form of cohabitation for women in
their forties, and few women remain in consensual cohabitation
as 'common-law' wives past their 54th year. (56)

The serial distribution of these alternative mating forms as normatively appropriate or inappropriate at successive phases of the adult life cycle is inevitably identical for both sexes, except that men typically begin their mating careers rather later than girls, are typically some 5 years older than their current partners, and generally die first, leaving their legal or consensual widows with or without children and kin at home.

Ideally in those peasant systems that institutionalize all three conjugal alternatives, a young couple may convert their relation from visiting to consensual cohabitation and so to marriage at their own discretion. Alternatively a young girl may marry one of her earliest suitors, who is then generally several years her senior. Both possibilities are rarely realized, and as a rule adults of either sex move through these successive phases of their mating careers by unions of varying form, length and fertility. Some women never cohabit, but maintain visiting relations with a succession of men whose children they bear, as for example in the case of Nesta described below. (57) For various reasons, this type of adaptation is also relatively rare. So are reversions from marriage to "common-law" cohabitations, which are strongly disapproved in settled peasant communities whose age-graded status structure ensures elders the immunities required to act as spokesmen for the local mores. Thus, as individuals increase in age, social maturity, parental responsibilities and local prominence, they are normally constrained by individual and social conditions to convert their non-domiciliary liaisons into stable consensual cohabitation, and in most peasant communities of Jamaica and Grenada, to convert these 'common-law' unions into marriage during middle or late middle age, marriage being institutionalized as the appropriate mating status for senior members of the community.

In rural and urban proletariats this serial order by which these alternative mating forms are integrated with advancing social maturity in the individual life cycle has limited validity, though many rural immigrants use it to orient their conduct. In these proletarian contexts, of which Sugartown is an excellent instance, all forms of mating are always simultaneously available to anyone, without normative restriction; and, if my data from Grenville are valid and generally representative, under these conditions marriage lacks finality, and after their desertion, separation or widowhood, men often revert to consensual cohabitation. (58) In such conditions many cohabitations are 'non-purposive', 'companionate' or 'keeper' households in contradistinction to the 'faithful concubinage' characteristic of peasants during and after their thirties. Likewise, in these proletarian contexts, non-domiciliary relations are often casual and promiscuous rather than sexually exclusive and durable. By comparison with settled peasant communities, among these proletariats the proportionate incidence of single-person households is generally higher, together with the ratio of 'denuded' households, especially those consisting of women, their children and/or grandchildren; but, while the ratio of households containing three generations declines, the ratio of households based on cohabitation remains constant at about 40 per cent, although the proportional incidence of marriage falls sharply. (59) In short, increased instability of mating organization in proletarian contexts is associated with increasing fragmentation of nuclear families and with the dispersal of their elements in smaller households of shallower generation depth. It is also associated with a general increase in the diversity and instability of household groupings.

This analysis demonstrates the orderly arrangement of alternative conjugal forms in a series integrated with advancing social maturity and status at successive phases of the individual life cycle in these peasant communities. It serves to show how differences in local systems of mating underlie differences in the domestic and familial organization of these communities; and it also shows how these family structures vary in consequence of differences in the complement, organization and incidence of these conjugal alternatives. (60) For illustrations immediately to hand we need only compare the proportionate distributions of households classified in Appendix 9 by family type and by the conjugal status of their principals at Sugartown, Orange Grove and Mocca. The relevance for studies of marital stability and fertility of these differing community mating structures, which are clearly integrated with the local systems of status allocation, has lately been shown by Stycos and Back. (61)

7

Recently also K. F. Otterbein has attempted to show how imbalances in the adult sex ratios of local populations, produced by movements of men to seek wage employment, 'determine' the 'family systems' of Caribbean communities. (62) To demonstrate this determinism, Otterbein calculates correlation coefficients between adult sex ratios on the one hand, and percentages of consensual unions in local cohabitations and of homes with female heads, on the other. Both calculations yield high positive correlations, indicating close associations between the variables concerned; and both are vitiated by unnecessary errors or inappropriateness in the data on which they are based. For example, to derive ratios of homes with female heads in Sugartown, Mocca and Orange Grove, Otterbein selects from Appendix 9 below the percentage ratios of denuded and single-person households classified as 'female', and simply sums them. Thus, although Edith Clarke expressly refrains from classifying domestic groups based on conjugal couples by the sex of their head, Otterbein treats all such households as units having male heads. Likewise he assembles the wrong data on the percentage of consensual unions among cohabiting couples from my survey analyses. (63) However, these errors of data compilation are more easily corrected than the conceptual blunders on which his analysis rests.

Briefly, Otterbein assumes the detailed and uniform constitution of the family system whose 'major determinant' he identifies as imbalances in the adult sex ratio. It is easy to show that this procedure and analysis is empirically and theoretically invalid. For example, in my rural Jamaica sample where the adult sex ratio was virtual parity (1 male: 1.04 females), 30.1 per cent of the households had female heads and 41.2 per cent of all cohabitations were consensual. In Latante and Grenville, Grenada, and in Carriacou, where sex ratios were considerably less equal (1:1.24, 1:1.29, and 1:1.92, respectively) consensual cohabitation accounted for 26.4 per cent, 42 per cent and 8 per cent of all domestic conjugal units. (64)

Otterbein's argument assumes stable ratios of 'single' males and females engaged in extra-residential mating *inter se*; and it also assumes that all other extra-residential relations hold between married men and 'single' women, most of whom presumably live in homes with female heads. But clearly the relative incidence of extra-residential matings and cohabitations, whether legal or consensual, is a function of the mating organization rather than of simple shifts in the adult sex ratios. The addition of another 50 men in a population of x adults with a previous surplus of 100 females will leave the percentage ratios of homes with female heads and consensual cohabitation completely unchanged if this male increment is accommodated in extant units, and if they remain celibate, mate extra-residentially, or contract consensual and legal cohabitations in already current proportions. Alternatively, this increment may decrease the ratio of households with female heads if its members establish so many single-person units, as for example at Sugartown where 34 per cent of the households surveyed contained single individuals, 110 men and 41 women. (65) In such a case, this change in the ratio of households with female heads proceeds without any corresponding change in the ratio of consensual unions. The point surely is that increases or decreases in the adult sex ratios depend for their familial effects on the local patterns of mating, kinship and domestic organization which accommodate them and regulate their effects. That a large surplus population of adult women need not entail the presence of any households with female heads whatsoever would be apparent to anyone who has studied an African polygynous society. (66) To say that such African comparisons are irrelevant merely indicates that the 'determination' of West Indian family systems by differential sex ratios presumes the specific patterns it seeks to account for. If West Indian societies institutionalize consensual cohabitation and other modes of mating together with female household headship, these are surely features of the social organization rather than simple functions of demographic and economic structures. Consequently shifts in the relative incidence of female household headship or of common law unions represent changes or adjustments of the domestic organization, and may proceed without any changes in the local adult sex ratios.

These demographic factors cannot possibly 'determine' the 'family system'—by which Otterbein evidently means the statistical distribution of certain arbitrarily selected features of the domestic organization—for the obvious reason that family systems and demographic ratios are drawn from quite different levels of social organization. For example, in Carriacou, St Helena, and the Long Bay Cays, Bahamas, the marginal incidence of consensual unions is clearly a function of distinctive kinship and mating structures rather than the 'demographic-economic' variable to which Otterbein appeals. (67) Indeed, his entire argument rests on the cultural prescription that men should own their homes in order to undertake marriage. This institutional prerequisite is said to motivate male migration in search of the necessary money. If so, the resulting disbalances of adult sex ratios are themselves 'determined by' the mating and familial organization whose conditions and variability they are then employed to explain. Otterbein's argument is another illustration of the deficiencies of 'causal' analyses of unfamiliar systems in terms of inappropriate extrinsic variables.

8

Another favourite method for such extrinsic causal analyses involves the interpretation of West Indian family organization by reference to economic conditions. This tradition has persisted from Macmillan onwards. (68) In general, these 'economic interpretations' concentrate on 'explaining' the variable incidence of marriage and common law unions by reference to differences of income and economic situation; and sometimes the present text is cited as evidence of this relation. Certainly Edith Clarke dwells on the economic preconditions and correlates of marriage in contrast to those of concubinage. Thus she says, 'in general marriage is associated with a higher economic status ... [and] by and large concubinage is an institution of the poor'. (69) But besides stressing the similarities between 'purposive concubinage' and marriage, Edith Clarke insists that the incidence and stability of unions of either type is a function of the community organization; and she observes that 'in Sugartown and Mocca, there is, in fact, no apparent real association of marriage or concubinage with the economic status or class structure'. (70) At Orange Grove 'marriage ... is part of the class structure'. (71) Elsewhere it 'occurs ... as a later stage in an association begun in concubinage ... the seal of a proven conjugal union'. (72)

Other students who have closely investigated the relation between differential mating forms and economic levels have come to similar conclusions. (73) These are most succintly expressed by Cumper, who concludes a detailed analysis of these relations in Barbados with reservations about the influence of economic conditions on family organization, due to the presence of intervening 'cultural prescriptions'. (74) For Jamaica, Stycos and Back have also tried to measure the associations of alternative conjugal forms with such variables as age, community type and employment statuses of husband and wife. They find salient differences in the distributions of these conjugal alternatives between women of identical age groups settled in different types of communities; and also between women of differing age groups in the same type of community; but they fail to find any direct evidence of correlations between marriage rates and the 'occupations'—by which they refer mainly to differences between wage and own-account employment—of these women's partners. Such differing incidences of marriage as these writers find in the unions maintained by men of differing 'occupations' are complicated by differences in the average age of these groupings. 'Age is still a most important correlate, marriage increasing and visiting decreasing with age in every instance. The woman's employment status is also important. . . . The occupation of husband is still related, but its relation is neither as pronounced nor as clear-cut as the other two variables.' (75)

These scholars then investigate relations between the marital and employment status of women of different age groups whose 'spouses' are classified as wage or own-account employed. They conclude that, irrespective of the woman's age and of her 'husband's' employment status, marriage is associated with higher rates of female unemployment than other forms of mating; but this conclusion is only borne out by their data for women in their thirties. Among women aged between 15 and 24 years, few legal wives are found among the unemployed; and in the succeeding age-group, 25–29, 'common law' and legal wives are represented equally among unemployed women. Thus even as regards the women's employment status there is no evident difference between legal and 'common-law' marriage before the 30th year, by which time most women are busy with children and home.

Stycos and Back also investigate the system of economic support for non-domiciliary mates and for the children of broken unions. They report that over 85 per cent of the 1,359 women in their sample who were engaged in extra-residential mating received economic support from their mates. Excluding their current partners, many women also received external support for their children, generally from their own kin or from the children's fathers; but as the woman's marital status changes from 'single' to consensual and to legal cohabitation, the contributions received from these absent fathers decline, and it seems quite clear that many men contribute little towards their children's care after their conjugal unions have ended. Even so, more than one-third of the current mates of these women, and close to two-thirds of their extra-residential mates over 40 years of age, contributed to the support of 'outside' children. Approximately one-half of all the men aged over 40 with whom these women were mating contributed towards the support of at least some of their children by former unions. Stycos and Back conclude that 'a remarkably consistent picture of adjustments of the family system to the exigencies of the fluid pattern of mating and childbearing emerges, a system in which resources are pooled in order to provide economic and child rearing support for children occurring out of wedlock.' (76)

9

Its normative character and status present yet another important focus of current interest in the study of West Indian marriage and family systems. T. S. Simey and Madeline Kerr both explored this problem in different ways, but perhaps Henriques first expressed the central issues most cogently. He described Jamaica as 'a society in which there is a contradiction as regards conjugal unions between what is legally accepted as the norm for the whole society and what is socially accepted. This contradiction or opposition between legal and social acceptance applies to other institutions as well as the family.' (77) On other grounds also Henriques dismissed the social distinctions between legal (Christian) and 'common-law' marriage as 'official and legal but quite useless sociologically'; (78) but although treating stable common-law unions and legal marriages as functional equivalents, he distinguished between the familial and household groupings they identified.

Following Henriques several writers, including Edith Clarke, have documented this thesis of normative dualism and institutional alternatives in mating and family organization of West Indian societies. (79) In general these analyses have confirmed Henriques' observation that among the West Indian 'lower classes' 'the attitude towards legal marriage is ambivalent. . . . Although no social stigma attaches to the unmarried state and "living in sin" is not a term of reproach, marriage is often regarded as an ideal which is not within the woman's reach.' (80)

On these questions among others our most systematic data lie in this text, in chapters 3 and 4. This shows clearly how folk attitudes to marriage and its alternatives vary in the different communities that Edith Clarke studied; and it also shows that while legal marriage ranks above other forms of mating in folk opinion, in some communities, e.g. Sugartown, there is 'no social disapprobation of concubinage nor bias towards marriage.' (81) Although at Orange Grove, 'concubinage is disesteemed', at Mocca 'the conjugal pattern is concubinage for life.' (82) Nonetheless, though these communities differ in the norms that they institutionalize and in the weight and sanctions that they attach to their observance, in all areas 'sexual exclusiveness is the ideal mode of behaviour, whether in marriage or concubinage'. (83) In extra-residential relations women are also required to remain faithful to their partners; and it is by reference to these norms of sexual exclusiveness that adultery and unfaithfulness are distinguished from casual or promiscuous intercourse to which no such conditions attach. (84)

That the normative dualism identified by Henriques is not restricted in Jamaica to modes of mating is further evident from Edith Clarke's discussion of family land in Chapter 2, and from the distinction she draws between social and legal legitimacy (85) and between adoption and the rearing of 'schoolchildren'. (86) But many instances of this pervasive normative dualism could be cited from other fields of social life, particularly religion, politics and social stratification.

However, Judith Blake has recently asserted that marriage is the only form of mating which Jamaican women of the 'lower class' approve and desire; (87) and by so doing, she has concentrated current interests in the normative structure and integration of West Indian society directly on the analysis of mating and family norms among West Indian folk. In discussing R. T. Smith's work above we have touched on another aspect of this basic problem.

Blake rests her analysis on replies to questionnaires on attitudes to mating and fertility which were administered to 99 women and 53 men in Jamaica in 1953–4 by a staff of 'trained' interviewers drawn from the local 'middle class'. The appropriateness of her sample and field procedures has already been criticized; (88) but her conclusions are also suspect on other grounds. Briefly, Blake's thesis is that Jamaican 'lower class' women regard legal marriage as a norm and disapprove morally of illegitimacy and extra-legal mating in all its forms. As evidence, she cites her questionnaire responses which indicate the women's expressed preferences and attitudes; and she refers to the familiar increases in the ratios of married persons as age advances. (89)

To account for the grave divergences between actual behaviour and expressed preference or 'norm'—an inference or equation for which Braithwaite properly criticized her (90)—Blake relies on two major arguments, both supported by her questionnaire replies. First she tries to show that young Jamaican girls become pregnant in their early liaisons through innocence and ignorance about sex, in consequence of their inadequate and misguided socialization and their exploitation by philandering males. (91) Secondly she argues that in consequence of these early errors, 'the bargaining position' of these unmarried mothers deteriorates 'in the courtship market', (92) since no men want to marry such women and to bring up other men's children. The woman is thus driven by economic need and by her expressed desires for marriage into a further series of extra-marital unions of visiting or co-residential types, in each of which she willingly risks further pregnancies in the hope of 'cementing' the current union and 'earning' its conversion into marriage. (93) These are the two basic arguments by which Blake seeks to account for the observable gap between women's expressed 'ideals' or norms and their actual conduct.

Though these Jamaican lower-class women are said to express active discontent and hostility to extra-legal associations and to the bearing of illegitimate children, we are informed—somewhat inconsistently—that whereas these women put the 'median ideal age' of marriage at 20 years, they put the 'median ideal age' of their first union—defined by Blake as any association involving sexual contact from rape to lifelong marriage—at 18.4 years; and that in fact half of them began mating during or before their sixteenth year, the median age of first union for Blake's sample being 17.0 and of (actual) marriage 25.6. (94) Thus to adopt Blake's method of reasoning, these women clearly distinguish sexual intercourse (unions) and marriage at both the ideal and behavioural levels. Instead of identifying, they segregate them, and apparently they regard premarital intercourse as a normatively indispensable prerequisite for marriage. Under such conditions, granted the virtual absence of any attempts to prevent conception, their premarital pregnancies seem inevitable, and it is thus pointless to attempt to transfer the responsibility for these developments to licentious males or to inept and restrictive parents, as Blake tries to do. In short, Blake's questionnaire responses themselves reveal the normative dualism she seeks to disprove.

Moreover, both the arguments by which Blake seeks to accommodate the evident discrepancies between these women's expressed 'norms' and actual behaviour are controverted by the data furnished by Stycos and Back. These writers show that only one-half of the women in their much larger sample became pregnant during their first unions, which they carefully define as 'sexual association lasting for more than 3 months', thereby excluding casual liaisons. (95) Even so, very few of these women entered their second union in marriage. Accordingly it appears that these young girls are not entirely the victims of innocence and ignorance, male exploitation and parental folly, as Blake would have us believe; and this, coupled with their expressed desires for premarital intercourse, disposes of her argument from 'ruined innocence'.

Furthermore Stycos and Back conclusively show that in Jamaica the chances of lower class women securing marriage on entering each successive union are unaffected by the presence or absence of children by previous unions. (96) This finding disposes of Blake's second assumption, and her supplementary argument of the 'deteriorating bargaining position' of unwed mothers by showing that in the local 'courtship market' this condition is irrelevant for marriage. Indeed, if Jamaican men prefer to seduce and abandon virgins, and refuse to marry unmarried mothers, it is difficult to see how anyone ever got married in the island at all.

There remains the statistical pattern of increases in marriage ratios with increasing age, which Blake cites in support of her thesis that women are normatively committed to marriage as the *only* morally appropriate basis for reproduction and family life. In doing so she commits precisely the same methodological sins of which she accuses Simey, Henriques and others, (97) but more grossly. W. J. Goode, who employs the same argument, at least commits no overt inconsistency in the process. (98)

Clearly Blake's elaborate argumentation rests on serious misconceptions of the meanings of 'family' and 'marriage' among her respondents—with whom indeed she had very little, if any, personal contact. As marriage is evidently neither normatively prerequisite for mating, nor parenthood, and as most couples marry late in life, often after the woman's reproductive career has ended, many married couples lack common children although either partner may have several by previous matings. These simple facts—that 'lower-class' Jamaicans begin mating extra-maritally at an early age and typically marry rather late in life after having had several children—should indicate to anyone that the folk conception of marriage differs sharply from that of the local upper classes, for whom it is the essential precondition of procreation and family life—at least in class-endogamous matings. Blake however has chosen to give these folk concepts of 'marriage' and 'legitimacy' their standardized middle-class meanings in American and West Indian middle-class society, thereby creating the false problem of apparent differences between conduct and norms at which she addresses her dialectic in a futile effort to 'prove' that marriage is the only 'norm' recognized by Jamaican women, who are the unwilling victims of social circumstance, forced against their will to mate and bear children outside of wedlock, and thus neither responsible for their actions, nor deviant from their own moral convictions.

This is precisely the pattern of self-vindication which Madeline

Kerr identified as distinctively Jamaican and perhaps West Indian; and the administration of Blake's questionnaire which left respondents free to attribute responsibility as they willed, without any objective checks, and to misrepresent or rationalize their attitudes, motivations, goals, experiences and circumstances, provided a perfect opportunity for these women to demonstrate by their vicarious self-exculpations the validity of Madeline Kerr's psychological analysis. It is therefore interesting that throughout her discussion Blake should ignore the much-publicized Mass Marriage Movement which was still under way in Jamaica in 1953 during her visit, and with which her respondents may quite well have confused her questionnaire enquiries, especially because the topics and personnel engaged in both campaigns were strikingly similar. Surely if Jamaican lower-class women were as fervently committed to marriage and as hostile to other forms of union as Blake asserts, this Mass Marriage Movement under militant if misguided leadership, backed by a well-organized Federation of Women with access to ample funds, should not have proved such a dismal failure. But then neither should the 'median ideal ages' of marriage and first sexual intercourse be so sharply separated by these female respondents.

Rodman has stressed the dangers of applying 'middle class' meanings and assumptions to such common terms as marriage, family, legitimacy and land ownership in sociological studies of West Indian folk. (99) Blake's analysis merely demonstrates the relevance of Rodman's caution. All our data presently go to show that whereas marriage, household and family are often congruent, their association is neither ideally prescribed nor empirically modal among West Indian Creoles of the folk or 'lower class'. Many, perhaps most, individuals and couples throughout Jamaica and other West Indian territories bear and rear children outside of wedlock; and in such Jamaican parishes as St Thomas and St Catherine, rates of consensual cohabitation have remained equally high and stable from 1943 to 1960. (100) On such evidence it is not merely meaningless but misleading to predicate a uniform 'lower-class' regard for marriage as the normative basis for family life. Mocca, described in this book, is a quite representative instance of those communities in which marriage is not prescriptively institutionalized. In urban proletariats and plantation areas such as Sugartown, marriage, despite its high public esteem, can neither be regarded as a local ideal, nor as the binding and morally obligatory rule of conduct which corresponds to the accepted sociological meaning of 'norm'. Among the West Indian upper and middle classes there is no doubt that marriage is normatively requisite in their matings with one another, though taboo in their matings with the folk; and, with due exceptions, among West Indian peasants in general, marriage is institutionalized as the appropriate personal status and basis for cohabitation during middle or later age. It is thus rather as an essential condition of maturity and social status in these rural communities than as the basis or 'context of social reproduction' that marriage has its decisive and distinctive significance for the West Indian rural folk; but of course, once this is realized the apparent divergence between expressed norms and actual conduct on which Blake and Goode both dwell, simply disappear. There is in fact no contradiction between statements that marriage is preferred or required and participation in premarital unions during early and middle life—provided only that marriage is usually reserved for later years. Likewise there is no contradiction between normative emphases on legitimacy and high illegitimacy ratios in the annual birthrates, provided only that we distinguish as Edith Clarke does, between folk concepts of social legitimacy which require free acknowledgment of paternity, and legitimacy as defined by law and the upper classes. (101) In most West Indian rural communities, marriage is indeed valued as the appropriate status for mature and independent couples of middle or senior years. The unmarried age-mates of these elders lose social status by their failure to fulfil these norms where the community institutionalizes marriage in this way. Thus in these West Indian communities marriage has dual meanings, as a condition of personal status, and as the most esteemed form of mating, though neither the sole nor the obligatory one. Its association with parenthood and the family accordingly varies individually and for couples as an effect of differences in their community situation and in their individual mating careers. In consequence its general equation with 'common law unions' among these people is a major sociological error, as Edith Clarke carefully indicates. (102) This is so because the people concerned distinguish these conditions sharply, and invariably ascribe marriage higher status. Moreover, as we have seen, differing communities may institutionalize the alternative patterns of mating in differing ways.

10

In summarizing these recent developments in the study of family organization among the West Indian folk or Creole 'lower class' I have touched on no subject that is not treated concretely and with insight in this book, but perforce I have omitted several topics, such as the dispersion of children, diversity of parental roles and surrogates, differential fertility rates associated with differing types of mating, land tenure, and recent changes in family organization associated with urbanization, and increases of social mobility. Several of these topics have been studied by others; but undoubtedly much work remains to be done, especially in the critical areas of social economics, psychology, education, legal reform, fertility control, and in the study of the processes and conditions of socialization begun by Madeline Kerr nearly twenty years ago. In attempting to review these recent developments and advances in this branch of Caribbean sociology, I have dwelt rather on the strictly sociological issues of method and theory, in an attempt to summarize the present state of our knowledge and to indicate recent advances in West Indian family studies by elliptic discussions of certain central themes and controversies. Perhaps there are few other tropical areas in which family organization presents as many academic and practical problems and opportunities as the West Indian area; and perhaps in no other comparable region has the family been studied so extensively over the past decade. Inevitably these later studies have raised new issues and interpretations, some of which have been mentioned here; but they also rest on earlier work; and in this context the present book, which provides the most careful and systematic account of this family system and its principal variations available to us, holds a central position.

M. G. SMITH

University of California
at Los Angeles

REFERENCES

1 Morton Klass, *East Indians in Trinidad: A Study of Cultural Persistence*, 1961, Columbia University Press, New York, pp. 93-136.
R. T. Smith and C. Jayawardena, 'Hindu Marriage Customs in British Guiana', 1958, Jamaica, *Social & Economic Studies*, vol. 7, no. 2, pp. 178-94.
R. T. Smith and C. Jayawardena, 'Marriage and the Family amongst East Indians in British Guiana', 1959, Jamaica, *Social & Economic Studies*, vol. 8, no. 4, pp. 321-76.
R. T. Smith, 'Family Structure & Plantation Systems in the New World', in *Plantation Systems of the New World*, 1959, Washington D.C., Social Science Monographs VII (Pan American Union), pp. 154-5.
G. W. Roberts and L. Braithwaite, 'Mating among East Indian and Non-Indian Women in Trinidad', 1962, Jamaica, *Social & Economic Studies*, vol. 11, no. 3, pp. 203-40.

2 J. Mayone Stycos and Kurt W. Back, *The Control of Human Fertility in Jamaica*, 1964, New York, Cornell University Press.

3 R. T. Smith, 'Culture & Social Structure in the Caribbean: Some recent work on Family and Kinship Studies', 1964, *Comparative Studies in Society & History*, vol. 6, no. 1, p. 42.
G. W. Roberts and L. Braithwaite, 1962, *op. cit.*, pp. 207-12.

4 M. G. Smith, *West Indian Family Structure*, 1962, Seattle, University of Washington Press, Table 17, p. 239.

5 Edith Clarke, *My Mother Who Fathered Me*, 1957, London, Allen & Unwin, pp. 127-33, and Appendices 5-8, 16 & 17.

6 Morton Klass, 1961, *op. cit.*; R. T. Smith and C. Jayawardena, 1959, *op. cit.*

7 Stycos and Back, 1964, *op. cit.*, pp. 318-24; Roberts and Braithwaite, 1962, p. 205; Dept. of Statistics, Jamaica, *Population Census*, 1960; *Some Notes on the Union Status, Marital Status and Number of Children of the Female Population of Jamaica*, no date (? 1962), pp. 15-16, 21; O. C. Francis, *The People of Modern Jamaica*, 1964, Jamaica, Dept. of Statistics, Ch. 5.

8 C. Jayawardena, 'Marital Stability in Two Guianese Sugar Estate Communities', 1960, *Social & Economic Studies*, vol. 9, no. 1, pp. 78-81; R. T. Smith and C. Jayawardena, 1959, *op. cit.*, p. 368; G. W. Roberts and L. Braithwaite, 1962, *op. cit.*, pp. 204-17.

9 Edith Clarke, 1957, *op. cit.*, pp. 97-111, 159-64.

10 *West India Royal Commission Report*, 1945, London, H.M.S.O., Command 6607, pp. 220-2.

11 *Digest of Statistics, no. 13*, 1953, Jamaica, Central Bureau of Statistics, p. 5.

12 Madeline Kerr, *Personality & Conflict in Jamaica*, 1951, Liverpool University Press, p. xi.

13 *West India Royal Commission Report*, 1945, p. 424.

14 C. A. Moser, *The Measurement of Levels of Living with Special Reference to Jamaica*, 1956, London, H.M.S.O.; M. Kerr, 1951, *op. cit.*, pp. 74-84.

15 *Ibid.*, pp. 115 ff., 165-74.

16 M. Kerr, 'The Study of Personality Deprivation through Projection Tests', 1955, Jamaica, *Social & Economic Studies*, vol. 4, no. 1, p. 83.

17 G. E. Cumper, 'Two Studies in Jamaican Productivity', 1953, *Social & Economic Studies*, vol. 1, no. 2; M. G. Smith, 'Education and Occupational Choice in Rural Jamaica', 1960, *Social & Economic Studies*, vol. 9, no. 3; M. G. Smith and G. J. Kruijer, *A Sociological Manual for Extension Workers in the Caribbean*, 1957, Jamaica, Extra-Mural Department, U.C.W.I.

18 See George Cumper (ed.) *Social Needs in a Changing Society: Report of the Conference on Social Development in Jamaica*, 1962, Kingston, Council of Voluntary Social Services; *Children of the Caribbean—Their Mental Health Needs: Proceedings of the Second Caribbean Conference for Mental Health*, 1961, San Juan, Puerto Rico.

19 E. Franklin Frazier, *The Negro Family in the United States*, 1937, Chicago University Press; Melville J. Herskovits, *The Myth of the Negro Past*, 1941, New York, Harpers, pp. 145-88.

20 T. S. Simey, *Welfare & Planning in the West Indies*, 1946, London, Oxford University Press, pp. 50-1, 79; Fernando Henriques, *Family & Colour in Jamaica*, 1953, London, Eyre & Spottiswoode, p. 103.

21 T. S. Simey, 1946, *op. cit.*, pp. 53, 85-7; F. Henriques, 1953, *op. cit.*, pp. 84-119.

22 F. Henriques, 1953, *op. cit.*, pp. 103, 111.

23 T. S. Simey, 1946, *op. cit.*, pp. 82-3; F. Henriques, 1953, *op. cit.*, pp. 105-7.

24 R. T. Smith, *The Negro Family in British Guiana*, 1956, London, Routledge & Kegan Paul.

25 R. T. Smith, 1956, *op. cit.*, pp. 51-2, 94-5, 108-13, 146, 257; R. T. Smith, 'The Family in the Caribbean', in Vera Rubin (ed.), *Caribbean Studies: A Symposium*, 1957, Jamaica, Institute of Social & Economic Research, U.C.W.I., pp. 67-8; R. T. Smith, 1964, *op. cit.*, pp. 30-4.

26 R. T. Smith, 1956, *op. cit.*, pp. 97, 167-8, 178-9.

27 *Ibid.*, pp. 147, 153, but see also p. 258; R. T. Smith, 1957, *op. cit.*, pp. 71-3.

28 R. T. Smith, 1956, *op. cit.*, pp. 102, 142, 150, 223-4; *op. cit.*, 1957, p. 70.

29 R. T. Smith, 1956, *op. cit.*, pp. 108-22, 228, 257; 1957, *op. cit.*, pp. 69-71.

30 R. T. Smith, 1956, *op. cit.*, pp. 142-3, 221, 226-9; 1957, *op. cit.*, pp. 67-75.

31 R. T. Smith, 1956, *op. cit.*, pp. 51, 108-10, 184-5, 223-4.

32 R. T. Smith, 1956, *op. cit.*, pp. 181, 195-6, 210-12, 223; v. also 39-47, 191-220.

33 R. T. Smith, 1956, *op. cit.*, pp. 199-200.

34 R. T. Smith, 1959, *op. cit.*, pp. 153-9; 1964, *op. cit.*, pp. 41-3; R. T. Smith and C. Jayawardena, 1959, *op. cit.*

35 R. T. Smith, 1959, *op. cit.*, pp. 158-9; 1964, *op. cit.*, pp. 42-3.

36 R. T. Smith, 1956, *op. cit.*, pp. 45-6, 89-90, 208, 223; v. also 203-20.

37 R. T. Smith, 1956, *op. cit.*, pp. 183 f., 203-6.

38 R. T. Smith, 1956, *op. cit.*, pp. 116-19, 178-81.

39 R. T. Smith, 1956, *op. cit.*, p. 182; v. also p. 259.

40 M. G. Smith, *Stratification in Grenada*, 1965, Berkeley & Los Angeles, University of California Press, pp. 49, 158, 237; M. G. Smith, *Kinship & Community in Carriacou*, 1962, New Haven, Yale University Press, pp. 59-84; M. G. Smith, 'Community Organization in Rural Jamaica', 1956, *Social & Economic Studies*, vol. 5, no. 3, pp. 306-9; E. P. G. Seaga, 'Parent-Teacher Relations in a Jamaican Village', 1955, *Social & Economic Studies*, vol. 4, no. 3; M. G. Smith and G. J. Kruijer, 1957, *op. cit.*, pp. 34-45; Melville J. Herskovits, *Life in a Haitian Valley*, 1937, New York, Knopf, pp. 86-7, 123-35; S. Sylvain-Comhaire, 'Courtship, Marriage and Plasaj at Kenscoff, Haiti', 1958,

Social & Economic Studies, vol. 7, no. 4, pp. 227-232; Remy Bastien, 'Haitian Rural Family Organization', 1961, *Social & Economic Studies,* vol. 10, no. 4, pp. 496, 502; George E. Simpson, 'Sexual and Familial Institutions in Northern Haiti', 1942, *American Anthropologist,* vol. 44, no. 4, pp. 661-3; Melville J. and Frances S. Herskovits, *Trinidad Village,* 1947, New York, Knopf, pp. 30-7.

41 Edith Clarke, 1957, *op. cit.,* pp. 28-31, 113; Nancie L. Solien, 'Household and Family in the Caribbean', 1960, *Social & Economic Studies,* vol. 9, no. 1; M. G. Smith, *West Indian Family Structure,* 1962, Seattle, University of Washington Press, pp. 6-11, 20-3, 221-5; Sidney M. Greenfield, 'Socio-economic Factors and Family form', 1961, *Social & Economic Studies,* vol. 10, no. 1.

W. Davenport, 'The Family System in Jamaica', 1961, *Social & Economic Studies,* vol. 10, no. 4, pp. 452-4; G. E. Cumper, 'Household & Occupation in Barbados', 1961, *Social & Economic Studies,* vol. 10, no. 4, pp. 410-17; K. F. Otterbein, 'The Household Composition of the Andros Islanders', 1963, *Social & Economic Studies,* vol. 12, no. 1, pp. 78-83.

42 R. T. Smith, 1957, *op. cit.,* pp. 67-71.

43 T. S. Simey, 1946, *op. cit.,* pp. 80-8.

44 F. Henriques, 1953, *op. cit.,* pp. 85-7, 103-19.

45 Edith Clarke, 1957, *op. cit.,* p. 182.

46 *Ibid.,* p. 26.

47 *Ibid.,* p. 92.

48 *Ibid.,* p. 62.

49 *Ibid.,* p. 27.

50 *Ibid.,* p. 98; v. also p. 82.

51 *Ibid.,* p. 115.

52 M. G. Smith, 1962, *West Indian Family Structure,* pp. 198-242.

53 J. M. Stycos and K. W. Back, 1964, *op. cit.,* pp. 318-41.

54 Edith Clarke, 1957, *op. cit.,* pp. 104-5; M. G. Smith, 1962, *Kinship & Community in Carriacou* (note 40), pp. 105-16, 221-6; M. G. Smith, *Dark Puritan: The Life & Work of Norman Paul,* 1963, Jamaica, Extra-Mural Dept., U.W.I., pp. 34-5; M. G. Smith, 1962, *West Indian Family Structure* (note 41), p. 251; K. F. Otterbein, 'The Courtship & Mating System of the Andros Islanders', 1964, *Social & Economic Studies,* vol. 13, no. 2; S. M. Greenfield, 1961, *op. cit.;* W. Davenport, 1961, *op. cit.;* S. Comhaire-Sylvain, 1958, *op. cit.;* Remy Bastien, 1961, *op. cit.;* Melville J. and Frances S. Herskovits, 1947, *op. cit.,* pp. 81-6.

55 Edith Clarke, 1957, *op. cit.,* pp. 82, 121-3; O. C. Francis, 1964, *op. cit.,* Ch. 5, pp. 7-11; J. M. Stycos and K. W. Back, 1964, *op. cit.,* pp. 327-30.

56 M. G. Smith, *West Indian Family Structure,* Table 7, p. 147.

57 Edith Clarke, 1957, *op. cit.,* pp. 58-9, 103, diagram p. 72.

58 M. G. Smith, *West Indian Family Structure*, Table 7, p. 114.

59 *Ibid.*, p. 242.

60 M. G. Smith, *Kinship & Community in Carriacou* (1962), pp. 116-22, 189-94, 216-21, 311; M. G. Smith, *West Indian Family Structure* (1962), pp. 198-265.
K. W. Otterbein, 1964, *op. cit.*; R. T. Smith, 1964, *op. cit.*, pp. 41-3.

61 J. M. Stycos and K. W. Back, 1964, *op. cit.*

62 Keith F. Otterbein, 'Caribbean Family Organization: A Comparative Analysis', 1965, *American Anthropologist*, vol. 67, no. 1, pp. 66, 77.

63 *Ibid.*, p. 72, Table 1; Edith Clarke, 1957, *op. cit.*, pp. 205-6, Appendix 9; M. G. Smith, *West Indian Family Structure*, 1962, Table 22, p. 242.

64 *Ibid.*, pp. 226-7, 243.

65 Edith Clarke, 1957, *op. cit.*, p. 205.

66 M. G. Smith, *The Economy of Hausa Communities of Zaria*, 1955, London, H.M.S.O., pp. 17-26; Vernon R. Dorjohn, 'The Factor of polygyny in African demography', in W. R. Bascom and Melville J. Herskovits (eds.), *Continuity and Change in African Cultures*, 1962, Chicago University Press, pp. 87-112.

67 Keith F. Otterbein, 1965, *op. cit.*, p. 72, table 1; p. 78, footnote 2; K. F. Otterbein, 1964, *op. cit.*, pp. 282, 299; M. G. Smith, *West Indian Family Structure*, pp. 245-6; R. T. Smith, 1964, *op. cit.*, p. 42; G. W. Roberts and L. Braithwaite, 1962, *op. cit.*, pp. 207 ff.

68 W. M. Macmillan, *Warning from the West Indies*, 1938, London, Penguin Books, pp. 49-53.

69 Edith Clarke, 1957, *op. cit.*, p. 109.

70 *Ibid.*, pp. 28, 105.

71 *Ibid.*, p. 27.

72 *Ibid.*, p. 84.

73 R. T. Smith, 'Family Structure and Plantation Systems in the New World', in *Plantation Systems of the New World*, 1959, Washington D.C. (Pan American Union), pp. 148-60; G. E. Cumper, 'The Jamaican Family: Village & Estate', 1958, *Social & Economic Studies*, vol. 7, no. 1, pp. 76-108; G. E. Cumper, 'Household & Occupation in Barbados', 1961, *Social & Economic Studies*, vol. 10, no. 4, pp. 386-419; S. M. Greenfield, 1961, *op. cit.*; W. Davenport, 1961, *op. cit.*

74 G. E. Cumper, 1961, *op. cit.*, p. 414; v. R. T. Smith, 1964, *op. cit.*, pp. 37-41.

75 J. M. Stycos and K. W. Back, 1964, *op. cit.*, p. 330, and Table 133 on p. 331.

76 *Ibid.*, p. 338; v. pp. 332-9.

77 F. Henriques, 1953, *op. cit.*, p. 106.

78 *Ibid.*, p. 106; v. also pp. 86-9.

79 Edith Clarke, 1957, *op. cit.*, pp. 77-84, 104-5, 108-10, 157-8; M. G. Smith and G. J. Kruijer, 1957, *op. cit.*, pp. 52-60, 242-50; Lloyd Braithwaite, 'Sociology & Demographic Research in the British Caribbean', 1957, *Social & Economic Studies*, vol. 6, no. 4, pp. 542-5; W. Davenport, Introduction in Sidney W. Mintz and W. Davenport (eds.) 'Caribbean Social Organization', 1961, *Social & Economic Studies*, vol. 10, no. 4, pp. 383-5; W. Davenport, 'The Family System of Jamaica', 1961, *Social & Economic Studies*, vol. 10, no. 4, pp. 425-35; J. M. Stycos and K. W. Back, 1964, *op. cit.*, pp. 99, 122-3.

80 F. Henriques, 1953, *op. cit.*, p. 107; v. also p. 86.

81 Edith Clarke, 1957, *op. cit.*, p. 82.

82 *Ibid.*, p. 92.

83 *Ibid.*, p. 77.

84 See W. Davenport, 1961, 'The Family Systems of Jamaica', *Social & Economic Studies*, vol. 10, no. 4, pp. 425-35, for a particularly sensitive presentation of these issues and the relevant data.

85 Edith Clarke, 1957, *op. cit.*, p. 30.

86 *Ibid.*, pp. 174-7.

87 Judith Blake, 'Family Instability and Reproductive Behavior in Jamaica', *Current Research in Human Fertility*, 1955, New York, Milbank Memorial Fund; Judith Blake, *Family Structure in Jamaica: The Social Context of Reproduction*, 1961, Glencoe, Ill., The Free Press.

88 L. Braithwaite, 1957, *op. cit.*, pp. 541-51; R. T. Smith, Review of J. Blake, 'Family Structure in Jamaica', 1963, *American Anthropologist*, vol. 65, no. 1, pp. 158-61; Hyman Rodman, 'On Understanding Lower Class Behaviour', 1959, *Social & Economic Studies*, vol. 8, no. 4, pp. 441-50; see also Judith Blake, 'A Reply to Mr Braithwaite', 1958, *Social & Economic Studies*, vol. 7, no. 4, pp. 234-7.

89 Judith Blake, 1961, *op. cit.*, pp. 110-11, 133, 170-1, 180.

90 Lloyd Braithwaite, 1957, *op. cit.*, pp. 541-5; v. also H. Rodman, 1959, *op. cit.*, pp. 444-9.

91 Judith Blake, 1961, *op. cit.*, pp. 51-2, 56-7, 76-109, 135, 146.

92 *Ibid.*, pp. 134-5, 142-3, 146-8, 160, 168.

93 *Ibid.*, pp. 134-5, 146-69.

94 *Ibid.*, on unions, v. pp. 14 footnote, 50-1, 135; on median and actual ideal ages of marriage and first intercourse, v. pp. 45-7, 50-1, 135.

95 J. M. Stycos and K. W. Back, 1964, *op. cit.*, pp. 110, 134-7, 145-6.

96 *Ibid.*, pp. 345-9.

97 Judith Blake, 1961, *op. cit.*, pp. 19, 110-17, 133, 170-2.

98 William J. Goode, 'Illegitimacy in Caribbean Social Structure', 1960, *American Sociological Review*, vol. 25, no. 1, pp. 21-30.

99 Hyman Rodman, 1959, *op. cit.*

100 Dept. of Statistics, Jamaica, *Population Census, 1960. Some Notes on the Union Status, Marital Status and Number of Children of the Female Population of Jamaica.* Jamaica, pp. 7-11.

101 Edith Clarke, 1957, *op. cit.*, p. 30; Lloyd Braithwaite, 1957, *op. cit.*, p. 542; M. G. Smith and G. J. Kruijer, 1957, *op. cit.*, p. 54; M. G. Smith, 1962, *Kinship & Community in Carriacou*, p. 93; v. also Bronislaw Malinowski, 1962, *Sex, Culture & Myth*, New York, Harcourt Brace & World, p. 63.

102 Edith Clarke, 1957, *op. cit.*, pp. 29-30, 73-7, 108-9.

CHAPTER 1

The Background

———

I

THE year 1938 may well come to be recognized by historians as marking the beginning of a new phase in the social and political development of Jamaica, if not of the West Indies as a whole. Inevitably the emergence in Jamaica, in that year, of a labour movement, aggressively expressing the needs of the working class, and the beginnings of Trade Union organization, meant the direction as never before of public interest to problems of work and wages, unemployment and poverty.

Alongside the political activity there were new and important developments in the voluntary social services. In particular, the formation in 1936 of Jamaica Welfare Limited under the dynamic leadership of Mr Manley marked the beginning of a new approach to welfare work with the emphasis on an improvement in the standard of living of the working classes through self-help. (1)

Inevitably the inquiries which were set on foot attracted attention to wider aspects of the organization of society and particularly to the structure of the family. In this respect it was clear that both ideals of behaviour and actual practice varied widely between different social classes: the principles which operated in the upper and middle classes were not even accepted as ideals in peasant and working class society.

Popular interest concentrated mainly on two closely related aspects of family organization: the fact that among the poorer

Jamaicans concubinage was a substitute for marriage, and the high rate of illegitimacy. It was also very widely believed that a rate of population increase which was regarded with alarm was directly related to sexual promiscuity, parental irresponsibility and the looseness of conjugal ties.

There followed a dangerous, because sterile, approach of seeking to explain dissident elements in contemporary social institutions in one of two ways: either by reference to the historical facts of slavery or in terms of both the cultures which have contributed to Jamaica's history—the European and the African. Thus the 'maternal' family was said to be characteristic of Jamaican peasants either because West African societies were supposed to have been matriarchal, or because during the period of slavery Negro children were wholly dependent on their mothers; the existence of concubinage as a socially recognized relationship was accounted for sometimes as a local version or adaptation of African polygamy and sometimes as a consequence of prohibition or discouragement of marriage between slaves. To many of those who were giving sincere and anxious thought to the problems of the family in Jamaica, it appeared simply as the European family 'gone wrong' owing to a series of historical events, the chief of which was slavery.

It is true that the principal features of slavery had the effect, intentionally or unintentionally, of obliterating African institutions and that at a later period there developed a coloured middle class which not only adopted European values but was highly sensitive to any reminder of African antecedents. It was largely from this class there came criticism of comparative studies which aimed at isolating the different cultural strains either in institutions, myth or folklore. To many, the different class patterns appeared as the result of a choice between two cultural traditions: the European, defined in terms of Christian monogamy and stress on the father role, and the 'African', defined in terms of the maternal family, concubinage, illegitimacy, etc.

Even if we reject those theories which explain contemporary institutions in terms of elements derived from parent cultures, we must take into account those historical events which have clearly influenced family life in Jamaica.

There was, under slavery, no room for the family as a parent-child group in a home; still less for the development of those stable relationships among a wider circle of kin such as can be maintained only if kinsmen live in permanent contact or are able to travel freely and visit one another. The residential unit in the plantation system was formed by the mother and her children with the responsibility for their maintenance resting with the slave-owner. The father's place in the family was never secure. He had no externally sanctioned authority over it and could at any time be physically removed from it. His role might, indeed, end with procreation. Occasionally a father was able to undertake responsibility for his family to the extent of supplying them with food from land which he cultivated but he was only able to acquire such land through the benevolence of his owner. In general, he was not the source of protection and provision for mother and children. This might come directly from some other man or from the system itself which, while a woman was of child-bearing age, secured to her and her children at least their minimum material necessities. It is against this background of the weakness of the father role in the system of family relationships that those of mother and grandmother assume particular importance. (2)

It would be a mistake, however, to stop here in our analysis. The fact of Emancipation did not in itself create a set of conditions, social or economic, in which the freed Negro could at once assume the role of father and husband in the new society. While, at Emancipation, the slave owners were compensated for loss of property by the British Government, so far as the slaves were concerned the assumption apparently was that they should remain as wage-labourers on the estates to which they had been attached. The British Government in the nineteenth century was not concerned to interfere in the social and economic adjustments created by the new situation. The local administration, representing the planters as it did, was still less prepared to introduce measures which, by giving the newly created peasantry an alternative to wage labour, would have threatened to deplete their labour supply.

Nevertheless conditions in Jamaica differed in an important aspect from those in the Southern States after Emancipation, where the ex-slaves were still tied inevitably to the old plantations and to wage labour at rates fixed and conditions prescribed by their previous owners. (3) In Jamaica they had not only the right to move but there was somewhere to which they could move and start a new life. Many trekked to the 'back lands' of the plantations, unsuitable for cultivation and unused by the planters, others established themselves as squatters on the Crown lands and in the forest reserves. Others gradually bought small holdings helped by the early Land Settlement Schemes of the Christian missions. Others, still, received grants of land from their ex-owners to own in perpetuity. The concept of family land and associated theories of inalienability and the right of 'all the family' to inherit are fully explained in a later chapter. But from the period following Emancipation, because it was felt to give the greatest freedom from white domination, a special value came to be attached to 'owned' as distinct from rented land. It became one, if not the most important, indication of improved, higher status.

There thus developed an association of certain ways of life and of earning a livelihood with status and class structure: as also with the patterns of behaviour accepted within the higher class. For example 'ownership' of land and marriage came to be associated with the highest class status, and manual labour or working for wages as 'a common labourer' with the lowest.

As far as the family was concerned, Emancipation, by making it possible for a man to own land and sell his produce, or offer his labour where he pleased, created conditions in which he could assume the role of father and husband without the threat of external interference in these relationships. Family patterns were, however, already prescribed by status and class structure. The slave-owners, in opposing the teaching of the Christian Missionaries on marriage, as inappropriate for the slaves, were in fact primarily concerned with the possible effect of this on their right of free disposition of their chattels. But they also appeared to be arguing that Christian monogamy was the prerogative of the white man, and associated with the caste structure. But, in fact, the white man's monogamy almost invariably had concubinage as its concomitant. White planters often accepted responsibility for their children by negro mistresses. Not only were the status and material conditions of the mother better in these cases, but the children often had the advantage of a better education than would otherwise have been available locally for them. They moved up in the social structure, becoming small landowners or entering one or other of the professions.

Thus was created a coloured middle class which Lord Olivier, writing in 1907, saw as the liaison between the two races through which cultural homogeneity would eventually be achieved. (4) The emerging coloured middle class, from the outset, aligned itself with the white upper class, adopted its systems of values, both in regard to occupation and marriage as opposed to concubinage, and stood aloof from the peasantry and the landless field-labourers, who, in their turn, developed both suspicion and distrust of the 'brown man', with his superior advantages. It was not until the turn of the century that the mutual resistances broke down sufficiently for this middle-class to emerge and be accepted by the workers as leaders, both in the political and Trade Union fields.

So far as the family is concerned there are still profound class differences in form, in household structure, in the basis of the union in marriage or concubinage and in the parental roles. And it is our thesis that these differences are not explicable either by reference to the different inherited cultural patterns or solely by the historical facts of slavery.

The important point for an understanding of the contemporary situation is that conditions which make it impossible for men to perform the roles of father and husband as these roles are defined in the society to which they belong, *persist in present-day Jamaica* and it is in conditions as we find them today that we shall most profitably look for the explanation of the 'unstable' features of family life to which such prominence is being given.

For this reason we set ourselves the task of investigating the different types of family structure in Jamaica. Finally, we made it our task to describe the actual relationships covered by the terms 'marriage' and 'concubinage', both between the couple and with reference to the children born to them.

We assumed the existence of the family as a social group: in other words we assumed that children were born and nurtured in some form of social institution. We did not, that is, expect to find that mating was truly casual and unorganized or that there was no parental responsibility—as Margaret Mead has put it, that there was 'no set of permanent arrangements by which males assist females in caring for children while they are young'; though if this should prove to be the case, we should consider that such a unique situation would all the more merit study. (5)

II

The three communities which form the basis of my research, Sugartown, Mocca and Orange Grove, show important differences. The first is in regard to size. Our records show the number of households in Mocca and Orange Grove to have been approximately the same—119 and 117 respectively—whereas we have 433 family records for Sugartown without taking into account the interviews recorded with 170 men and women who arrived during the early part of our stay seeking work, the majority of whom had no fixed place of abode, and 315 who came in daily from the neighbourhood villages to their jobs. The total population for the three Centres is shown in Appendix 2 to be: Sugartown 1,191, Orange Grove 677, and Mocca 412.

Sugartown, unlike the other two, was a township imposed upon a post-Emancipation settlement where the families lived upon family land and practised subsistence farming. The urbanization began in the beginning of the century with the turn over from banana and coconut production back again, as in the old days, to sugar. Present-day Sugartown centres about the factory, surrounded by thousands of acres of cane. Along the main road are the shops. The few two-story wooden houses are the Chinese grocery and rum shops, where the family live on the upper floor. Small one-, or at most two-, roomed shops are owned or rented by the local butcher, cake-maker, shoemaker, bicycle repairer and the like. On the pavement outside the grocery shops, the women higglers spread their trays of fruit and vegetables for sale. On two or three of these small shops is the red and white striped barber's 'pole', although one of the barbers plied his trade in the open under a large tree. Behind this main road run narrow footpaths leading into the family holdings which are now congeries of one or two-roomed thatched huts with here and there an old wooden house, in the last state of disrepair, inherited from the 'old people'.

There is a middle-class section where housing conditions are better, situated on a steep lane on one side of the village and within the estate compound the company houses for junior and senior staff. On the side of the main street facing the factory are the estate barracks; long wooden ranges divided into single rooms with outside kitchens, intended by the Company only for seasonal male workers, but in our time, owing to the housing shortage, occupied in fact by couples, sometimes by whole families, sometimes by two men and one woman. The management, it is only fair to say, were anything but complacent about these conditions. Some years previously they had offered ninety acres of land to the Government for a housing scheme and the use of their bulldozers to clear the sites, but up to the time we were there their gift had not yet been accepted. When it eventually was, the offer of the bulldozers was refused because, it was said, of the necessity to provide relief work, with the result that the cost of development put the houses beyond the means of many of the people who had applied for them. None of this, however, happened while we were there and over-crowding in the one- and two-roomed wattle-and-thatched shacks made any sort of decent home life within them impossible for the majority of the population. The family in Sugartown lived in the family 'yards', ate in the tiny smoke-blackened wattle kitchens, and drew water for all domestic purposes from the Company stand-pipe outside the barracks in the main street. Babies and small children were washed in pans in the yard; adults and the older children bathed in the river, where, also, the women did their laundry.

The special pattern of society in Sugartown derives from conditions of work in the sugar industry. It requires a large labour force for some seven months and only limited numbers for the rest of the year. There is no difficulty in getting the additional labour required owing to the extent of unemployment and much larger numbers than can be absorbed begin to pour into Sugartown from the beginning of 'crop' as the busy season is called, both from the neighbouring villages and from other parts of the Island. The incoming population creates, as it were, a recurrent social revolution transforming the ordinary routine and rhythm of life. The housing shortage is aggravated and the newcomers create changes in the constitution of households and both set up new, and alter existing, conjugal relations. Earnings fluctuate from a relatively high level in the crop season to bare subsistence level, or below it, in the *tempo moto* (slow time) as the slack period is graphically described.

The population of Sugartown is too large, too mixed and too mobile for the development of any strong community sense. What associations there are tend to be sectional and do not provide a relational system which involves continuous mutual co-operation and interdependence. The largest and most influential organization is the Trade Union, but it is an organization of sugar-labourers, and mainly confined to men. Other sectional associations are the Cane Farmers' Association and the Rice Growers' Association. The dances held occasionally on the Masquerade Ground bring another section of the community together—mainly the younger folk. The largest non-sectional gathering while we were there was on the occasion of the death of a prominent citizen. During the Nine Nights ceremonies which followed the funeral, a large and diverse section of the community participated at one time or another in the feasting and singing. But there is nothing in Sugartown to compare with the kinship solidarity of

Mocca, or the opportunities which occur regularly in Orange Grove for the entire group, men, women and even children to meet together and act as a corporate whole.

In Mocca, where there is neither a source of employment nor land for mixed farming, there is no mobility of population. No one comes into the village; only a few of the younger folk move out. The community is historically as old as the original village of Sugartown on which the estate pattern has been imposed. Houses, in Mocca, are built on family land and family and kindred cling together, united in the struggle to find a means of livelihood in a hostile environment where the process of mechanization and changing industrial conditions have passed them by.

Although the village is only ten miles by road from Sugartown its men do not seek employment in the factory or canefields during crop, and in fact we found few contacts between the two Centres.

The Mocca folk are agriculturalists at heart. They produce what foodstuffs they can on the family land on which their houses are built. Here, also, they keep their small stock—pigs, goats and chickens. A few own cattle which they graze on the roadsides or run surreptiously on the back-lands of adjoining properties. As many as can rent 'grounds' on which they grow foodstuffs for the local markets and for home consumption. These 'grounds' may be, and in fact generally are, situated many miles away from Mocca and much time is wasted in travelling to and from them. They are usually visited at regular intervals, for planting, bushing and weeding, and then at the reaping period. Inevitably, the culti-vator suffers from praedeal thieves and invariably the crops suffer from lack of regular care. Tenancy is on a short-term basis. They have no training in any trade; the only work on the sugar estate for which they would be qualified would be as cane-cutters and this does not attract them. Their poverty is extreme and varies little with the seasons. By far the majority of the homes are one- or two-roomed wattle-and-thatched houses, which do not keep out the rain and are expensive to maintain. The diet consists almost entirely of home-grown starchy foods seasoned with salt-fish bought at the shop. The principal families are all connected by marriage or concubinage and the village is tiny enough for the members to be acutely aware of each other's affairs. Most of the inhabitants trace their ancestry back to the founders of the village. One or two people who have come in since then are still called 'strangers' (the local term is 'bluefoot') although they have lived there most of their lives.

One's first glimpse of Orange Grove is a red dirt roadway running through a fertile valley of farms with neat citrus groves and solid, well-built houses, often with an upper story, set among flower and vegetable gardens. Some of the farmers own horses, practically everyone has at least one cow, donkey, goat or other small stock. Eggs are sold through a co-operative marketing organization, and milk supplied to the Condensary. They are subject to the vicissitudes of farmers everywhere; but their mixed farming is competent, their orange groves well-cared, the soil is fertile, the climate healthy and temperate, and they have a market at satisfactory prices for whatever they produce. Levels of income are relatively high and there are no violent fluctuations as in Sugartown. This Centre is larger than Mocca, but the community sense is highly developed and there are recurrent occasions, such as meetings of the Crop Associations, when the community can exchange views on matters which concern them all. It was interesting to note that at the monthly meetings of the various organizations, in the Community Hall, the programme always included songs and recitations by the young people so that even the children in the village participated.

Land has a particular meaning for the people of Orange Grove since it is the sole means of livelihood for everyone and the whole life of the farmers, their wives and children are bound up with it.

To summarize, in Sugartown there are fluctuations between relatively high earnings and bare subsistence living, in Orange Grove there is a more even and relatively high level of economy, and in Mocca there is consistent and extreme poverty. These are the general economic backgrounds of the three Centres.

It is important to have these differences between the Centres in mind because they are obviously influential when we come to consider the forms of conjugal union and kinship roles. For example we shall later be showing that there are certain pre-requisites which have to be fulfilled before marriage can be considered. A man should, in the ideal at any rate, be able to offer a wife, as distinct from a concubine, an assured social position. He should, if a wage earner, be in a position to buy his own house and land on which they can make a permanent home or have inherited land or house, and be regularly employed, even if this does not in fact imply relatively higher actual earnings.

In Orange Grove the possibility of fulfilling these requirements exists. It is probable that only the better off farmers in Orange Grove derive as high an income from their farming as do the best paid sugar-workers. But their income is more evenly distributed over the year; and is demonstrably the result of the amount of foresight, energy and intelligence they themselves put into their work. They are sure of a market for whatever they produce and they have the land they need. Their ambition is to improve their farms and add to their stock; emulate their neighbours in the better furnishing of their homes and provide for the future of their children.

These are all incentives to saving. In Sugartown the labourer feels that he is at the mercy of forces over which he has no control; the demand for his labour is always less than the manpower available. The principal incentive to thrift—the possibility of buying house or land—is lacking. There is no land to buy. The period of crop and high wages is like a boom following an acute depression, and it has all the instability of a boom. Part of the new wages go to pay off debts accumulated during the *tempo moto*, part in replenishment of a depleted wardrobe, and much of the rest is dissipated in gambling or drinking.

For this reason alone, it is not surprising that Orange Grove has the most stable form of family life and highest marriage rate in any of the Centres. But there is also the fact that, if we may so phrase it, marriage induces marriage. In Orange Grove it is part of the class structure and is reinforced with strong social sanctions which do not exist in either of the other two communities. Concubinage in Orange Grove is practised by the poorer families, or those of the younger folk who have broken away from strict parental control, but it is regarded with disfavour by the respectable farmers and their wives. Where an irregular relationship results in pregnancy marriage generally takes place.

Where there are not the clear-cut class distinctions, such as we find in Orange Grove, to reinforce the legal or religious basis and outlaw the irregular union, and where the method of earning a living and the conditions of employment do not in general allow of the realization of the ideal which is associated in people's minds with the institution of marriage, the ratio is much lower. Whereas in Orange Grove these unions represent a falling away from the accepted social standards, and can be co-related with other social and economic factors, there is no such observable distinction in the other two Centres. In Sugartown and Mocca there is, in fact, no apparent real association of marriage or concubinage with economic status or class structure.

III

The anthropologist in search of the family *sees* first the house, surrounded by other houses in yards on family land: separated by barbed wire fences, along village streets or country roads; appearing as a thatched roof in the distance, emerging between trees of breadfruit, ackee or mango on the edge of a yam field; or as a white painted wooden cottage behind regular lines of orange trees with their green and yellow fruit. Within that house, be it hut or cottage, is contained, for some time of the day or night, part of the group which he is about to study.

But what part of it? Will he find the majority of these households to contain parents and their children; or mothers only with their daughters and their daughters' children; or a man and woman with some only of their offspring? Or, instead, will he find a heterogeneous collection of kin, brought together by some new pattern of association, based on a system of relationships fundamentally different from that found in other societies elsewhere?

Before we can answer these questions it is necessary to be quite clear as to the meaning of the terms we shall be using to describe different types of relationship, since it is largely the loose use of language which is responsible for the existing confusion and false assumptions on the subject of family relations in Jamaica.

The terms to be defined fall into three categories: those which describe types of union, those which describe types of grouping based on kinship, and those which describe types of grouping based on residence.

It is particularly in regard to the first that language is popularly used in a misleading way. The meaning of *marriage* is clear: it is a conjugal and domestic union formally entered into in the manner prescribed by the law and approved by the religious authorities, and involving the implicit or explicit recognition by the parties of duties towards each other and towards their children. Where only one form of conjugal union has the sanction of law and religion, all others are correctly described as *irregular*. But these are of many different kinds and it is of the greatest importance to be able to discriminate between them.

In popular discussion, and in some published work, terms like concubinage, common-law marriage, prostitution, promiscuity and polygamy are applied, without distinction, to any type of irregular union. For our purpose these terms need to be either clearly defined and differentiated or else abandoned.

We may deal first with the two terms which are sometimes used to describe irregular unions in Jamaica but which do not correctly describe any of the unions which we have observed. The first is *common-law marriage*. This term is used without definition in the 1943 Census of Jamaica and also by Henriques, who defines it as 'the union of a man with a woman which lasts indefinitely without the full sanction of law', and adds that the distinction between Christian marriage and common-law marriage is sociologically useless. (6) Common-law marriage is a legal term describing a type of union which at one time was recognized by the law as marriage although it had been entered upon without all the formalities which the law prescribes. It is therefore not appropriate to apply it to unions which are clearly distinguishable from marriage, both by the partners and by the society at large, and, in my experience, it is never used of any type of union by the Jamaicans who are themselves participants in these forms of union.

Polygamy, the second term, is the legal marriage of a man to more than one wife at the same time. Henriques' definition of polygamy as 'a man or woman co-habitating with more than one of the opposite sex' would not be accepted by anthropologists in general. (7) If standard usage is followed, polygamy can only exist where the law recognizes it.

Of the terms which can appropriately be applied in Jamaican conditions, we define *concubinage* as the conjugal union in co-habitation of a man and woman without legal and religious sanction. *Casual mating* is a sexual congress without co-habitation or any intention to form a permanent relationship. *Promiscuity* is indiscriminate casual mating. *Prostitution* is the practice of promiscuity for payment.

Groupings based on kinship can be divided into the *simple family*, consisting of parents and children, and the *extended family*, which includes, in addition, kin of a higher or lower generation.

In regard to legitimacy: the law recognizes as *legitimate* only children born in wedlock; but in the case of couples living in concubinage it is necessary to distinguish between children of the union and other children of either partner. We have used the terms *socially legitimate* of the former and *outside* of the latter.

In differentiating between residential groupings, or household types, we may distinguish, first, *simple family households* and *extended family households*. *Consanguineous* households include (a) *denuded family* households in which there is only one parent and which may be of either the simple or extended type, and (b) *sibling households* in which adult brothers and sisters live under one roof. Finally there is the *single person* household and households of unrelated men living together or women sharing a room, which are common only in Sugartown. (8)

This was, of course, a broad classification. For it to be useful

in the later stages of our inquiry, into the behaviour patterns
between members of the household and the kin outside the household, we had to make a number of distinctions within the groups.
For example, in *simple family households* we distinguished between
couples with children of their own and those which included *outside* children of either the man or the woman, or both. By this
means we were able to show, for example, that outside children in
the home were more likely to be those of the woman than of the
man; that they were most likely to be included where the current
union was childless and where that union was based on concubinage rather than marriage.

In the preceding pages we have placed particular emphasis on
the importance of the type of land tenure and use as a criterion in
the selection of our Centres. In addition to the reasons already
given it may be said that ownership, and the type of ownership,
of land has an effect also on the constitution and stability of the
household group and on the behaviour pattern between husband
and wife or concubines. Before proceeding to our analysis of
family relationships, therefore, it is proposed to attempt to discover the underlying systems of beliefs and practices in regard to
land and to follow this by an account of the legal and social
aspects of the two forms of conjugal union—marriage and concubinage.

FOOTNOTES TO CHAPTER I

1 For a history of Jamaica Welfare Limited (now the Jamaica Social Welfare Commission) see *Social Welfare Work in Jamaica* by Roger Marier.
2 See Franklin Frazier, *The Negro Family*, and Professor T. S. Simey, *Welfare and Planning in the West Indies*, 1946, pp. 79-80.
3 See Frazier, ibid.
4 Olivier, *White Capital and Coloured Labour*.
5 Margaret Mead, *Male and Female*, 1946, p. 188.
6 F. M. Henriques, *Family and Colour in Jamaica*, 1953, pp. 84, 106.
7 Henriques. Op cit., p. 84.
8 For the distribution of these types in the Centres and a detailed analysis of their structure see Chap. 5 and Appendices.

CHAPTER 2

Land Tenure

———

THERE has never been, since Emancipation, nor is there now, any legal discrimination in Jamaica on the basis of race or colour in regard to ownership of land—nor indeed in respect of any other right of citizenship. So far as land is concerned there is not, nor ever has been, any territorial segregation of black or coloured from white. Even before Emancipation land was owned by slaves who had been given or bought their freedom and, under the Consolidated Slave Acts, legal sanction was given for slaves in respect of usufructuary rights in garden land, and time to work in these gardens. They had the right to keep stock and to sell the produce of their gardens at market rates to their masters. (9) We must distinguish between a colour-bar, which legalizes inequality and is ultimately based on the conception of 'higher' and 'lower' races and colour prejudice, and class distinction bound up with a caste system and arising from the social organization in time of slavery. It would be erroneous to conclude that colour and racial prejudice cannot exist within a free society or to minimize its effect in the West Indies on the relationships between groups in the community. What is important is that the expression of prejudice, where there is equality before the law, is controllable. Thus the absence of differential legislation in Jamaica has had far-reaching effects on the social development of the community and has left the way open for an evolutionary progress towards homogeneity.

After annexation by the British all land became the property of the Crown and was granted by Royal Patents to English colonists subject to the payment of Quit Rents. Failure to pay the Quit Rents resulted in forfeiture and shortly before Emancipation 70,000 acres had reverted to the Crown. By 1838 out of 3,404,359 acres of Patented land, 815,303 were in arrears for Quit Rent and taxes. Some of this land was resold to small settlers but after 1838 the practice of forfeiting land for non-payment of taxes was dropped as unprofitable. The land in question was invariably 'back lands' running up from the plantations to the mountainous interior of the Cockpit Country. Much of it had been irregularly squatted on and rents were collected or not collected as circumstances might determine. (10)

In addition to these lands and to privately owned land which might be bought or rented there remained the Crown land—the land which had either never been granted out in Letters Patent or which had been forfeited to the Crown for non-payment of rents and taxes. The first category consisted mainly of the central ridge running east-west across the Island and known in the west as the Cockpit Country, rising in the east in the Blue Mountains to a height of 7,500 ft. This was suitable only as a forest reserve and had never been alienated. On these lands some of those who had not money to buy established themselves as squatters. Some of the forfeited land was marginal and even in slavery times had been used for subsistence cropping.

While, therefore, at Emancipation no land was set aside for the creation of an independent small farmers' community there were three categories of land available on which, theoretically, a peasantry might establish itself: the forfeited lands which might be purchased from the Crown, and which attracted many of the most independent and ambitious of the freed slaves who had saved money, the marginal lands which might be purchased or leased from the estate owners by wage earners on the property; and the mountainous forest reserves which might be squatted on. (11)

There was thus a far-reaching difference in the situation at Emancipation of the slaves in Jamaica as compared with those in the Southern States of America, where, according to Frazier, 'the masses of Negroes were doomed to continue their dependence upon the white landlord; while a minority through their thrift and self denial gradually acquired title to relatively small holdings in a region dominated by the plantation system and cotton culture'. In Jamaica they did not remain wholly dependent upon their ex-masters, either for wage labour or for an alternative means of livelihood. In this situation a special social value came to be attached to the ownership of land. It acquired importance as a symbol of freedom and independence. 'For the vast majority [of emancipated Negroes] who were concerned with the everyday problem of making a living, land ownership was of paramount importance. Their desire to acquire land and their expectation that the Government would provide them with "forty acres and a mule" has generally been derided as a naïve and childish hope. On the contrary, their hopes concerning land ownership indicated that they had sound ideas concerning the real meaning of freedom.' (12)

Olivier quotes a statement in the British Parliament by one of the Commissioners who inquired into the Morant Bay outbreak of 1866 that 'there was a general idea among the black population that all the "back lands", as they were called, had been originally the property of the Queen, and that the Queen, by some grant which had been concealed from them by the manoeuvres of the white population, had made these back lands over to the Negroes. . . . There persisted at the back of the Negroes' minds, and very distinctly among those who had themselves come from Africa, the essentially sound fundamental axiom of African law, that land belongs to the King (or Chief) as trustee for his people, that whatever degree of private property in land may become established by custom and law such rights apply to beneficial occupation only, and that the rest of the land is to be held available for, and will be assigned by, the King to families for whose support unoccupied land is required. That principle had, of course, also been the foundation of English law, long overlaid by Parliamentary usurpations on the part of the landlord class, and by the ingenuities of their lawyers. But the principle had actually been maintained in the original settlement of Jamaica and reinforced by the local legislation making effectual and beneficial occupation as well as the payment of quit-rent a condition of the retention of proprietary rights in the land'. (13)

The trek to take up lands for cultivation wherever available and to establish a community of independent cultivators threatened to disrupt the economy of the Island, built up as it was on the sugar industry. The peak demand for labour on a sugar estate coincides with the two seasonal planting periods. The planters found their labour supply diminished at the precise moment when it was most needed.

'In January 1836, the Colonial Office advised that to protect the planters in respect of the supply of labour, facilities for obtaining land by the people when emancipated be diminished, that the occupation of Crown lands by persons having no title be prevented and that a price be fixed on such lands as to place them out of the reach of persons without capital. . . . The object is not to force the cultivation of the present staples by depriving the Negro of every other resource for subsistence but merely to condense and keep together the population in such manner that it may always contain a due proportion of labour.' (14)

Although the right to acquire land could not be impeached, steps were taken to control encroachment on unoccupied land— not, at that time, with a view to preventing misuse of land, so much as to protect property and ensure a fluid labour supply for the estates. (15)

There is evidence to show (not least of all in our own research in the field in all our Centres) that individual planters made grants of land to their ex-slaves. Such grants were the origin of the category of 'family land'.

In addition, the practice, begun in slavery, of granting back lands on the estates either free, or at a peppercorn rental, for subsistence farming to employees, continues to the present day. Thus in Sugartown a total of 1,200 acres were made available by the management (theoretically only to its employees) at a peppercorn rental of a shilling per acre per annum. Of this, 600 acres of back lands were taken up by small cane farmers who were registered to deliver their canes to the factory and the rest given out for sub-sistence farming. The practice began, and continues, as an attempt to palliate the peculiar socio-economic problem of the sugar indus-try—namely, that the bulk of its labour force is seasonal and can be employed for only five to seven months of the year. Labourers were also permitted to build their houses on estate lands and allowed to cut timber and thatch for the purpose. In cases of ab-sentee proprietors, where there was often inadequate local super-vision, the peasants settled on the back lands of estates and estab-lished squatters' rights.

It is clear from the evidence, however, that not only was there no official programme for settling the people on available land but that, on the contrary, the policy of the Government was primarily directed to ensuring a plentiful supply of labour for the sugar plantations. In this way the rigid black-white class structure of slavery was carried over into Emancipation. (16) That this class structure has not, in the subsequent history of the Island, devel-oped on racial or colour lines is due to the fact that, in spite of coercive measures, there was never legal sanction for discrimina-tory practices between racial groups in the population. No one was excluded from owning, inheriting or transmitting property to their descendants and the laws for acquiring or alienating land based on the English Common Law were applicable to all people in the Island.

Moreover, although there was no official policy of land settle-ment, the Christian Missions continued after Emancipation to do what they could to improve the living conditions of the Negro population, in the matter of land as well as education. The earliest land-settlements in Jamaica were the work of these missions and in particular of the Baptist Churches. An example quoted by Lord Olivier was John Clark's settlement of twenty or more villages in St Ann including fifteen to sixteen hundred families. 'This system of forming independent villages has been extensively carried out in all parts of the island; . . . until at least two-thirds of the whole population possess their own little properties.' (17)

II

The British Colonists, who received grants of land by Letters Patent from the Crown after annexation of the Island, were given Common Law Titles by the Crown. Although there was not compulsory registration of these titles in Jamaica, I am informed that most were subsequently recorded at the record office. These properties were not surveyed, as is now a pre-requisite to acquiring a Registered Title. (18)

In the absence of much more intensive historical research than is attempted here, it is not possible to state what happened in the case of the small parcels of land which were bought by the slaves prior to and after Emancipation. It is known that such transfers took place, and there is evidence in our work in Jamaica that at least some slave-owners made free grants of land to their slaves. If these pieces of land were formally conveyed, and if registered or Common Law Titles were obtained, it should be possible to trace these transactions in the archives at Spanish Town and the figures would give an indication of the extent of early peasant settlement. In our own fieldwork we never came across any such documents although some of the land in our 'old districts' had been inherited by the present occupiers from forbears who received it as a grant at the beginning of the nineteenth century. Considering the importance attached to any official 'paper' and the way such 'proofs' of ownership are treasured these would undoubtedly have been shown us had they survived. (19) It is probable that in most of these original purchases or free grants, there was a Conveyance from the landowner. There is evidence, however, that a good deal of 'squatting' took place, not only on the back lands of properties, but also on the Crown lands in the pockets of soil in the Cockpit Country. With the absence of adequate patrolling of the Crown forest reserves, these 'free tenants' were left unmolested for years and in some cases established squatters' rights which could be upheld under the terms of the Statute of Limitations. (20) Where a man has neither a Title nor a

Conveyance for his land he may, under this Statute, establish ownership by proving undisputed possession for a minimum of twelve years.

As will be seen from the account which follows, very few of the holdings 'owned' or occupied by the peasants were more than a few acres in extent and many more are measured in 'squares'. The value of the land in terms of money (apart from its social value) is small. The cost of taking out a Registered Title which entails paying for a survey and employing a lawyer, is prohibitive in the majority of these cases.

According to the Law of Inheritance, in the case of Intestacy the eldest legitimate son is the legal heir to all property. Illegitimate children are not recognized as having any legal rights. (21) Failing the establishment of a legitimate heir, the land is forfeit to the Crown and is administered or disposed of by the Administrator General.

There is a considerable body of current belief in our community which does not easily adapt itself to this legal framework. We found, for instance, that three documents are popularly believed to establish proof of ownership: (i) *a Receipt* from the vendor when the land is purchased, stating the amount paid and the area, and, in some cases, setting out the natural boundaries; (ii) *a Tax Receipt* in the name of the man or woman for payment of the Land Tax, and (iii) *a Will*, bequeathing the land to a particular member of the family.

The only real value or use of the first two of these documents in a Court of Law would be as evidence of possession. A Will indicates nothing more than the testamentary desire of the previous owner and does not, as is popularly believed, *per se* establish anything. But, if proved, it would be a good source of title. (22)

This may not seem very important; few laymen in any country fully understand the intricacies of their own legal system. But English Common Law, based on precedents, in so far as it relates to land tenure (which is what we are here concerned with) grew out of the native theory and practice over generations of evolutionary experience in Britain. In its translation to Jamaica, it was a comprehensible system to the English settlers. Once, however, peasants began to buy and use land, another layer of experience, and a different set of traditional beliefs in regard to land, handed down from parent to child, began to appear in the practice of inheritance and transmission of land, and, among the peasantry where it operated, to give a specific (and as we shall show, a different) meaning to such terms as 'ownership', 'right', 'claim', 'use', which do not easily fit into the pattern of English experience as expressed in the legal code.

Thus we found that a distinction exists in the meaning of the word 'ownership' when applied to land which a man acquires by purchase (*bought land*) and land which he, generally together with other members of his family, inherits (*family land*). There is also another distinction within this category of inherited land. Thus not *all* inherited land is '*family land*', though there appears to be a tendency so far as the controls on transmission and alienation are affected, for it to become so in the second and third generation.

Again, in contradistinction to the law which recognizes the eldest son as the rightful heir where there is no testamentary disposition, we found the principle of joint inheritance by 'all the children' generally recognized and it is by no means apparent that any discrimination is practised against illegitimate children. But the peasant theory of land tenure, based on African principles, came into conflict with English Law chiefly in the matter of joint inheritance and of what are regarded as the equal *rights* of all the family where family land is concerned, and its corollary that family land is not 'owned' by any one member of the family, but belongs to all the family and, secondly, in the traditional proscription on the alienation of family land. (23)

Moreover, temporary non-exercise of a claim on family land does not, in the traditional system, preclude a subsequent exercise of that right. For example, a brother may return to the family land, occupied by his other brothers and sisters, after years of residence elsewhere and it would still be recognized by his family that he had the right 'if he had the need', to erect his house on the land and share in the crops of any fruit trees planted by his forbears.

It is admittedly a confused situation, and not always clear in individual cases, but the evidence of a consistent system and of its social sanction is, I think, irrefutable. The position is not made happier by the fact that among the younger generation one member of the family may attempt, and sometimes succeed, in enforcing a claim based on the legal code, in violation of the customary system, and, strong as public opinion may be against such procedure, it is inevitably ineffectual where there is recourse to law. But it is obvious that the difference between the customary practice and the legal code creates a situation in which there is plenty of room for dissension to arise.

It is now necessary to examine the material on this subject collected in our Centres and endeavour to formulate the theory more specifically on the basis of this evidence.

III

We have first to consider the concept of *family land* and the system of rights in regard to inheritance and use which govern it. The term now, as we shall show, is commonly applied to all *inherited land* as distinct from *bought land* but in its primary meaning family land is land inherited from an ancestor who acquired it by gift from the slave-owner at Emancipation.

The first evidence that there existed a customary system of land tenure emerged from the accounts given us of the founding of the old districts in two of our Centres: Mocca and Sugartown. Later we found the principle restated in the history of the transmission of family land generation by generation from the original head of the family to the present holders.

In Sugartown, when we arrived and were trying to distinguish the ecological features and differentiate between the new Estate village and the old settlements, we were told that three of the districts—Yaccatown, Springfield and Mountainview—had been founded after Emancipation.

The account given by a member of one of the old families of

the origin of the old districts is as follows: 'The whole of Yacca-town had originally been land granted after slavery to the freed Negroes. The people then were not very wise which was why we (the descendants) have not got enough land. They did not look ahead (he touched his forehead with his finger). The lower part of Springfield and of the Neighbourhood village into which it runs, has the same history. You could say it was all family land for it had been handed down from generation to generation. It could never be sold. Family land could not be sold. The members of the family had a right to a house spot on it and to reap the produce. Even though one member paid the taxes, and had it registered in his name, he was only a trustee, he did not own it, and he could not dispose of it. They would say "too many people are involved".'

According to my informant these descendants now formed twenty-six families all of whom were related or linked by con-jugal unions. On another occasion he stated: 'Family land cannot be sold. It is inherited. It cannot be willed by the descendants. If the original owner left a Will then that would be followed. People have a right to come and live and use the land if they are of the family. If there was room they would be given a house site. For instance if one of my family came here and asked permission to stay on my land, and if there was room for him to put up a little house, he would ask to do so, until he could find his own place, and I would let him. You know, my brother lives here.'

The origin of Mocca was similar to that of the old parts of Sugartown. The whole land area is owned by a number of fami-lies, closely knit by kinship or intermarriage or interconcubinage. The lower part of the village is still called 'Bungotown' or 'Africa land'. This land is administered by the head of the family whose grandparents were given an acre of land by their mistress after Emancipation. The old man himself did not live in the village but in an adjacent one on another piece of family land. Nonetheless, he was still in control of the family settlement in our village. While some of it was inhabited by his descendants he retained his own claim to a share of it by leasing a portion and collecting the rents. His grandparents came as slaves from Africa. He did not remember what part they came from. But when they were freed their mistress (whose name he took) gave them a piece of land which they have free of taxes for ever. It is about an acre. This land is situated in Mocca. Part of it he leases to tenants; one tenant pays rent because he is a stranger, but the others do not pay rent because they are living with women of the family. He would never sell the land. 'You see I don't pay taxes. The mistress of the property gave it to my people free. I am not free to sell it. When there is nobody of the family to live on it, it will stay as no man's land if the property don't take it. The land is left to reap generations.'

In Sugartown we were given a definition by an old lady of what family land meant 'in the old tradition'. This woman traced her ancestry back to grandparents who came from Africa. The land belonged to her father who inherited it from his father and in his turn left it to her and her brother. The land is in two pieces, one in Sugartown, containing the family house and the graves of the ancestors, was occupied by her. The other, two and a half acres, was situated in one of the Neighbourhood villages. Her brother lived there and they jointly cultivated it and reaped the produce. Although they exercised all rights of use she was emphatic that they held it in trust for the family and that absent members had not pretermitted their rights through lack of occupation. According to her statement, she and her brother 'regard this land in the old family tradition. Neither piece could or would ever be sold by her or her brother. Her father taught her that in their country the land would always be for any of the family— they could come there and reap anything. That is why she had built the second room in her house so that any of the family coming would have a room to stay. With the younger ones it might be different. They might not want to live there. The younger ones preferred to live in Kingston but that was not so in the old times. They had the African tradition. For instance, any of the family who came to see her would be free to go and pick a coconut from the trees on the land. That was what the older people told them. Her father left no Will—all this was understood'.

In regard to family land in its primary meaning, or 'in the old tradition', the fundamental principles are (1) that it is inalienable, (2) that it passes to all the children, and (3) that any member of the family 'through the name or through the blood' has rights of use which are not lost through non-exercise for any period.

It is evident, however, that a distinction is made between family land in this primary sense and land *bought* by an ancestor in more recent times. In theory it would appear that all inherited land is subject to the prescriptions and proscriptions which govern family land. In practice, however, individual rights might be established by a Will or verbal bequest and alienation, in certain circumstances, occur. An examination of such cases reveals at the same time that any deviation from the traditional pattern was regarded with disfavour by the older people and stubbornly resisted. The pressures on the traditional system are increasingly strong, arising from the defects inherent in the system within the context of the social structure of Jamaica today. Family land, in the process of transmission and use has in the main long ceased to have agricultural value, apart from the economic trees with which it is usually well stocked. It represents security in the sense that any member 'in need' can erect a hut on it and live rent free and, as we shall show later, has a bearing on the type of household and the status of the woman where the family is matrilocal. On the other hand it runs counter to the ambition to own land and the dislike of usufructuary communal rights only. Disagreements between members of the family over family land are in Jamaica one of the most common causes of litigation and invariably the reason is the attempt of one or more members to establish an individual right by exploiting the conflict between the unwritten traditional system which is current in one segment of the society and the legal code which is applicable to the whole society.

The first principle to be modified is that of inalienability. Inherited or family land in this derived sense may be sold by agreement between the family. At the same time the family, in this context (as we were told by the head of Bungotown in Mocca and by the Sugartown informant already quoted), includes, besides all living members traceable through the blood or the name, wherever they may be, the generations to come, who can obviously not be consulted. Its sale is also a breach of faith to the dead who left it to the immediate occupiers as trustees for this larger group. Immediate as well as distant forbears are invariably buried on family land and this is another bulwark against alienation. The graves are generally 'tombed' and even where the family now lives in considerable poverty tombstones are often elaborate and expensive, engraved with the person's name, age at death and a text from the Bible, and the spot surrounding the graves carefully tended. The most serious and impressive religious rituals in Jamaica are those associated with death and burial and there is still a strong belief that the ghost of an angry or neglected forbear will return to haunt his descendants. (24)

Although the family may consent to one of its members selling his inheritance it is regarded as a wrong thing to do. This applies however small the holding and however dire the man's need. Family holdings rarely amount to more than an acre or so and are more generally measured in square chains. In one instance in Sugartown, the family inheritance consisted of half an acre and a small house, left to a man and his sisters. The son had left the home to practise his trade of cobbler and wrote his sisters to ask permission to sell a square of the land to pay off a man to whom he owed £4. They allowed him to do so, but by this act he had 'forfeited his right to any more of the land and they could keep him away, if they wanted. He was a bad brother'. In this case, although the land was described as family land it had been inherited from recent forbears who had bought it. It was not land acquired at or before Emancipation and handed down intact since that date to descendants of the original ancestor. We came across no case where the sale of family land in this primary sense was permitted.

Theoretically *bought land* is not immediately subject to any restrictions and the purchaser has the right to dispose of it by sale, gift or testamentary disposition as he wills. Any such action is always, however, resented as cutting across the natural expectation of his children to inherit. A typical expression of resentment came from a Sugartown man whose parents both had land: the mother one acre and the father four and a half. The mother sold the place 'to spite her children'—he did not know why. When she got old they had to rent a room for her to live in and she died in the poorhouse. His father also sold his land so that there was nothing for the children to inherit.

The process of *creation* of family land in the present day was observable in Orange Grove where the land had been purchased within the last half century either by our informants or their fathers or elder brothers. The term *family land* in its primary sense is not applicable to any of these holdings. Prior to the settlement there had been holdings on the backlands running up into the mountain behind the valley in which Orange Grove lies, and some of our farmers were descendants of the original owners of these holdings. Some of these were family land in the primary sense. For the most part they had abandoned any claim on them, however, in favour of the fertile lands in the valley to which they had freehold title.

In Orange Grove there appeared to be two processes at work. One was towards fragmentation and individual ownership, the partition, that is, of the inheritance among each child. The process of fragmentation is illustrated in the story of John Willis who lived with his wife on a six acre farm inherited from his father. In addition John acquired by purchase two separate two-acre lots and other pieces totalling eight acres from his brothers and sisters, which they had inherited from their father. He and his wife died leaving seven adult children: Sam, Jane, Mary, Ann, Fred, Ella and Sue. During his lifetime John had disposed of some of his property. Thus on Ella's marriage he sold three-quarters of an acre to her husband. The reason given was that by this time John and his wife were failing in strength, the sons had their own holdings and the old couple needed help to work the land. They did not want Ella to go away with her husband to another district. He also sold an acre to Fred and an acre to Mary's husband. When he died his Will was read and it was found that he had disposed of his remaining property as follows: To Ella, one acre adjoining the piece already sold to her husband; to Sam the six acres and the house inherited from his father; to Fred two acres; to Jim one and a half acres; to Sue one acre; to Mary one and a half acres and three-quarters each to Jane, Ann and Ella. He also left one acre to his illegitimate son Jim, and half an acre to the illegitimate son of his daughter, Jane. The remaining portion went to Sam 'as the heir at law'. Jim, the illegitimate son, died and, with Sam's permission, Fred was allowed to take possession of the acre bequeathed him by his father. (25)

The practice of making gifts of land, or fruit trees on the family holding, to individual children during the lifetime of the head of the household was common in Orange Grove. Families here were large, and sons in particular tended to stay with their parents and assist with the farm work. There was not yet overwhelming pressure on these farms: the acreage was adequate to maintain the family in the first and second generations at a relatively high standard. The soil was fertile and had not previously been used for peasant agriculture: the methods of cultivation were competent, as was the selection of crops and their rotation. It was only by looking into the future that one foresaw the inevitable deterioration that the system of inheritance would create. In the present, however, it was justified as ensuring the security and independence of the members of the family. One of the most respected farmers in Orange Grove referred to the bad custom in Jamaica of keeping children dependent on their parents so that they 'had no strength to give you when you are old'. On the contrary, he said, 'I give them from now. I gave land to my daughter and she cultivate it herself, alone. She makes up the land and plants without assistance'. He had also given her four coconut trees and four breadfruit trees. He said that he valued these trees at five pounds each so that he considers he has given her forty pounds and he has told her it is her dowry. (26)

Although there was no record of any sale of land in Orange

Grove to an outsider, portions were sometimes sold to landless kin. There were cases of a man with a holding larger than the immediate needs of himself and his family selling part of it to a younger brother or nephew and in all such cases the price asked for was considerably below the market value of the land. There was little formality in these transactions, though a receipt would be given for the sum paid.

One other form of alienation of family land may occur when it is forfeited to Government for non-payment of taxes. This was likely to happen when the joint heirs lived in other parts of the country or were off the Island and tenure was exercised by an aged man or woman unable to use the land or, alternatively, earn money to pay the tax.

IV

The dictum that succession to family land was either 'through the blood' or 'by the name' needs to be clarified since it establishes the principle of legitimacy so far as land is concerned. (27) Legitimacy in this context has no reference to marriage or concubinage. Where inheritance is 'through the blood' there is no differentiation between a woman's legitimate and illegitimate children; her heirs are all those who trace descent from her. Similarly, where inheritance is 'by the name' a man's heirs are all his children whether by the present wife or concubine or by other women in previous unions and (in theory at least) regardless of whether these offspring do or do not form part of his household. Children of these women by other men do not participate in the inheritance even if living in the home.

A woman, whether wife or concubine, has no customary 'rights' to land inherited or bought by her spouse. She is not, according to the traditional system, as distinct from the legal code under which she has the same rights as in British law, in any circumstance his heir. If there are no children of their union, the property reverts to his brothers and sisters and their descendants. At the same time it is generally conceded that the wife or concubine has a right to live in the family home and on the land during her lifetime. Such provision may be made in the man's will or verbally. Not infrequently there is the direction that the right of use lapses if she remarries or takes a concubine. But even where there is no will, it would be rare for the family to dispute her right, whether as the mother of his children or not, to live on the family land.

These principles were inherent in statements made to us by the descendants of the old families in Mocca and Sugartown. They subsequently emerged tortuously from the accounts given us of the transmission and inheritance of land. In the present generation the principles were sometimes challenged. There were one or two cases of individuals who said they had abandoned their claims on the family inheritance because they thought 'all that sort of thing foolishness'.

Dissatisfaction with the traditional system most commonly occurs, however, where one of the descendants of an old family has prospered and moves in a social group within which a different set of ideas is operative. The Campbell family in Sugartown were a case in point. Mr Campbell began work as an apprentice at the Estate. During the war he went to America as a farm labourer. He was regularly employed during crop; and out of crop he 'traded'. He had built himself one of the best houses in the village, consisting of a sitting-room, two bedrooms and hall with a verandah overlooking a trim, well-kept flower garden. The house was expensively equipped with shop furniture and a radio. Mr Campbell was very conscious of his social status in the village and it was some time before he opened up and gave any information at all. He refused at first to admit that he knew anything about his father. He preferred not even to give his name. It was only when I had expressed my regard for 'the old families' that he acknowledged his descent from one of them. His reticence was, in part, due to self-consciousness about his illegitimate birth, concerning which he was plainly embarrassed. He did not introduce the lady with whom he had lived for ten years and referred to the thirteen-year-old girl who lived in the house as her niece. It was only after many social contacts that we were able to get a reasonably clear account of the inheritance.

His maternal grandmother, Jane, and her sister, Caroline, were 'caretakers' for an old man who left them half an acre of land. The sisters built their houses on it. Mr Campbell's grandmother Jane had two daughters, Sara and Mary; Caroline had one son. Mary, our informant's mother, married and went abroad and her son was brought up by his grandmother. When she died she left her house and share of the half acre of land on the traditional principle to 'all her children', viz. her two daughters and her grandson. Mr Campbell proceeded to take out title to 'his share' and produced the document which showed the area to be approximately five squares. He indicated Sara's piece on which there was an ill-kept garden and a heap of old zinc sheets and cheap boards, the ruin of a hut which had once stood there. Sara, he said, now lived in barracks on the estate, but he either could not or would not say where, and, although this fact was later confirmed, we were never able to trace her and get her account of the inheritance. Caroline's portion was occupied by her granddaughter, Mrs Murray, who was also interviewed. According to her the land was family land and could not be sold. She (or her husband) had built a very superior house on the site and her husband also rented land, besides having a regular job on the Estate. She had had her portion surveyed and according to her it consisted of two and a quarter acres, whereas according to Mr Campbell the total inheritance was only half an acre. The discrepancy was never reconciled since the breach between the members of the family, none of whom was on speaking terms, excluded any possibility of a joint interview. What was unquestionably evident throughout was the underlying sense of conflict created by the deliberate flouting of the traditional system. At the same time the process of *re-creation* of family land out of bought land with the associated concepts of inalienability and the rights of all the family to inherit—generally by individual 'share' rather than joint use as in the case of John Willis of Orange Grove—was continually going on.

While it is permissible to make special provision for a son or daughter who has given special care and attention to an aged parent, or in some cases for the eldest son, there would be strong resentment against the exclusion of any socially legitimate heir. A Sugartown woman inherited a tiny plot of land—three-quarters of an acre to be exact—from her father. Before he died her father told her that in no circumstances should she part with the land: it should go from her to her children and her children's children.

There are thus two principles of distribution of family land. The first, associated with family land inherited from the ancestors who acquired the land at or before Emancipation (family land in the primary sense), is where the land is left to all the children, reckoned in either the paternal or maternal line, and is used by them according to their need, as a group. Even in the case of family land in this primary sense we found *individual rights of use* recognized and respected although no power to alienate or bequeath outside the proper line of descent.

The second principle of distribution is where certain children or kin are selected from within the inheriting group and given, either verbally or by will, a share of the family inheritance. While these principles are not mutually exclusive it would appear that, where family land in its primary sense is concerned, the process of sharing does not abrogate the principle of group inheritance and the prohibition on alienation either by sale or gift even within the family. Individual inheritance is, in theory at least, permissible only in the case of bought land where the line of descent has yet to be established. In practice it was found to occur in the case of inherited land or family land in the secondary or derived sense. It is possible to interpret some of our evidence to mean that the eldest son has a superior right—provided he is in the right line of descent. The case of John Willis just cited is an example. More usually, however, a son or daughter was singled out because of care given to an aged parent. Thus a Sugartown man told us that 'he was not the first child but he was born on the land and looked after his father, so he inherited it'. Where the proposed beneficiary was not a son or daughter or only one of a number of socially legitimate heirs, the gift inevitably caused friction and might be converted to a right of use only or abrogated. A Sugartown woman claimed the land and house in which she lived was hers. Subsequently it was shown that it was one of two parcels of family land, the second piece being occupied by her brother. The two were not on speaking terms but it seemed probable that the land had been passed down in the male line. The woman had a girl living with her whom she referred to as her step-daughter. In fact she turned out to be her paternal uncle's daughter. She wished to leave the land to this girl at her death but said that it would depend on who cared for her in her old age. Whoever did this would have a claim on her. In any case she did not intend to leave this 'step-daughter' out. If we were correct in our assumption that the land passed 'by the name' the girl would have no more than a life interest in the family land and could not pass anything on to her children. What emerged from this and other records was that a kinsman who cared for an aged relative was recognized as having a claim to participate, if only to the extent of a life interest, in that relative's family land.

One of the reasons for the difficulty in formulating the principles of tenure and inheritance was the impracticability of discussing the subject on a theoretical level with our informants. On many occasions we discussed a man's ownership and use of 'land' only to discover, when we had recorded a number of wildly conflicting statements, that he was concerned with a number of pieces, all held, owned or operated on different principles, and that the apparent contradictions were due, not to any lack of clarity in his mind, but to our own failure to appreciate to which parcel a particular statement referred. Such a case occurred very early in our field work in Mocca and it was in fact by laboriously disentangling this particular account that there finally emerged evidence of a systematic theory.

The farmer in question operated four different pieces of land: an acre of family land, three separate pieces of rented land in area six squares, twelve squares and two acres; and half an acre of land which he had bought. (This latter piece had belonged to his brother. He cared for this brother and his three children till he died and after his death the brother's family said he must take the land because of his care of the old man and his children. After a while they changed their minds and told him he must buy it.) He did not propose that this should be treated as family land: as soon as he had finished paying for it he was going to have it surveyed and put in his son's name. He did not anticipate any family dispute as a result. He and his children were very loving. He paid the taxes on the piece of family land and was solely responsible to all his brothers and sisters for it. 'Whenever I reap I distribute and who feel can come and reap.' He cultivated his part which was one acre. His brothers and all but one of his sisters, who lived outside the parish, also used the land. Although she never came he sent her, from time to time, gifts from his crops and her share of the permanent trees on the land: coconuts, breadfruits, bananas, plantains and cocos.

There is abundant evidence that it is where group inheritance is the rule that disputes most often occur due to the exclusion of one or other line of descent. This particular man lived with his wife and children in a house he himself had built on one piece of her family land. According to his statement her family had robbed her of her interest in another piece of family land.

His statement shows that his wife's father left four acres of land first to his brother, and at his death to his children. It was in three separate pieces: one acre went to one sister, an acre and a half to a brother and the other acre and a half to our informant's wife. There was another piece of family land: that on which the wife had lived with her father and the rest of the family until his death. On this land she had been born and it belonged to her family but 'the rest of them had robbed her of it'. The several statements obtained from this informant, though they remain confused, indicate that the land, in this case, passed by the name and that while our informant's wife had a life interest her children were not entitled to inherit. The second point of interest concerned the acre and a half share which had been left to his wife and which, he informed us, he had had surveyed—presumably with a view to acquiring title in his wife's name. It illustrates the second line of development, concurrent with the process by which bought land is being converted into family land: namely, the tendency for family land when 'shared' to be subject to a new line of inheritance. In this case passing from the paternal line to the maternal line.

Another source of confusion and conflict arises where there is non-use by one or more of the heirs of family land. This may occur where the heirs in question have settled in other parts of the Island or gone abroad or have other and more profitable means of support. Theoretically the non-exercise of their rights by any member of the family does not prejudice the right to return to the family home at any time if he or she 'has the need'. In fact, with family land shrunken in size by the process of 'sharing' and with its fertility exhausted by generations of misuse, such action appears to be rare and would only be made in duress. What cannot, however, be overstated, is the sense of security which an interest in family land gives to the man (or woman) who has a precarious livelihood and no permanent home of his own.

The word home, as a place one can go back to, may be said to be synonymous with a family holding. One might, not inappropriately, paraphrase the dictum about marriage and say, 'One does not *go home* to a rent house'. The nostalgia in the tone of a sugar worker who longed to 'go home' to his mother's land in a distant parish but could not until he had made good and could return with money in his pocket, is also reflected in the following account of a woman then living in a rented room and working in the canefields, whose longing is for the time when she can go back with her sons to her parent's land and make her home there. 'When she goes back her sons will go with her. They are all in sympathy with her. In their father's yard they regard themselves as being in the enemy's camp. At present she goes and comes and when she is coming she brings with her bags of food. When coconuts are reaped she gets her share after taxes have been paid. Her brother and sister look after the land. When she and her sons go back they will cultivate the land and build houses in which to live. She already has a zinc house on her mother's land but her sons will have to build thatch houses. She and her sons will come down to Sugartown to work in the Crop and when the Crop is over they will go back to their land.'

V

Houses are subject to the same principles of group and individual inheritance as operate for family land and may be transmitted in either the male or the female line.

In Sugartown, house sites have a special value owing to the demand for accommodation for sugar workers and the erection of additional huts on family land for the purpose of letting the rooms to single men was found to be the principal source of income especially for women members of the family. The right to build houses on family land and rent them may be exercised by members of the family who live elsewhere. The following is a description of one of the family compounds in our sugar centre, where each of the families had a separate house. The land, one-third of an acre in extent, with three small cottages, was left to all her children by their mother who inherited it from her mother and mother's mother before her. One cottage was left to each child. At the time of our visit there were on it five two-roomed houses, and a three-roomed one; one double kitchen and two single ones.

The mother had seven children by her husband, six of whom are alive. (Her husband had two outside children, one of whom is alive but is not legally entitled to participate in the inheritance.) Only the two younger sisters live on the land, the elder of whom occupies a two-roomed cottage (A) and is erecting another two-roomed cottage (B). She has her own kitchen. Her household consists of herself, her concubine and their son aged 5, the man's adult sister, and an adopted son aged 16. The second sister and her son, aged 12, occupy one room in a third cottage (D); she rents out a fourth (E) which she also owns, and one of the rooms in (F), a fifth three-roomed cottage which she inherited. She has her own kitchen. The other siblings, three sisters and a brother, live in other parishes and rent out their rooms; the brother rents out the second room in cottage (D); the two oldest sisters get the rent from yet another two-roomed cottage (C) and the third from the remaining two rooms in (F). These siblings send their own agent to collect the rent for them.

Where there is a large family house on family land and this is also left to all the family, the children who do not live in the home may rent the rooms which fall to their share.

While a life-interest in family land is one of the most evident bonds in the family pattern, there are obvious sources of conflict in the crowding together of numbers of adults and their children on a small piece of land. This is intensified in the case of joint inheritance of a house. Paradoxically, the element of conflict or discord between members of the inheriting group, may be as strong, if not a stronger factor, in perpetuating the system, and keeping the group together, as where there is complete trust and amity. In the latter case, the members can afford to live where it suits them and rely on the recognition by the land-using group, of their 'claim' and 'right'. Where there is any question of infringement or an intention to exploit the non-exercise of these claims or rights, then joint residence becomes necessary.

The following is an example of such a case. Incidentally it is also an illustration—though admittedly an extreme one—of the effect which this joint inheritance of family land and houses by all the children may have on the type of household. It occurs in Sugartown. No similar case occurred in Mocca where none of the original family homes remained and all houses were wattle and daub thatched huts which had periodically to be renewed. As it is a complicated family organization comprising two household records and three separate pieces of family land a diagram may help to clarify the story of the inheritance. (28)

Our informants were Nesta and Winston in Household 1, and Mr and Mrs Brown and Celeste in Household 2. Although we had many interviews with all the interested parties, saw them continually in our rounds of the village and went over the ground (both literally and figuratively) many times, the statements remain contradictory. Even as to the total area of land there was disagreement but it appears unlikely that more than three or four acres were involved.

Both Winston and Nesta said that this land had originally been bought by their father and 'a brother of his', George Brown. The genealogy as supplied by Cyril and Celeste shows that they were actually half-brothers, James, the elder, being an outside child of Jane's. Celeste added that Jane had been a co-purchaser with her sons. We are left to decide whether to discount Celeste's statement because of her age (at 77 she spent most of her days dozing in the sun on the doorway of her room) or credit it, on the ground that, like many of our oldest informants, her memory of the past was clear and vivid. The point is important, since James and George were the sole 'ancestors' a division of the land between their descendants each individual having his 'share' would be in accord with the customary practice, and, except by their grace, Celeste would have no share in the inheritance. If, on the other hand, Jane had participated in the purchase, then Celeste would have a claim on the inheritance.

James Dixon died when Winston was eight years old, his wife having predeceased him. He left, according to Winston, an apiary from which he had been making nine barrels of honey annually, and owned horses and donkeys. Winston was left in his uncle's care and they all continued to live on the family land. But according to Winston his uncle treated him badly. Although he was sent to school till he was thirteen he was frequently beaten, and worst of all his uncle 'made away' with the apiary, including the machines for extracting the honey, and all his father's stock, so that when he came of age there was nothing left. This was the beginning of discord.

At the time of our stay in the village, Nesta, Winston, Princess and their children (or some of them) lived in the house built by James while Cyril and his wife and family lived in the three-apartment house built by George. Celeste had her own room in this house, but had at one time had 'her own house on the premises', i.e. on the family site. During our nine-month stay in the village, Cyril completed fencing off the site on which his house stood from the rest of the family property, but could not be drawn into any explanation. He would never discuss his relatives in Household 1.

The ownership of the 'rest of the land' (said by Princess to be two and a half acres) was not at any time referred to by Cyril but, according to Nesta, it is divided between herself, her sister and their brother. Again, according to her, they three alone 'are bound up in this', i.e. the inheritance was between them equally and does not concern Cyril or any descendant of George.

Winston, on the contrary, claims that 'all this land' is really his 'as the only son of his father' (his only brother being dead) and that his sisters live there 'rent free'—the implication being that this is by his goodwill. In regard to his cousin's share, Winston considers that all Cyril has a right to is the house site which James gave to George during his life time. This again conflicts with the statement that George and James together bought the land which would give Cyril every right to inheriting his father's portion.

It is certain, however, that it is the brother and sisters in Household 1 who solely *use* this 'remainder'. Princess told us that her share was one square and that she leases it at 7s. 6d. per quarter. Winston rents out five house sites, of one square each, at 9s. per quarter and it is indicative of his disregard for kinship claims that one of the tenants from whom he exacts rent is his cousin—'the son of another brother of his father'.

This case is a striking example of the effect which an interest in family land has in keeping the family together, as much where the conflict is overt or suppressed as when there is solidarity. The family inheritance includes a home, and the fear of the sisters that, if they do not occupy and use the home, their brother may attempt and even succeed in establishing individual ownership, has its result in their separation from the several fathers of their children. For both sisters are at present consorting with men (G and O in the diagram) whom they cannot bring into the home because it is already full to capacity. Yet they cannot go and live with their lovers because they are fully aware of their brother's intention to oust them especially now that he has taken a concubine, has one child and 'another on the way'.

Princess's eldest son 'would live with her if he could but the home is not convenient' so he rents a room in the village. But, although he works at the factory, she is still responsible for him. She cooks his food for him and he gives her something. It is not a definite amount but last Saturday he gave her 12s. She herself has been out of work for three months but she has a gentleman with whom she is friendly. He helps her with the children though they are not his. He is a carpenter, although he is not trained. In crop he gets work at the Dump. The Dump is the deep place in the factory where they dump the cane for feeding the machine. It is deep, and when they dig it out they find it is floored with boards. His house is small, so small that they cannot live there. She prepares his food and sends it to him and he comes to visit her but does not sleep at the home. He gives her 15s. a week. She hasn't got a garden but around the house she reaps from the plantains, the bananas and the coconuts, when there are any. Also she has her share of one square of the family land at Springfield.

Nesta is also still in company with the father of her two youngest children. He lives in Springfield. While the interview was going on his young daughter (by another woman) came and stood at the kitchen door waiting for her father's dinner while Nesta fried the fish.

It was very noticeable in Nesta's account that although she knew the whereabouts of all her children and chatted about them at length, visits them and is visited by them, she volunteered nothing about the formidable number of their fathers. It is almost certain that these unions were matrilocal and, in this particular, follow the usual practice where the woman has an interest in family land.

Where a woman has such an interest, but does not own a house, the house may be built by her concubine, so that there is the further complication that the man owns the home but that it is erected on the woman's family land.

The genealogy in footnote 28 shows that beside her children

by George, Cyril's mother had children by two other men who are not said to have any part in the land left by George. This ties in with the statement by the Patriarch of Mocca, already quoted, that inheritance follows 'the name', i.e. goes in the paternal line. This underlies much of the conflict between Winston and his sisters. Nesta's children bear no less than six family names and all that Nesta would—or might—be able to transmit to any of them would be *her own individual share* if she could establish to everyone's satisfaction that her father had in fact made any such bequest, verbally or by Will. The respect paid to a verbal bequest during a life time, or to a will, may override normal accepted procedure.

VI

We may conclude, therefore, that there is, common to all these communities, a customary system of family tenure, inheritance and use, supported by a body of traditional beliefs and a system of values and reinforced by strong social sanctions. There is good reason to believe that the system in its entirety is common throughout Jamaica. This traditional system of tenure distinguishes three categories of land, family land, inherited land and bought land, and governs the process of their transmission and inheritance. It will be useful at this stage to summarize our findings.

The term family land is applicable to all land inherited from the ancestors. In its historical or primary sense it takes its origin from the pre- or post-Emancipation grants of land to freed slaves, grants made by the donor probably to individuals but interpreted by the recipient and the members of that family as including all the family in perpetuity.

The principle governing 'ownership' and transmission of *family land* is explicitly stated. It belongs to all the family and it is held in trust by one member for the family; is inalienable and is transmitted to 'all the family'.

'Bought land', a generic term in common use applied to land purchased by a man or woman, is not subject to any restriction on alienation or transmission. This freedom tends, however, to become qualified in practice as a result of two things: one is the high place of land in the scale of social values; the other the deep-rooted conviction (on the part, let it be said, of both parents and children) of the 'right' of all the children to inherit. In practice, therefore, bought land is often left to 'all the children' and when this happens the land may be said to acquire, in the next generation, the character of family land and be subject to the appropriate restrictions.

We had thus, in recording the distinction explicitly made by some of our informants, to recognize a third category of land, viz. 'inherited land which was not family land', where both the theory and the practice of tenure and inheritance was complicated by its traditional character. Thus there were cases where bought land inherited by a man or woman was left by them to all their children and other cases where fragmentation occurred.

We have seen, however, that even where the principle of joint inheritance is applicable, in practice only one or some of the heirs might in fact inherit. This was generally the result of conditions which made effective occupation or use by some members impossible or unattractive, and did not invalidate the principle. It was unequivocally asserted that members who did not exercise their right to live on land did not thereby lose their right to do so at a later period. Non-residential heirs might draw on the land by reaping the fruit of permanent crops on the holdings (such as breadfruit or coconut) or by renting rooms or house sites upon it. And always their right to return and live on it was acknowledged. These privileges also extended to their recognized heirs.

This brought us to the next problem of defining 'legitimate heirs'. Was descent bilateral or unilateral; what precisely was meant by 'all the family' inheriting—a particularly confusing aspect of the problem in view of the numbers of step-brothers and sisters in any family.

We found that we could get rid of one complicating element without much difficulty and assert with confidence that the question of legitimacy (whether legal or social, that is between children or married parents or parents living in concubinage) did not affect the inheritance. Secondly that there was no sex discrimination: daughters were equally eligible with sons to inherit.

It was not so easy to resolve the statements made to us in regard to the tracing of descent 'by the name' (i.e. through the father) and 'through the blood' (i.e. through the mother).

In Mocca, where we had the advantage of drawing on the aged descendants of the original ancestors, the pattern was predominantly patriarchal. Descent and inheritance were traced 'through the name' and since children invariably took the name of the father even when illegitimate, this excluded children of daughters from the line of succession. In Sugartown, where the occupiers and trustees of family land were more often than not found to be women, it was the blood that counted and not the name. Thus a woman's heirs might be of two or more different names (i.e. fathers). Children having neither the blood nor the name of the ancestor to whom the land belonged, had no presumptive right to inherit, even when brought up in the home. And this had nothing to do with the fact that they were or might be illegitimate.

In other words where land is inherited from the father it passes to sons and daughters of the name, i.e. any of his children by any woman; but children of any of these spouses by another man, even though they may live in the home would not be regarded as eligible for the inheritance. In the same way if the land is transmitted by the mother, her children, whatever their paternity, would be of the family but outside children of her husband and concubine would not be. In this sense, therefore, illegitimate and outside children in a home may be said to be differentiated against, although this has nothing in common with the legal prescription against inheritance by illegitimate children when there is, or may be, a legitimate heir, a prescription which, on the contrary, conflicts with the traditional system and when enforced in the courts creates a sense of deep injustice and indignation. In fact were this legal principle enforced it is obvious that a large portion of smallholders in possession of inherited land might be discovered to have no title to their land which could be upheld in a court of law except such as they were able to establish under the Statute of Limitations.

We pass thus to a need for definition of the term 'family' so often used in statements quoted in this chapter to refer to the heirs to family land. This term is obviously not extended indefinitely to all members of the name or the blood. Apart from what we may call fortuitous limitation, that is, where members for one reason or another, refrain voluntarily, or by force of circumstances are prevented from exercising rights, there is also the limitation imposed by the size of the inheritance and the physical impossibility of its containing all the potential heirs. From the examples which we have quoted it is clear that the inheriting unit is the offspring in line of descent, whether through the mother or the father, of the progenitor from whom the land is inherited. Thus for the purpose of inheritance of land, the term family excludes 'outside' children of the spouse of the parent through whom the inheritance passes. Where brothers jointly own land, and the children of both siblings inherit, the process of individual division is unusually accelerated.

Finally we have shown that the theory of joint inheritance by all the family, specific in land inherited from the ancestors who are buried on the land, tends to become attached to all land acquired, and that once there has been joint inheritance by all the family, the principle of inalienability is also invoked.

It was clear from our research that the position in regard to land tenure was not a static one and that there were continual pressures both from within and without, operating on the one hand to reinforce the traditional beliefs and practices and on the other to modify or undermine them.

The system of family land and joint inheritance by all the children may be regarded from the functional point of view as a conservative force, ensuring that the inheritance is kept intact and contributing also to family cohesion and solidarity. Joint occupation and use not only keep the kinship group together but link the individual members of the family in a series of repetitive activities which of necessity call for co-operation and mutual adjustment. Agreement must be reached in regard to living accommodation; sharing of the economic trees planted by the ancestors; of the area which can be planted in food crops for the separate households; of the yard containing the individual kitchens and (often) the communal toilet. The children of the families play together in this yard, while their mothers perform their daily individual and separate household tasks within sight and sound of each other. There is the continual 'borrowing' and lending that is so much a part of the pattern of Jamaican life and the ideas of hospitality.

Contact is also maintained with absent members of the family, involved in joint ownership of the land, living in other parts of the Island. When the crops are reaped baskets of food stuffs are sent from the home cultivation to these relatives working in Kingston or elsewhere, and in return those who can reciprocate with small sums of money or gifts of clothing.

With the increasing scarcity and irregularity of employment and the corresponding insecurity of the wage earner as well as the pressure of population on the land which the small man can buy or rent, a few squares of family land in which one has an interest come to have great importance and the internal forces are all against any division of the family holdings or enforced consolidation. The few pounds received in compensation is no recompense for the satisfaction to be got from the knowledge that there is a place to which a man or woman can go when the worst happens and be permitted 'to build his house and live there'.

At the same time active pressure from within, directed against joint inheritance and towards individual ownership, is evidenced by the increasing practice whereby heirs are given their individual shares either in a will or by joint agreement among themselves. The traditional principle of joint inheritance runs counter to the very strong ambition of the peasant to own his land and house. This emphasis on ownership colours the whole attitude to land use under tenancy systems. The demand for 'land room'—an expression commonly used in Jamaica—remains a present obsession and the panacea for all ills. The demand is always for land which can be bought, not leased. A Sugartown field worker told us that 'if he had his wish he would call a public meeting and incite the people towards the progress of the community', which, in his opinion, could only be achieved by their being allowed to purchase land to live on out of crop. The land must, however, be individually owned; every man must have his own piece: 'community ownership' would only cause trouble. In Sugartown the urge to own land and a house was the strongest incentive to industry. The majority of the incoming workers came with the expressed object of earning enough to buy their own holding or acquire capital to develop land already owned. In part, these conditions explain the antipathy to leasehold. But it would be unwise to assume that mere remedy of the defects in the system (necessary as this is) would satisfy the peasant for whom land has not only a real but an almost mystic significance. It may be said that in this desire to own his land, the Jamaican peasant is no different from peasants in Britain, or Europe, or any other part of the world. There are, however, intensifying elements in the Jamaica situation. First, as we suggested in our historical analysis, land acquired during slavery a social and status value, and, after slavery, became in a sense both the symbol and the reality of freedom. Secondly, the religious association of land is strong: the spot on which the ancestors are buried is sacred and land containing their graves should not be permitted to pass into alien hands. Thirdly, in the economy of the Island, ownership of land is believed to be the only real and permanent source of security and of the means of satisfying the normal expectations which operate between men and women as prospective parents and between them and their children. And this has no connection, be it stated, with the income which the land can provide. There is a deeply ingrained suspicion that jobs, however well paid, are insecurely held and this feeling of insecurity grows with the increasing pressure of population on available jobs, the failure of education and practical training to keep pace with this increase of population, and the steep climb in the rates both of unemployment and of unemployability.

We saw that, from within, there came pressure both to conserve the traditional system of joint inheritance and inalienability, and, at the same time, movements toward division into shares and individual ownership.

The external forces are all against conservation of the traditional system. First it is unrecognized by the law of the country and, I am told, unknown in all its complex implications to most practising lawyers and solicitors.

From another angle, the system is discreditable as a perpetual source of dispute. We have referred to the stabilizing and cohesive effects of the system on the family, but we have equally shown that the congregation of families on family land and in family houses with communal ownership is also a frequent source of contention and disagreement, although, from one point of view, even these disagreements were a factor in keeping the group together. There is thus where the desire is to effect amicable agreement (and the monetary value of the inheritance is rarely sufficient to make litigation worth while to anyone) a great temptation to do this by cutting the Gordian knot and forcing a division or sale. Secondly, the legal recognition of legitimacy as a principle governing inheritance, which has no counterpart or reality in customary ideology or behaviour, and the legal concept of an individual heir-at-law, defined in terms of age or sex, all mitigate against the social stability of the traditional system in a society where the several sub-cultures are continually encroaching and reacting on one another. Thirdly, there is the impracticability of the system in the modern social evolution of Jamaica. From the aspect of land use it is inevitably wasteful and incompetent. A good deal of family land is under-used, occupied by the old people, who are physically unable to develop it. Other multiple owned holdings are completely unproductive save for the food trees planted by the ancestors. When adjacent to a town or an industrial centre (such as Sugartown) they fully justify their existence as house sites. But in rural or depressed areas where they are expected to carry a large kinship group having no other means of subsistence, they may, and do, keep the family together, but for no profitable purpose. Misuse of land in the form of exhaustion or neglect, under-use because of lack of capital, or multiple owner-ship restricting development, are all practical results which have to be weighed against the strong sentiment and the high values attached to the system.

On the other hand we have, as illustrated in Orange Grove, the opposite practice of division of the land among the children not to mention sales at lower than economic prices to landless kin. Although the community of Orange Grove in its present form was only some three or four decades old, our records show that few if any of the original units were intact. Considering the size of the families and the strength of family sentiment this process of fragmentation gives rise to some anxiety for the future of what is, at the moment, one of the most prosperous, progressive and well integrated farming communities in Jamaica.

The publication of the first draft of this chapter in 1953 (29) was occasioned by two local events which showed the urgent need to understand the beliefs and practices in regard to land tenure. One was the appointment in 1951 of a Committee to pre-pare schemes for re-housing the thousands of persons made home-less by the hurricane of 1951, the money for which was largely contributed by the British Government, partly by free grant, partly by interest free loan. This brought to public attention the difficulty of granting loans either for housing or agricultural credit, where in the large majority of cases no titles existed for small holdings or house sites, and resulted in a demand for im-proved facilities for rapid registration of titles. The other was the publication of a year later of the report of the International Bank of Reconstruction and Development (30) which made recommen-dations for a survey of land tenure, agricultural practices and resources. My article pointed out that unless the current beliefs, common throughout the farming communities and equally strong-ly held by the landless wage-earning population, as they have been described in the preceding pages, were fully understood and due regard paid to the tenacity with which they held and the senti-ment which attaches to them, changes which in themselves seem altogether admirable and which, in any case, are inevitable under the pressure of modern economic conditions and population growth, may be unduly held up if not ultimately defeated.

Reforms in the system of tenure, inheritance and use are bound to have far-reaching effects. The current practices profoundly affect the family—the form of household, the conjugal tie, the system of kinship roles and duties. They are a vital factor in preserving the sense of mutual responsibility and interdependence of kin and in keeping the family together. Moreover, they have had the strength to survive in spite of changing economic and social conditions and pressure on the land available for small settlers, and in spite of the fact that they are largely unrecognized in the legal code.

To insist 'once for all' on Registered Titles for all holdings as a preliminary to any sponsored system of housing or agricultural loans or credits has a nice, tidy sound to it and, indeed may ultimately be necessary and beneficial. But such wholesale registration should only be undertaken with a full realization of the effect of insistence (a) on the principle of individual ownership (and use) where it runs counter to the traditional theory of the rights of the kin; and (b) on defining the individual heir without appreciating the two possible lines of legitimate inheritance—through the blood or by the name. Family land is inherited by 'all the children' and may be used jointly by the appropriate group of kindred, regardless of the name that appears on 'the tax paper' (i.e. who pays the land tax). Alienation outside 'the blood' on the one hand, or the paternal kin on the other, is prohibited. It is a wrong against the family, living and unborn. If this idea is as deeply rooted as we believe, and if the concept of family land attaches, in the process of transmission, to all 'bought land' there is a further difficulty, which challenges this 'once and for all', of perpetuating the reform and controlling subsequent fragmentation or partition. Even the principle of joint-registration of holdings, which is legally permissible, is not a simple solution since it would require the agreement of large numbers of kin not only scattered about Jamaica but in other parts of the world.

There is another complex question: the principle to be followed in determining the rightful heir in the case of intestacy or where the family, or any member of it, resorts to law to settle an attempt at innovation or attempted exploitation by one member of the kin. In current practice 'all the children' may include descendants of both the parents or those of one parent only; it may also include siblings or lateral kin of the relevant side. There is no recognition of an exclusive right to inheritance or use by any one member of the family, no prior right based on sex, on seniority or legitimacy in the legal sense. Any such distinctions would seem to our informants to strike at the very root of kinship solidarity. And however 'weak' and 'unstable' we may find conjugal relationships to be, one of the most significant facts which our research shows is the strength and tenacity of kinship bonds.

FOOTNOTES TO CHAPTER 2

9 M. C. Smith. *Social Structure in the British Caribbean.* Social and Economic Studies, Vol. 1. No. 4. August 1953.

10 Olivier. *The Myth of Governor Eyre,* 1953. pp. 176-7.

11 Olivier. Op cit. Chapter IX.

12 Franklin Frazier. *The Negro Family in the United States.* pp. 140-1.

13 Olivier. Op cit. pp. 175-6.

14 W. L. Burn. *Emancipation and Apprenticeship in the British West Indies,* 1937. pp. 305 et seq. See also the *Reports* of the Jamaica House of Assembly on the subject.

15 See Olivier. *Jamaica, the Blessed Isle.* pp. 261 et seq., for evidence given by the Rev Henry Clarke, M.H.R., the author's grandfather, before the Royal Commission of 1897.

16 See M. G. Smith, op. cit., for an elaboration of the thesis that 'status was even more important than race and colour in the structure of British West Indian society at this period'. See also R. A. J. Van Lier, *The Development and Nature of Society in the West Indies,* 1950, and M. Kerr, *Personality and Conflict in Jamaica,* 1952, Chap. X.

17 Olivier, op. cit, pp. 113 et seq.

18 The Jamaica Registration of Titles Law, based on the Australian 'Torrens Law', was not introduced until 1888.

19 The oldest document shown us, seen in Sugartown, was a title deed, dated 1854, 'between Dame Isabella Bell-Cooper of Isleworth House, Middlesex, England, by Alexander Barclay, . . . her Attorney' and our informant's grandfather, 'whereby for the consideration of the sum of Nine pounds, Twelve shillings lawful money of the said Island, truly paid, etc. etc. the said Dame Isabella granted, bargained, sold, alienated, remised, released, enfeoffed, conveyed, and confirmed and by these presents did grant, bargain, sell etc. to our informant, his heirs and assigns one rood and nineteen perches of the said Island.' (Sugartown.)

20 The Statute of Limitations provides that squatters rights are established on Freehold Estates and Crown Land by undisputed possession for 60 years.

21 The Law of Inheritance has recently been amended by the act of 1937.

22 The Wills Act of Jamaica is based on the English Act.

23 The concept of 'equal rights of all the family' and of 'inalienability' are not foreign to English Law. There is, for example, the Estate-tail, directed to keeping land in a family for generations. There is a functional difference here, however, since in England this was associated with the principle of primogeniture and operated to prevent fragmentation. In regard

to joint inheritance, Mr Carberry has drawn my attention to no less than four types of joint estate. He suggests that the important difference is that in England these tenancies are usually deliberately created—most often by a Will—and do not normally arise on intestacy, though intestate inheritance of this type still obtained as, for example, in gavelkind where the land went to all the sons equally, up to the early part of the twentieth century.

24 See *The Death and Burial of Mrs Malcolm* at end of book.

25 The importance attached to a Will is indicated in Sam's account: Sam's father's executor was Mr A. who is known to be an honest and strict man. One Sunday evening the Will was read to Mr A. in the presence of the Rev Mr X., sealed and handed over to Mr A. with instructions that no one must be allowed to know the contents till after the death of both Mr Willis and his wife. The wife did not know the contents of the Will. Sam thinks it is always wise not to let any of the dependents of the person in question know the contents of his Will. Some people make the executor one of their own sons but that is dangerous if that son is not independent. Some men will make their wives their executors. That is also dangerous because the wife might love one of the children more than the others. This chapter was originally published in an earlier draft as an article entitled 'Land Tenure and the Family.' in *Social and Economic Studies*, Vol. 1, No. 4, August 1953. On page 109, paragraph 3 of this article it is stated that Fred was younger than Sam. Re-examination of the record shows that this was not correct and that Fred was in fact the eldest legitimate son.

26 In Ashanti, where land was inalienable, the gift of trees to a son did not confer any title to the land on which they grew. See Rattray, *Ashanti Law and Constitution*, 1929, p. 15.

27 The Ashanti word for clan is *abusua* and this word is synonymous with *mogya* (blood). . . . Descent is matrilineal, i.e. a man or woman belongs to the clan not of his father but his mother . . . the clan persists as long as the direct female descendants last, but is immediately lost in the children of any male. . . .' The word *ntoro* meaning spirit (or semen) is inherited by the man from his father and transmitted by him to his offspring. 'Just as the *abusua* is passed down the female line as long as there are females to transmit it, so the *ntoro* is passed on through the male line as long as there are males, but is immediately lost as soon as it comes into the female line, for a female, while having the *ntoro* she derived from her male parent, is not able to transmit it to her children who will inherit a different *ntoro* from their father.' R. S. Rattray, *Ashanti*, 1923, pp. 35-7.

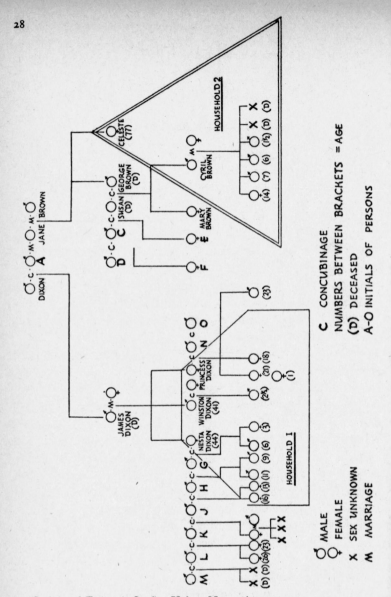

29 *Social and Economic Studies*, Vol. 1, No. 4, August 1953.
30 The International Bank of Reconstruction and Development. The Economic Development of Jamaica, 1952.

CHAPTER 3

Marriage

———

I

THE legal regulations governing marriage in Jamaica are similar to those in England. (31) The couple must be over the age of consent; they must not be within the prohibited degrees of consanguinity and affinity; and neither must be already married. A breach of the prescriptions in regard to age and consanguinity makes the marriage null and void and might subject the persons involved to penalties. Bigamy renders the second marriage null and void and is also a criminal offence.

Marriage may be solemnized according to such form and ceremony as the parties see fit to adopt; but certain requirements must be fulfilled. The ceremony must be performed by a properly constituted Marriage Officer appointed by the Government. In addition to civil marriage registrars, ministers of the recognized churches (Anglican, Roman Catholic and Nonconformist) may also be, and generally are, so appointed. Where this is the case there is no need for an additional civil ceremony provided the other legal requirements are duly fulfilled. These requirements are: (a) the couple must appear before a Marriage Officer, civil or religious, and swear before two witnesses an affidavit that there are no impediments to the marriage, that is that they are of legal age, are not already married and do not come within the prohibited degrees of affinity; (b) prior notice must be given of the intention to marry by the posting of the certificate in some public place, either outside the Registrar's office or in the church. Where the ceremony is to be a religious one the banns may also be called

73

in the church; (c) the solemnization may then take place either in a church or a registery office as the parties desire, provided the religious rite includes a prescribed formula similar to that used in the secular ceremony. Finally, once the marriage has been solemnized it is the duty of the marriage officer to have it registered.

The law makes the usual provisions for divorce or separation on the grounds of desertion for seven years, adultery or cruelty. It authorizes the wife to sue her husband for failure to maintain her. Marriage legitimizes the children of the couple, whether born before or after the marriage, and in this respect discriminates between them and any children born to either partner in previous unions of other types. In the eyes of the law only the right of legitimate children to inherit property would be recognized in the absence of testamentary disposition in favour of others. In cases of intestate succession the law also differentiates between the eldest and younger sons and recognizes no rights of daughters. These principles run counter to those followed in the customary transmission of rights in land. Few people, however, seem to be aware of them.

II

The facts that marriage is monogamous, is intended to be a lifelong association and that a husband is liable for the support of his wife and their children are fully appreciated. It is often explicitly stated that because of these mutual responsibilities, enforceable at law, marriage is something to be entered into only after the couple have got to know each other thoroughly, in a preliminary period of cohabitation, or to be rejected by the man as something he cannot afford.

The law's distinction in favour of legal issue has, on the contrary, no counterpart in the social reality of behaviour or relationships. This applies as much to the predominantly middle class society of Orange Grove as to the peasantry of Mocca and the proletariat of Sugartown. It is true that the exclusion from the household of outside children of either parent was more

74

marked in the case of married couples than in families based on concubinage, but what was more striking was the higher ratio, whether in marriage or concubinage, of outside children of the woman who were included in the home, as compared with those of the man; in other words, the marked tendency for women to keep their young children with them wherever it was possible, and the rejection by the stepmother of her husband's children by another woman. (32) This is not to say that we did not hear in Orange Grove for example (as one hears in middle-class society everywhere) a good deal of outspoken condemnation of the practice of concubinage and of the prevalence of illegitimacy; and this cannot be disassociated from the belief that marriage endows a union with attributes of respectability and carries with it a higher class status. In certain classes a couple might feel their reputation for respectability jeopardised by the presence of their illegitimate children in the home. I think there is evidence for this in the larger proportion of outside children in families based on concubinage, although couples living in concubinage are less able to bear the expense. Another reason unquestionably is, however, that if a man allows the woman with whom he is living, whether she be wife or concubine, to bring her children by another man into the home, he is legally responsible for them while they are under age. (33) The invariable existence of these children by previous unions is thus one of the reasons against marriage since even if he does not have them in his house, he is always suspicious lest some of his slender earnings may be diverted to their support.

It is not clear how far the prohibition against marriage between persons within certain degrees of affinity are seriously regarded. Our collection of genealogies enables us to trace a few cases of incestuous mating but these were not cases of marriage but of concubinage. It is difficult to believe, in view of the wide dispersion of step-siblings, unknown to one another, that there are not a great many more incestuous unions than were traced by us, and many where the fact of near kinship is not suspected by the persons concerned. In one case, however, we heard of a man going so far as to change the surname of his children to 'erase' the fact that their mother was his cousin. This appears to indicate that the marriage of cousins within the paternal line, where *the name* is inherited, is not approved.

The formal procedure and the requirements that both the intention to marry and the fact of a marriage be published (the 'gazetting' of the marriage as it is referred to) with its implications that the ceremony and the vows taken by the couple are witnessed by others, are well understood and approved. They fit in with the love of formality and ritual which is a marked feature of Jamaican behaviour.

One prescription of the legal code is, however, probably less well understood. In general a religious ceremony, performed in a church by a parson, is preferred to a secular one. This is consistent with our findings that religious considerations provide the strongest single motive for marriage. It also gives great opportunity for display and dressing up in contrast to the drabness of the ceremony in a registry office which does not offer an occasion for associating the group of kinsfolk, friends and neighbours in the event. On the comparatively rare occasions when a marriage is celebrated in a registry office, it is usual for it to be followed by a religious ceremony and feast, or even with a feast alone, in which the social importance of the event is emphasized, the vows reaffirmed in the presence of kinsfolk and friends, and God's blessing invoked. Or the bride and groom, bridesmaids and 'godparents' may attend an ordinary church service dressed in their wedding finery. This is referred to as a 'Turn Thanks' ceremony.

The rule that a marriage service may be performed only by a legally constituted marriage officer is not generally known. My impression is that any clergyman is assumed to be qualified to perform the ceremony. If I am correct in this, there may be cases of a 'marriage' being invalid without either of the parties being aware of it.

The husband's liability for the maintenance of his wife and his responsibility for her debts are fully understood. Hardly an issue of the daily newspaper appears without a notice from a husband repudiating the debts of a wife who has deserted him. This responsibility is one reason why men say they live in concubinage because 'marriage is not for the poor man'—though this also refers to the initial cost of the display in clothes and entertainment considered appropriate for the occasion.

It is recognized that marriage is monogamous and should be for life and this is an argument in favour of late marriage and of a preliminary period of concubinage which leaves the parties free to separate at any time should they so desire. At the same time sexual exclusiveness is the ideal mode of behaviour whether in marriage or concubinage. 'Unfaithfulness' on the part of either the man or the woman is one of the most frequent causes for the break up of irregular as well as of regular unions. But whereas in concubinage the injured party can simply dissolve the union, marriage is regarded as a serious contract to break. Its dissolution involves loss of face and where the religious sanction is operative, it is regarded as a violation of the marriage vow. There is a local superstition that adultery brings seven years bad luck. Moreover, although it is known that the law provides for divorce, the actual procedure required by the law is by no means clearly understood. To take legal advice involves expense which often cannot be afforded and generally it is simpler for the dissatisfied partner to 'disappear' and, if he or she so desires, live in concubinage with the next partner. A type of advertisement which commonly appears in the newspapers implies a belief that divorce can be effected by the mere fact of notifying the public of a separation. A characteristic form of notice which often appears in the daily newspaper is the following: 'This is to notify the public that my husband has left me from September 1953. I know nothing of his whereabouts. He is therefore not responsible for me any more'. Similar notices are inserted by husbands.

III

In our search for our informants' own distinctions between marriage and concubinage it became clear that these institutions were not regarded as alternative forms of conjugal association between which any individual was free to choose. In contrast to concubinage which begins as an informal arrangement and involves no conjugal or parential ties that cannot be easily broken, marriage is regarded as a serious and responsible step. Moreover marriage cannot be considered at all unless the conditions proper to it are fulfilled or appear capable of fulfilment. And some of these conditions place marriage beyond the reach of large numbers of the population, while others make it necessary to postpone marriage until after a preliminary period of cohabitation.

The first set of these conditions are economic. It is not considered correct for a man to propose marriage unless he owns a house and, preferably, a bit of land. 'A man should not marry and live in a rented house.' The cost of the wedding itself, with the extravagant expenditure on clothes, finery and food for the wedding feast often exhausts all the man's savings. But what is more significant is that he is expected to support his wife in a higher status than that which is accepted for a concubine. Concubinage is recognized as a partnership in which there is equal responsibility between both partners in practical affairs. It is considered right and proper for the woman to do any form of work to assist in the maintenance of the home. Marriage, however, is expected to bring about 'a change of life', to release the woman from the anxiety and drudgery of earning her living, to transform her 'from a common woman to a lady'. A married man told us that his wife left him after six months 'because she did not want to cook and wash for him but to sit like a lady'. It is worth mentioning that this man's chief source of income was from two squares of land which he cultivated. It is derogatory for a wife to 'go out to work'. A Sugartown man told us proudly that he stopped his wife from working because he wants to see her in the home when he comes from work. Another boasted proudly that his wife did no work at all. A wife also may expect to be provided with a servant to help in the home. (34) A widow whose husband 'would not mind her' had taken off her wedding ring: 'what was the use of a wedding ring if she had to work for herself?' The wife of a

Sugartown labourer complained that she had to be wife, maid and nurse. It wasn't right. She ought to have a maid to cook and one to look after the child so that when he came back from work she would have had time to tidy herself and sit with him.

Orange Grove was the only one of our Centres where the majority of the population had the necessary social and economic security to satisfy these expectations. It is no accident that marriage was the rule here as it was the exception in Sugartown and Mocca. (35) Although some of the smaller farmers in Orange Grove had probably a smaller net income than regularly employed sugar workers, their way of life offered greater security and they suffered none of the vicissitudes of the man dependent on casual labour. Even when food crops failed through bad seasons there was always enough to eat for the family and grass for the cattle and, above all, there was never the necessity of finding cash for rent since all the farmers had their own houses on their own land. Housewives in Orange Grove, by looking after their homes and the needs of their families, assisting in some of the work on the farm, relieved their husbands of some responsibility and were fully occupied. In Sugartown and Mocca where the majority of homes had only two small rooms, and furniture and equipment were the minimum, a woman's housewifely tasks did not occupy her for long and she had considerable time on her hands. Very few make their own clothes. The weekly wash, which would not take a competent laundress more than a few hours, is spread over days and the mornings spent at the river or spring for this purpose were social occasions, the work being done with no sense of urgency. When, therefore, the expense of marriage was given as a reason for postponing it or preferring concubinage, the man had in mind the fact that a wife was often an economic liability whereas a concubine was an asset, and was unwilling to 'put the ring on her finger' until he was sure that she would continue to be a helpmate. We were frequently told that 'the decision for marriage' rested with the man. The advantages to the woman were more apparent. A woman who had lived for eleven years in Mocca with the same man said that she had 'rushed' him about marriage but he just said nothing—'*I* can't marry—the poor woman can't marry—the man must marry me!' There are, of course, exceptions to the generally accepted pattern of wifely behaviour. We had a case of a wife whose husband praised her because when times were hard she had gone out daily to work as a domestic servant, coming home at nights. He allowed this, although he did not like it, and described her as 'faithful and economizing'.

While concubines invariably told us they did not know how much the man earned and had to be content with whatever he chose to give them, a wife expects to receive her husband's full confidence in this matter and a reasonable share of his income. In one case a husband said that he handed over all his weekly pay packet to his wife and received back some of it as 'pocket money'. It was, he thought, the wife's duty to do the saving.

Both men and women are fully aware that a neglected wife may have recourse to the courts so that if a man's position deteriorates after marriage this is a far more serious matter than if he were living in concubinage. 'Marriage has teeth' and a 'bad woman' may take him to court or bring public disgrace upon him by threatening to leave him and exposing his inability to support her in a proper manner.

It is not to be assumed that there were not exceptions to the general rule that marriage should not be entered into unless the economic pre-requisites were fulfilled. Young men and girls, in love, set up house together and might decide after a very short period of cohabitation that they could trust one another sufficiently to risk marriage even although they would both have to work hard to make ends meet. Invariably, however, in such cases, one or other party was previously disposed towards marriage as against concubinage for one of two reasons: a religious conviction that sweetheart life was not acceptable in the sight of God, or that it is not respectable. In Sugartown and Mocca we were told by cult leaders that 'concubinage life is against Christian principles' and that 'you cannot live in concubinage and do the will of God'. Persons living openly in concubinage are not admitted to full membership of the recognized churches. Marriage, without the preliminary trial period of concubinage (though not necessarily without previous sexual intimacy), most frequently occurred among young people who 'grew in church together' or whose parents were church members.

But marriage has also class associations and is not only the respectable form of union but one of the indices of upward movement in the social scale. There is also a myth that 'in the old days' marriage was the norm and that then even unions based on concubinage were meant to be lifelong. An old lady, born in 1884 whose husband was five years her senior, belonging to a respected Sugartown family in comfortable circumstances, gave the following account of the proper procedure to be followed, which, though doubtless to be taken with circumspection, is not a solitary instance. If two young people wished to be united the first thing would have to be for the families on either side to approve of each other. Not one member must have any stigma attached to his name. In her own case her lover went to her parents and asked for her hand, and his parents came and saw her parents, and they talked it over. In those days if a man married a girl and found her not to be a virgin, he would send her back to her parents and probably take them to court for breach of contract or some such thing. She was engaged to her husband for four years. In those days men had to force themselves on girls. She had loved her husband, but even after the engagement she would not even smile at him. She was not allowed to talk to him. If they were found, say on the street, talking, she would have been flogged. He used to come to her house and after paying his respects to her parents, he would go off to talk with her brothers. Their only speech together must be in the hearing of elders. Their only means of private communication was by writing. 'In those days young ladies had to "wait". But girls of today do not wait—they force themselves upon men. No young people lived in concubinage; only old people who more so wanted companions and couldn't be bothered with marriage.' The same old lady had had eight children by her husband. Two of her daughters had given her illegitimate grandchildren, but she said she 'never forced the issue for marriage because she did not think the men suitable. The girls had had their fun and were penitent and allowed her to handle the situation. They went away to forget the affair and left the children with her.'

To the question whether marriage is more likely to take place between the children of married parents our data gives an inconclusive answer. In some cases we were told that the parents' example had been the reason for a marriage in the next generation, but the reverse was as often true. A girl who had seen a promiscuous mother bring up a family without any help from their fathers sometimes took the example to heart and decided to seek the greater security of marriage. The experience of being herself left with a child to support unaided often led a girl to declare that this would not happen to her again unless the man promised marriage.

Only in Orange Grove among our Centres is society so organized that pressure can be deliberately exercised on the behaviour of individuals. Here marriage has the sanction of respectability and is also the hall mark of status. A small farmer who acknowledged having been promiscuous in his youth when he travelled about the Island said he would never have thought of marriage in those days, but when he returned to Orange Grove and began to farm he married 'to satisfy the public—if he had not, discrimination would have come right in their midst'. In Sugartown individual behaviour and personal relations were not subject to the vigilant criticism of kin or neighbours to anything like the same degree. Apart from the religious incentive, there was no social disapprobation of concubinage nor bias towards marriage among the workers or the old families. In Mocca, where family and kin are stressed, public opinion was exerted towards the maintenance of unions and the recognition of parental, conjugal and kinship responsibility, without any particular stress on marriage.

Before embarking on marriage, both partners are expected to show that they have finally ended any previous attachments, and they must also be given time to demonstrate what is generally described as their 'intention to live together' or their 'faithfulness'.

There is no question, however, of postponing cohabitation till this devotion has been tested. In fact it is firmly believed that the testing can be done only over a long period of living together. According to a Jamaican proverb, 'come see me and come live with me are two different things'.

The period of free cohabitation, following as it may a number of experimental unions, is rationalised as a necessary trial of compatibility which is not only expedient but respectable, since it ensures the stability of the marriage which follows. Great contempt was often expressed for a couple 'who just picked up themselves and married right off'. One woman criticizing such a procedure said that if she herself were to get married she would have to live with the man about three years first. Married people must not only believe but know from experience that they can trust one another, and this was impossible 'if you just butt up a man one day and marry him tomorrow'. The result of these attitudes is that the ceremony is often postponed until after the birth of all or many of the children. One marriage in our records followed a concubinage of 14 years during which six children were born.

During the trial period there are certain qualities for which the woman is 'tested'. Fidelity or the intention of being faithful is the first. A woman should show that she can be discreet and that she can justify the higher degree of confidence and trust which a wife has a right to expect. She should bear with poverty, if it comes their way, without discussing it with neighbours. She should not be familiar with anyone not her own equal. One man enumerated the qualities he looked for in a wife as speech, ability (in other words intelligence), and that she should have a good shape. He looked to see if she had ambition and if she was familiar with anyone—man or woman—who was not 'qualified as herself'. (This he explained as meaning 'people who do not look up'.) She must be able to cook, too, and wash and do housework.

Despite all this emphasis on practical qualities, it must not be assumed that, as one girl put it, 'love was not important'. We had a touching tribute by an old lady of ninety of her husband's devotion. He was her good husband she said, and excused her tears by explaining that when a man had been as good to you as he had been to her, you could not remember him without crying. He was faithful and a husband in need and deed. They were 'like kite and tail'.

IV

Marriage occurs, therefore, as a latter stage in an association begun in concubinage and is an indication that the economic conditions regarded as obligatory have been fulfilled. and that the contracting parties have approved one another sufficiently to risk the change in status and responsibilities which marriage implies. It marks the end of a free association which can be dissolved at any time at the will of either party and also the end of a period during which the woman may find herself left wholly responsible for the maintenance of the children of the union. The shared life and the birth of children gives the opportunity for the paternal role to be developed and marriage at this stage is an indication that this role has been learned and that the father accepts his responsibilities. After marriage a man stops wandering about the country and settles down. Marriage is an expression of the solidarity which has gradually been built up within the household. It is true that in discussions on this subject the emphasis is always placed on the change of status *in the couple:* and particularly on that of the woman. But whereas in concubinage of any type the children are in all respects mainly if not wholly dependent on the mother, marriage by confirming the permanence of the union between the parents emphasises the father-child relationship. It also gives the opportunity for continuity in the sibling relationships. Thus, in marriage, the primary kinship relationships suffer least disruption and are most strongly developed. Marriage occurring after a period of cohabitation is, in other words, the affirmation of stability; the seal on a proven conjugal union.

V

Marriage itself and the family consultations which precede it are formal matters which follow a prescribed pattern. We have a number of detailed accounts of marriage procedure. That which follows was given us by a Sugartown man who described it as 'the correct procedure as practised here'.

Once the couple have decided that they wish to marry the matter should, he said, be taken up with the two families concerned. The man takes the matter first to his mother and father. He says: 'Mother I am going to marry a girl for better ambition'. Then the mother says 'Bring her and let me see her'. If the mother does not like her she does not like her, but she cannot stop the marriage. But that certain amount of help that she would give she does not give. The girl then takes the man to see her parents and they give their approval. After these formalities the date is fixed and the couple go and see the parson and fix the date with him. All the family, both sets of parents, the godfather, the best man, the godmother and the chief bridesmaid must know the date before you give invitations to outsiders. After that is settled, when you go to the parson he will instruct you, and the godfather and godmother also can instruct you. You pick the line of clothes you want to wear and inform the godfather and godmother to wear similar.

If you give out invitations you get presents up to one month before the wedding. If you are going to marry in April you give the godfather and godmother notice from January and give out invitations to outsiders in February. The godfather and godmother must get their invite a month before the outsiders. Presents start coming and you get eggs from the guests. These are for the cakes. Our informant said his wedding cake took ten dozen eggs but nine dozen would be all right. You choose who you want to make the cake or the godfather will tell you who to give it out to.

The godmother goes with your wife to purchase clothes. The

godmother must be an older person who is married already. All godfathers and godmothers have to be married and must be older than you. If you are marrying in April, you start buying the dress from February and give it to the dressmaker. The same thing applies to the man and his suit. The godfather is supposed to dress the man and the godmother the bride.

Our informant had acted differently; he had done it in his own way. He had invited the tailor to the wedding to make him dress him. The dressmaker was supposed to dress the bride. The next thing is to 'fortify the home' and get a man and woman to look after the furniture. They have to be invited to stay days before the wedding. You don't pay them. They are called housemaid or housekeeper. They are guests whom you invite for the special purpose of keeping the house. They don't have to be married but they must be respectable people. You charter and fortify the house three months before the wedding and the housemaid has to visit from that time and keep it in order.

If you are young the parents handle the furniture but you choose it. The girl's parents are expected to aid financially but it is left to their mind and pocket—they are not compelled to do so. If they don't the boy's parents might feel funny but they would not let them know.

After the furniture is bought everybody slacks off but a week before the wedding they get busy again. They see that the clothes come in and the cake is given out to be made. One day before the wedding the cake comes in. If you are going to marry and come to your house everything is done there; but if you are going to marry and go to your parents' home everything is done there.

The night before the wedding is the 'set-up' night because people come from far and you have nowhere to put them up to sleep so everybody keeps up the night. In the early night you have the first prayer meeting. You sing and drink tea, cocoa and chocolate. You have bread, plenty bread, for the guests bring bread, even show bread. They also bring plenty of presents.

At this point our informant showed us a table crowded with

glassware which were presents he received at his wedding. He kept them, he said, as souvenirs and if a friend were getting married he would lend him some for the occasion.

At the set-up the boy can go to sleep under the care of the godfather. The girl can go and sleep with her friends but the godmother must know where she is so that she can find her for prayer meeting in the morning. At three o'clock on the morning of the wedding the prayer meeting begins. Before the prayer meeting they give instructions to the couple. The godfather, the godmother, the mother and father of both the boy and the girl are present. The couple are told you are going to meet trials, crosses and worries in the world. You must live a clean life, not to yourself but to God and man; and that is love. And in that love now, you must first love your wife, love your mother and your father and give the same to the world. Wife submit yourself to your husband, and husband submit yourself to your wife. Wife take heed from your husband, also husband take heed from your wife. Be not a hater to people in the world or to anyone because you would not be living a good life towards God. You must first love yourself and love your wife; also God will love you.

Here our informant interjected that that was a part of the general advice and admonishment given the couple and he was sure from it we could 'galvarate plenty', which was taken to mean that we could imagine the rest of the homily.

After all this they come out into the hall where all the friends are gathered and they pray for you and you pray for God's blessing on the match. This starts from three in the morning and goes on until 6 a.m. Then they drink tea and everybody begins to tidy for the church. After tea they take away the man and he does not see his wife again till at church. The godfather and godmother take the man to church and then return for the bride.

After the ceremony you go back home a new man and address the people, give a personal experience and the godfather and godmother encourage. Whatsoever happens to the couple the godfather and godmother are responsible. If they have any disagreement they have to come and thrash it out with them. The couple must never discuss their disagreements with any outsider but only with the godparents.

The party then moves to where the wedding feast has been laid out. Since the houses are too small to accommodate everybody the yard is prepared for the occasion. A booth is erected under which are tables and benches. The best man and the chief bridesmaid cut the cake. The best man sets the knife in the centre and counts one, two, three. After three the one that cuts first is going to marry first. They take off the crown of the cake, the size of a cup, uncut, and only the man and wife must eat that. The crumbs of the cake must not fall on the ground for a dog to eat it for if this were to happen the couple would not have a good life. But you can take some of the crumbs and burn it in fire and give to dog, and then if any drop and dog eats it it is all right.

The duties of the godmother and godfather are therefore to see that all the arrangements for the wedding are properly made and to take charge of the couple on the eve of the marriage. At the wedding ceremony itself the best man and the chief bridesmaid are the principal functionaries. In the account just given we were told that it was the godparents who took the couple to the church. The more usual custom, however, is for the best man and the chief bridesmaid to accompany them, and the best man to escort the bride and the bridesmaid the groom. If there is no father of the bride the best man gives her away. The best man and the bridesmaid sign the register. At the reception the godmother again takes charge and is assisted by the best man and all the bridesmaids. The toastmaster has no other function than to organize the speeches but both godparents address the couple and admonish them as to their duties to one another, to their respective families and their neighbours.

FOOTNOTES TO CHAPTER 3

31 *Revised Laws of Jamaica,* Chap. 122.
32 For a fuller discussion of this subject, including figures in regard to the number of legitimate compared with outside children present in homes based on marriage and concubinage in proportion to the number born to the parents, see Chap. V, p. 115 et seq.
33 Section 2 of Chap. 453, *The Maintenance Law.*
34 See Chap. VI, pp. 176-7, for an account of 'schoolgirl' domestic help.
35 The figures show that there were 75 couples living together in Orange Grove of whom 56 were married and 19 lived in concubinage. Comparative figures for the other Centres were: Sugartown 58 married couples, 161 in concubinage and Mocca 22 married, 40 in concubinage.

CHAPTER 4

Sex, Procreation and the Institutions of Concubinage

———————

I

ATTITUDES and practices in regard to sex and procreation vary considerably between our Centres. In Orange Grove marriage is predominantly the accepted form of conjugal union, the percentage of married couples being 75 per cent as compared with 35 per cent in Mocca and 26 per cent in Sugartown. The illegitimacy rate was low and there was nothing comparable with the casual concubinage and promiscuity of Sugartown. Families live in large, well-furnished houses which allow for the children to have separate sleeping accommodation from their parents. Among the upper class farmers and their wives it was difficult, if not impossible, to discuss the subject of sex. Whenever it was introduced it was shied away from, either with shocked surprise or a refusal to admit that irregular sex relations ever took place. The comment made on our inquiry by one Orange Grove citizen was that 'when he heard the rumour that we were asking sex questions he did not credit it for he thought we could not be so out of order'. The implication was that in the upper strata marriage was the invariable form of union and that concubinage and illegitimacy were only to be found among the lower middle class families belonging to the old settlement whose cottages clustered on the fringes of the larger modern farms. Casual sex relations, which did in fact take place, were surreptitious and usually carried on outside the village.

Marital infidelity was a serious breach of the social code whether

90

in wife or husband. Great emphasis was placed on proper 'discretion' in a wife. The husband of a woman who did not behave with proper decorum was not only commiserated, but blamed for having married her. It was said of a much respected farmer that 'in his youth he was a wild man and was caught and had to marry her'. The history of this particular couple shows that the indiscretions of men are not regarded with equal severity, at least by their own sex, though in his case some of the forbearance shown him was due to the position his family held in the community whereas his wife was an outsider of whom such high standards were not expected.

In Sugartown, by contrast, sex was a favourite subject of conversation with both men and women. Men enjoyed talking about their sexual prowess, the number of children they had fathered and the number of their conquests, referring with especial pride to any relationship with a virgin. Both men and women regarded sexual activity as a normal part of adult and adolescent life, and there was never any attempt to temper the discussion if children were present. Childish and adolescent precocity was, on the contrary, regarded with tolerant amusement and, in the case of boys, with admiration.

As was to be expected in a community where it was the pattern of the majority, couples living in concubinage showed no embarrassment about their status. There was reticence, however, among concubines no less than wives, about acknowledging any differences in parenthood of outside children in the home. This had first to be deduced when we learned of the discrepancy in surnames. Married couples rarely take their outside children into the home. One reason for this is the fact that the husband then becomes liable for their maintenance; another is that the presence of an illegitimate child would be regarded as a stigma in the enhanced social status which marriage carries with it. Even in homes based on concubinage, however, it was unusual for outside children to be present. One cause was the financial responsibility, since the Bastardy Law makes a man liable for their maintenance in such cases. But besides the man's reluctance 'to support another man's bastards' the women were jealous of the man's children by another woman and feared that it might perpetuate the previous association with the mother. They were also, not without reason, fearful where the child was an adolescent girl, of her stepfather's interest in her.

The figures show that there were considerable differences between the Centres. (36) In Orange Grove there were illegitimate children in only four married families and in six based on concubinage, or 13 per cent and 50 per cent of the total number of families where children are present. Here also the percentage of married couples among all conjugal unions was 75 per cent as compared with 35 per cent in Mocca and 26 per cent in Sugartown. In Sugartown the proportions were 14 per cent and 40 per cent and in Mocca 9 per cent and 21 per cent. Where outside children are included in the home it frequently causes friction and may lead to the break-up of the union. If the couple are childless, however, outside children, generally of the woman, may be happily included. In one interesting case in Sugartown a married couple had living with them four children of the wife all by different fathers. She would not discuss the subject but I learned from her husband that, although they had lived together for seven years before mariage, they had had no children and all those in the house had been born before they met. He said that he treated them as his own and tried to do his best by them, setting up both boys and girls in a trade.

In Mocca, where the conjugal pattern is concubinage for life, the family is all important and there was not the least hesitancy in discussing the outside children in the household nor any difficulty in getting particulars in regard to their different fathers. Here illegitimacy has no social significance. At the same time there is little open discussion of sex, and none before their womenfolk. The stress here is on kinship and any extra-conjugal relationships which threatened to disrupt an existing union would be regarded as a serious matter by the family of the injured party. Here, as in Orange Grove, promiscuous or casual affairs were surreptitious and furtive compared with Sugartown where they were carried on openly and where they had greater social importance because of the number of children born to couples who only came together for the period during which work was to be had on the sugar estate. It is important to appreciate the very different background to sex and family life in Sugartown as compared with either of our other Centres if we are to understand the differences between the 'concubinage' of Mocca and the casual parenthood of Sugartown and the meaning of kinship terms in all three communities.

Out of 'crop' when the boom of relatively high earnings ceased, and the bulk of migrant labour had departed, the pattern of life among the permanent residents was not unlike that in Mocca or among the poorer families in Orange Grove. There was great poverty but then few of the permanent residents participated in the higher wages; those who had received an income from renting rooms or huts on family land were temporarily the poorer and tradesmen, barbers, butchers and the like had both to extend, and live, themselves, on credit. But for the majority life returned to a norm which has existed for generations, where family and kinship ties were respected. The principal fact in the latter was the existence of family land and the rights of the kin in respect of it.

Against this background we have to take into account the peculiar features of crop-time life which create a different type of behaviour in regard to sex and procreation.

The male migrants who pour into Sugartown for the crop were either older men who had some alternative means of support at home, if only a small piece of land, to which they intended to return or men who had no regular means of livelihood anywhere. Some of these were youngsters just starting life, others had already, as their life histories showed, moved from one place to another for years. As one graphically phrased it: 'In the *tempo motto* I ping-pong around, one week on, one week off'. Many of the older men had left families at home. Many had had a large number of consecutive irregular unions in different parts of the Island. The majority arrived penniless or with only a few shillings in their pockets. Those who had a kinsman in the district were sure of receiving help until they got work. Others could rely on the hospitality of anyone who hailed from his own district or parish. The most pressing need was for somewhere to live and money to pay rent.

The immediate effect on the community was to increase the congestion in the existing huts and cottages. One if not the principal means of livelihood among the old residents was renting one-roomed thatched huts which they erected on family land or taking in lodgers in the family house. Both in the huts and in the barrack rooms, men, and in many cases men and women, shared sleeping accommodation. This often led to temporary quasi-conjugal relationships which relieved some of the immediate economic needs of the partners. They pooled their resources and shared living expenses. The man got someone to do his marketing, cook his food and wash his clothes for considerably less than it would cost him to pay for these services, an alternative which is in any case unpopular. (One man told us that 'after having had lots of sweethearts who treated him badly' he was reduced to having to pay a lady 9s. a week to cook for him). The woman was assured of her keep and a roof over her head. She continued her normal activities but could now spend whatever she earned on clothes and other necessities and send money to assist in the maintenance of any children she might have left at home. Although these 'house-keeper' arrangements as they are called may not be formed primarily for sexual reasons, it is normal for the parties to have sexual relations and for children to be born.

While some of the incoming women were genuinely seeking work on the sugar estate many flocked in with the hope of enjoying an easy life when 'the money began to flow'. We were warned by a local resident to expect this influx soon after crop began. 'Then men begin to talk big and there will be plenty of merry-making and love-making because there is plenty of money.' Another told us that 'every year a heap of women come with no intention to work but to get what they can out of the men. Three of them may take a room together and grab the first man that comes along'. These women are called by different names. 'One year it was "dill-dill", another "factory ranger", another "leggo beans".' The year we were there the term was 'pinks'. They had an effect on the local girls some of whom soon began to imitate them, 'playing coquette' as it was called. While the 'real professional' had a scale of fees the local girls prided themselves that they did not receive payment in money though it was correct for the men to entertain them at dances and make them presents of food or clothing. Because of the fear of venereal disease many of the men said they preferred to go with the local girls and would make advances to the more attractive and precocious adolescents as they paraded in the main street in their best clothes in the evenings. A number of women in Sugartown told us that they preferred a variety of lovers to having one man and being faithful to him. A girl in her twenties said she had broken with her family because her mother objected to her having many lovers and wanted her to settle down and get married and this she had no intention of doing. A nineteen year-old girl had borne her first child at fifteen and had had many affairs with men whom she 'did not love, because she wanted to—because it was nature'.

Not only is sexual activity regarded as natural: it is unnatural not to have had a child and no woman who has not proved that she can bear one is likely to find a man to be responsible for her since 'no man is going to propose marriage to such a woman'. Maternity is a normal and desirable state and the childless woman is an object of pity, contempt or derision. 'A child is God's gift' and 'nothing should be done to prevent the birth of a child'. A woman who does not have children is believed to suffer physically; she will also suffer from nervousness and headaches and may even go insane, if she does not have the full number that she is destined to have. A midwife told us that she was always asked after a birth how many 'knots' there were in the umbilical cord, as this is held to be an index to the number of children the mother was meant to bear. A barren woman may be referred to as a 'mule'. A man may even desert his wife because of her childlessness. There was a case in Orange Grove where the man left his wife because, although she had previously had a child, she bore none to him. In such cases the man may believe that 'he and his woman do not match'.

Just as a woman is only considered 'really' a woman after she has borne a child, so the proof of a man's maleness is the impregnation of a woman. There is, therefore, no incentive for either men or women to avoid parenthood even in promiscuous relationships: on the contrary, it is the hall-mark of adulthood and normal, healthy living. There is a very common belief that a man knows, in the act of coition, that he has impregnated the woman. The man is satisfied by the proof of his virility and does not necessarily accept any of the obligations and duties of parenthood. These are generally accepted as the woman's responsibility and there is no public censure if he does not acknowledge or fulfil them.

At the same time women are acutely aware of the economic burden which children represent if they have no male support for them. This fear has to be set against the desire for children as an insurance against old age. Once therefore a woman has demonstrated that she is able to bear a child she may seek to avoid having another by recourse to drugs or 'bush' medicines which are supposed to bring on menstruation. Such action was condemned by the men. One man said that 'plenty of girls took medicines to the disapproval of their men. They waited till the man had gone to work and then boiled the bush and drank it and when the man came home they would cry out for pains and tell him that they had had a fall or some such thing and he would have to believe it'. We were told that some 'bad mothers' took their young daughters to the dispenser and asked him to do away with 'the stomach' as pregnancy is described. In view of this attitude it was not surprising to find that we had no evidence of any use of contraceptives except in Sugartown where the men were said to use them in intercourse with the 'pinks', not with the object of avoiding impregnating the woman but of avoiding venereal disease. There was considerable fear of this which was one reason why men said they preferred to go with the local girls, many of the 'professionals' being said to be 'unsafe'.

In view of the general attitude to sex and the high value placed upon fertility it is remarkable that the first pregnancy of an adolescent girl, in Sugartown no less than in Mocca or Orange Grove, normally provokes from her mother a reaction which would imply general recognition of a much stricter code.

Throughout the innumerable accounts which fill our records of the girl's early training we repeatedly come across the statement—from women with a high record of promiscuity no less than from those living in marriage or life-long concubinage—'I was brought up strictly'. This, within the context, meant that girls were warned against having sex-play with boys at school, discouraged from casual relationships as they grew older, and punished when pregnancy occurred while they were still young and living at home.

In the overcrowded living conditions of the homes in Sugartown and Mocca children invariably acquired knowledge of sex at a very early age from sharing sleeping accommodation with adults of both sexes. What children did not learn from observation they picked up from other children at school. There were many accounts of boys and girls having intercourse at school (usually in the latrine) but in some cases their initiation was by a much older person. Seduction of young girls by older men was said to be due in some instances to the belief that intercourse with a virgin was a cure for gonorrhoea.

There was plenty of evidence that mothers warned their daughters against sex-play. In Sugartown, as compared with Orange Grove and Mocca, the society as a whole did little to reinforce her teaching. When, as we shall see, the girl became pregnant and was expelled from her mother's home, kinsfolk and neighbours alike intervened to effect a reconciliation. Moreover, injunctions to avoid premature sex and procreation were given by the mother only to her girl child.

It does not appear that girls were warned in advance by their mothers to expect menstruation or to associate it with sexual maturity. Although there were exceptions, it was more usual for a girl to derive her knowledge of this, as of sex in general, from other girls. In some cases menstruation began soon after sexual relations and was thought by the girl to be caused by intercourse. There was, however, sufficiently strong evidence of repugnance among adult women of intercourse during menstruation to believe that formal instruction was given as to the impropriety of this.

Sexual intercourse during pregnancy was regarded as necessary for the well-being of mother and child and to ensure easy delivery. There appeared to be some reluctance on the part of most women to resume sexual intercourse in the early months after childbirth but not enough evidence to suggest that there is any taboo. A Mocca woman told us that she kept away from her husband from three to six months after her children were born.

'Boys are not taught as much as girls.' They were not punished as are the girls if their early sex experimentation was discovered, nor did they receive any instruction from their fathers as to the responsibilities of paternity. Moreover, there was no adult pattern of male conjugal or paternal responsibility in the Sugartown community as a whole for the young boy to imitate or be influenced by. On the contrary, his early sex-play was regarded with amused indifference, if not admiration, by the older men and he early learned the general attitude of his seniors that children are primarily if not solely 'woman's business'. It was not part of the social ethic that he should provide for his girl and their children. In fact, his own personal home life as well as that of the majority of his playmates and companions, might demonstrate the exact opposite. There were, of course, exceptions, and important exceptions, among the old families and permanent residents of Sugartown. But on the whole it is to Orange Grove and Mocca that we have to turn to find examples of fathers lavishing care and affection on their children and carrying out their conjugal and paternal duties.

It is usual for the girl's first pregnancy to occur while she is still a dependant in her mother's home. The mother's behaviour when she discovers her daughter's condition falls into four almost ritualized stages. The girl's misconduct is always said to have been carried on surreptitiously without her knowledge and brought to her attention only when the signs of pregnancy become apparent. The discovery is greeted with noisy upbraiding, the girl is severely beaten, and in many cases turned out of the house. In the second stage the girl takes refuge with a neighbour or kinswoman. After a period, which may be quite short, the kinsfolk and neighbours intercede with the mother on her behalf, and the girl is taken back into her mother's home for the birth of her child.

In these cases the role of the lover varies but in general it rests with the mother to decide whether any recognition should be given to the baby's father. If it is a boy and girl affair he is unlikely to be in any position to support her or provide a home for her and his parents do not concern themselves with the affair. The mother takes over responsibility for her grandchild and may send her daughter away to a relative in order to sever all connection with the young man. If, however, he is an older man in a position to 'compensate the girl for spoiling her' her mother may keep her at home and urge him to contribute towards the birth expenses and the maintenance of the baby. In neither of these situations does the mother press for him to enter into any form of domestic relationship with the girl, partly because she is said to be too young and inexperienced and partly because the correct preliminaries—a formal courtship including asking the consent of her parents—had not been complied with.

It would be inaccurate to describe these pregnancies as occurring in a context of general adolescent promiscuity since in a large proportion of cases they were stated by the girl concerned to be the result of a first and exclusive sexual relationship with one boy. Such an incident may even sometimes be said to be an isolated episode in a girl's life. If the mother allows the relationship to continue it resembles a prolonged honeymoon, or a courtship including rights of sexual access generally understood to be exclusive.

During this period the relationship may become stable so that it is not dissimiliar to the trial period of the *purposive concubinage* to be described later.

Occasionally the boy comes to stay with her in her mother's house but this is rare. The young fellow whose irresponsible sex play has fortuitously resulted in paternity is no more anxious to accept the subordinate status which this would involve than he is to take responsibility for his child.

In the case of a girl's first pregnancy, therefore, her mother, after the traditional display of disapproval and the conventional reconciliation, normally takes charge of the baby and assumes responsibility for its care and upbringing. In subsequent pregnancies the procedure is generally different. Most women are too heavily burdened by their own domestic responsibilities to encourage grown-up daughters and their children to remain with them. Exceptions may occur where the grandmother is joint occupier of family land and the daughter has the right to build her own house on it. The girl, with her children, may then set up her own establishment, in a type of *denuded family household*.

The harsh parental discipline and premature responsibility imposed on her may shock the girl into avoiding casual relationships for some time. She may decide 'not to have anything to do with men any more' or if she does, to follow her mother's injunctions and try to find a man who is in a position to be responsible for her. This ambition may be strengthened by the experience of continued dependence on the limited resources of her mother or parents. For although the bearing of a child has social significance as marking the girl's transition from childhood to full womanhood, and the mother is now encouraged, by kinsfolk and neighbours, to recognize her daughter's new status and reshape her attitude and behaviour to her, the girl's economic dependence upon her may now be greater than ever. It is impossible, as we show later, for the single woman to keep herself and her children on her earnings and it is these circumstances that there develop the type of 'housekeeper' domestic arrangements which deserve to be classed as a form of concubinage. They must be distinguished from those forms which may be described as *purposive* where, as a result of a free and deliberate selective process, a man and woman decide to test their compatibility with a view to spending the rest of their lives together. In contra-distinction these relationships (most common in Sugartown) are entered into almost haphazardly, with no implication of permanence and are inevitably highly unstable. If the woman becomes pregnant the association invariably breaks up either immediately or after the child is born. Usually the woman goes back to her mother's home for the birth of the baby, and more often than not does not return. In other cases, the couple separate when the man goes away after crop.

These domestic or housekeeper arrangements are clearly recognized, by both men and woman, as implying a lower status for the woman than is attached to other types of conjugal union. The euphemistic term for the concubine is 'girl friend' or, for an older woman, 'Miss So and So'. In these cases the man will often deny that she is his 'lady' or 'wife' and refer to her as his 'housekeeper' or 'servant', or may simply say that she 'looks after' him. He would often deny that he knew her 'real' name. A single man, aged twenty-five, who had been in Sugartown two years told us that he had 'a lady' but insisted that her only function was to 'provide for him'. Not only is there a different emotional tone in referring to her, but her inferior status was often implicit in her behaviour when the couple were interviewed together. The woman would refrain from participating in the conversation or be evasive or shame-faced, and take the first opportunity of slipping away. There was none of the free give-and-take in discussion which characterized the behaviour where there was recognized equality. It was always difficult, for example, when the man was present to get any information from the woman as to her previous history and, in particular, about her children, if she had any, and where they were. If the woman was a stranger to the district the man neither knew, nor wanted to know, of any responsibilities she might have acquired from previous relations with other men. In no instance would she be permitted to have her children with her or send anything to them from the money she was given to run the establishment. For this reason, as much as any other she was never 'trusted' with any intimate knowledge of the man's earnings, nor given any fixed sum: 'she took what she was given because she might be told to go at any time'.

The distinguishing features of these non-purposive unions are, therefore, the fortuitous manner in which they occur, their transitory nature and the inferior status of the woman. She has little expectation that the arrangement will last or provide any permanent solution of her economic problems. Moreover, she cannot claim the man's exclusive sexual attention though if she were found to be going with another man she would certainly be turned out.

Nevertheless they do occasionally develop into something more mutually satisfying and last for some years. Thus one woman began a relationship which lasted eight years by meeting the man with whom her brother shared a room and acceding to his persuasion that she join them. 'She went and they began to like each other but the word had not been said between them. Being in the home she would do little things for him. She washed his clothes and looked after the house and little by little, as she had no one and he had no one they came together.' This is relatively rare, however, and depends not only on personal factors but on the man's getting regular employment. If he fails to do this and goes away at the end of crop, even if he returns the following year, it is by no means certain that he will take up with the same woman again—even if she has borne his child in the interval. In fact this added liability may well be the deciding factor in his seeking another woman. Nevertheless the repetition, in one life history after another, of some such phrase as 'I must seek a man to be responsible for me' leads to the conclusion that even the most casual-seeming concubinage is not without the hope, on the woman's side, that it may lead to a permanent domestic establishment.

III

A very different type of union is that which may be described as matrilocal. In one type of these there is no cohabitation. A girl whose parents have an interest in family land tends to remain on it and if she is still in her mother's home it is rare for the man to join her. Where she shares a family house with other siblings she may as in the case of Nesta, already described, have a long succession of lovers by whom she bears children, without any of the men ever joining the household. (37) Nevertheless the relationship between the couple is different from that which obtains in the boy and girl affairs in the situation of the first pregnancy. The woman performs many of the duties of the wife or concubine, such as cooking for her man, sending his meals to his home or work place, and washing his clothes. The fact that she owns the house, however, gives her the right to terminate the arrangement at her will. If she discovers that the man is going with other women or if he fails to make a contribution towards the maintenance of herself and their children, she can tell him to go.

In the more usual type of matrilocal union the man joins the woman in a separate house belonging to her on the family land, or she is given a house-site on which he builds their own house. In the latter case the woman is said to own the land and the man the house. Theoretically he would have the right to remove it if they parted but since it is usually only a wattle and plaster thatched hut it is rarely worth his while doing this. Moreover since the woman invariably assists in the building, either by doing some of the lighter work or by preparing the food when the work is done with the assistance of kin or neighbours on the partnership system, any such action on his part would be strongly resented.

In both these types of concubinage the woman has the companionship and the economic advantage of a man to help her and at the same time of establishing her right of use of the family land. The man has the security of a roof over his head and is not in danger of becoming homeless when he is unable to find money for rent.

When unions of this sort break up, the children remain with the mother. In accordance with the principle of succession they will inherit their right to the family land to which their father has no claim. Since the actual size of the holding may be no more than a few square chains, adult sons are expected to go out to try to earn a living but there is a tendency for the daughters to stay on and most of our grandmother households were formed in this way.

The significant feature of matrilocal unions as compared with patrilocal unions is their association with family land, not only in the denuded type of households but in those of the simple and extended family types. In Sugartown, in simple family type households, the proportions of matrilocal unions where there is land was 88 per cent as compared with 20 per cent in patrilocal households. In Mocca the proportion was 88 per cent to 45 per cent. In extended family types the proportion is 70 per cent and 32 per cent in Sugartown and 85 per cent and 65 per cent in Mocca. In Orange Grove as we have shown the great majority of farms are owned by the man. Matrilocal unions occur most frequently in both Sugartown and Mocca in extended family type households the proportion to patrilocal households being 47 per cent and 38 per cent respectively.

IV

The distinctive feature of what we have termed purposive concubinage is that the union is entered into after a formal courtship in which the man promises both the girl and her parents to look after her as she were his wife. It is not uncommon for him actually to promise marriage or give some indication that he may seriously intend to make her his wife if the trial period is satisfactory. We have a number of accounts from men in Sugartown of the difference in the approach they would make to a girl in the first instance if they were only 'playing round' or wanted her 'as a bed mate' and if they were seriously asking her to come and live with them. In the latter case, we were told, he would take time to court her, escort her from school or church and when he was satisfied that their attraction was mutual if she were young and living with her parents, he would ask her to invite him to meet them. He should then ask their consent to the 'friendship'—a term which is used to include sexual intercourse. If the mother is satisfied that his intentions are serious and that there is a likelihood of the young couple being faithful to one another she may give her consent without pressing for any formal union. While the couple do not set up house at once and may not do so even after the birth of two or more children, a relationship begun thus formally will, more often than not, develop into a domestic union and may culminate in marriage. Whether it does or does not depends a great deal on the mother's approval and it is evident from our records that she may sometimes break up such an association even against the wishes of the young couple.

In this type of concubinage the 'expectations' of the man and the woman differ in no way from marriage. There is the same insistence on the ideal of sexual exclusiveness and, in fact, many unions were dissolved by the woman no less than the man on account of unfaithfulness. Since we found it generally accepted that young men must have their fling it is probable, however, that women showed a good deal more forbearance than appeared from some of their statements. Only if the offence became blatant, so that the woman, besides having to share her man's earnings with another woman, lost face in the community, did her patience give out.

In concubinage, as distinct from marriage, however, the woman accepts the fact that she will have to contribute to the household budget by doing whatever work she can find, and neither she nor her man loses prestige by this. In Sugartown the man is expected to make his full contribution during crop when work is available. In the *tempo moto*, when he is unemployed or under-employed, the burden of making ends meet may fall largely on her. For her to do her share is regarded as normal and is only resented by her if the man spends too much of his earnings on outside pleasures or fails over long periods to get work. What was, however, never tolerated was that he should spend money on other women. Thus a woman described her first concubinage as having begun very happily. James was her first lover, and, to begin with, he treated her very well. 'He loved every thread that sewed my frock.' But after about five years he 'ceased to mind (support) me', began having other women, and sleeping out at nights. She had had two children by him in the nine years they lived together: 'both of us did love one another but as he would not mind me, I left him'.

The man for his part recognizes his obligations to support the woman while they are together but bitterly resents it if she makes unreasonable demands or deserts him when he falls upon hard times. In his view, the woman in concubinage should be obedient and shoulder her full share of the work; if she refuses he may accuse her of wanting to be a wife and leave her.

The majority of men also acknowledged that they had a responsibility for the maintenance of their children by a woman with whom they had cohabited for any length of time. In many cases men were said to continue to send presents for their children long after they had parted from the woman and even after both had entered into another union. This, however, is clearly the ideal. Actually the contributions made after the couple have separated are spasmodic, the amount and regularity of the payments depending on whether the man is working or not and also on his subsequent liabilities. In the man's view they should be regarded as voluntary gifts: 'if he has it he will give it' and he considers it to be both unreasonable and vindictive for a woman to attempt to force him by, for instance, going to the court for a maintenance order. She should know that he has now other responsibilities and that he cannot support two families. In no case does he accept responsibility for the concubine herself once they have separated.

While the most common causes for the dissolution of concubinage were said to be 'unfaithfulness' and 'non-supportance' of the woman, there were many accounts of couples separating after a violent quarrel over a relatively trivial matter. It was not the custom for neighbours or friends to interfere on such occasions, nor was there any protest or attempt at reconciliation by the family of either of the partners. In the same way as concubinage is entered into without any formal rite involving either the respective families or the society, but by the simple action of the woman moving into the man's home or vice versa, so its dissolution is regarded as the private concern of the couple and no business of anyone else. However serious the intentions of the couple may have been when they began to live together and however sincere their attachment, the characteristic of concubinage is that it is held by men and women alike to be a free association which may be ended at any time at the will of either party, nor is the existence of dependent children held to qualify this freedom. There is no evidence whatsoever that either party to the arrangement take any precautions to avoid parenthood while the union is still in its experimental stage. On the contrary, it is rare for childless unions to endure; as rare as for marriage to occur before the birth of children.

So far as children in lower-class working homes are concerned therefore, the majority live, during their most formative years, in danger of the disruption at any moment of the closest kinship ties. Although it is a general pattern and not a unique individual experience, the effect of this instability in the relationship between his parents has a profound effect on the development of parent-child roles, and particularly that between father and child. The child who sees his mother turned out of the home for another woman may give expression to his hostility against the father by openly taking his mother's side. More often than not the strongest recollection which he carries over into adult life is of paternal indifference, or strictness if not harshness and outright neglect. Consciously or unconsciously he learns that it is to his mother he must look for any security or permanence in human relationships. In accordance with the general concept that children are 'woman's business', when the union breaks up the children are normally regarded as her responsibility. If she is immediately left destitute they may be sent to relatives or given away to friends or strangers. They, or some of them, may rejoin her when she is able to make a home for them but these denuded family homes seldom contained *all* the women's children. If and when she entered into another conjugal union it was rare for her to be able to have them with her. Thus siblings and half-siblings were separated and often distributed among a number of widely scattered households.

V

Concubinage as a conjugal union, that is as a relationship between a man and a woman, is not recognized in the legal code, which provides no safeguards for the woman living in concubinage. Her concubine is not liable for her maintenance nor for her necessaries. Unlike the prescriptions for marriage there is no formality for entering into such a union; apart from the general prohibition against incest, no prescription in regard to affinity; no redress for the woman if she is ejected by the man or if he brings another woman into the house.

The Maintenance and Bastardy Laws of Jamaica (*Revised Laws of Jamaica*, Chapters 452 and 453) make a man liable for the support of his illegitimate children provided they are under age, but the operation of this Law presents so many practical difficulties that it is not surprising that it is invoked far less often than it might be.

In the first place paternity has to be established. *The Law for the Registration of Births* (Chapter 121, section 17) provides that the name of the father of an illegitimate child may be entered by the Registrar on the registration form if the mother and the person acknowledging himself to be the father of such child attend personally before the Registrar and request him to make such entry. In such cases both parents sign the form. If, however, the father does not attend, if only for the reason that it is too much trouble, the woman's name alone appears on the certificate. This means that when the necessity arises for the woman to claim under the Maintenance and Bastardy Law the onus of proof of paternity rests on her. Proof may not, by that time, be either easy or possible, since however willing he may have been, at the time the baby was born, to acknowledge the child, the mere fact that a Court Order is being sought by the woman implies that the man is trying to avoid his obligations. Even where a Court Order is obtained, there are still difficulties in the way of collection of the money. In theory the man is ordered to pay the amount stated in the Court Order to the Clerk of the Courts from whom the woman should collect it. In practice this rarely happens for more than the first payment. Where the distance is not too great the woman goes herself or sends one of the children to the man for the weekly allowance. But if there is 'bad blood' (and there always is resentment over maintenance orders) the man will seek to avoid payment by changing the place of his abode. He can then be sued for contempt of court but a summons has to be served on him by the police and this is not easy in face of the general conspiracy of silence on the part of the man's friends and the difficulty of tracing him when he moves from one parish to another. It is more difficult to trace the whereabouts of an unmarried than a married father. In general marriage is associated with a higher economic status. Either a man owns land or a house and cannot readily abandon them or is in regular employment which he would be reluctant to leave. He is therefore less mobile than the poorer man who is satisfied with concubinage or with casual relationships with women as he moves from place to place in search of work, or sometimes to escape responsibilities he cannot fulfil. This latter fact—that by and large concubinage is an institution of the poor— also affects the extent to which it is worth while for the woman (who is extremely realistic in the matter) to invoke the law either where the man is unemployed and without adequate means to maintain a family, or, alternatively, so seriously estranged that it is likely that he will evade his responsibilities by leaving the district.

At the same time no one with experience of these cases will deny that as a rule the police show little enthusiasm for this duty and there is, moreover, the fact that any such action is vociferously condemned by men as vindictive and inconsiderate and is not regarded with favour even by other women. One may quote the case of a highly respectable woman deserted by her husband (at the time in regular well-paid employment), who was advised by a Poor Relief Officer to sue for maintenance. She attended at the Courts Office and was then able to give the necessary information as to his whereabouts. The police officer failed to serve the summons immediately; the man learned of the action being taken, left his job and took employment in another parish. He was traced by the Poor Relief Officer who informed the police of his whereabouts, and the summons was duly served. He was ordered by the Court to pay a few shillings a week. He paid for a few weeks and then disappeared. The woman reported that payments had ceased and was informed that if any action was to be taken the man's address would have to be provided. With the help of the Poor Relief Officer she was again able to find out where her husband was working and returned with the information. She said the policeman and the Clerk of the Courts laughed at her and asked why she went on persecuting the poor man. She declared she would never go back to the Courts, she had been made to feel humiliated and shamefaced.

There is also the fact that a maintenance claim is generally made by a woman when the man has left her, and invariably in such cases, incurred new liabilities. A case in point was that of a man, over fifty, a carpenter by trade who had had jobs for short periods only in different parts of the Island and who, at the time when we interviewed him, was still irregularly employed. He had had six children by five different women in the course of his travels. He was then 'in company' with the mother of two of his children but had recently had a baby by another woman. When this woman took him to court he said she was 'wicked'. He used to give her 6s a week for herself and the baby but she said it was not enough. She did not seem to realize that it was not she alone he had to look after. 'A man don't have to tell me to support my child but she must realize it's not one child I have to support.' This case illustrates the futility of any legal distribution of responsibility where paying Peter inescapably means depriving Paul, in this case later families, of their means of subsistence.

It is more usual for mothers to try to get assistance under the Poor Law. The condition of eligibility for relief is still what it was when this Law was passed in 1889. A person is eligible if he or she is 'wholly destitute and unable for physical or mental causes to maintain himself'. This is interpreted as meaning that a person is not eligible for relief merely because he or she may be temporarily incapacitated from earning his living unless it can also be shown that he is wholly destitute. It also means that even though a man or woman may be incapacitated by age or sickness he or she is still not eligible for relief if they own property, unless they are prepared to hand over such property to the Parochial Board. Family land is sometimes lost in this way although, as we have explained, the party in question may be only one of a group with equal rights, or may be trustee for a number of relatives.

In the early part of this century, the Board of Supervision of Poor Relief in Jamaica attempted to temper this definition by ruling that a woman whose husband was dead, having three or more children whom she was unable to support, might be deemed to be destitute. Strictly, in the terms of this Circular, only a widow may benefit by the concession but this qualification is in practice generally ignored so that it is now possible for a young able-bodied woman, who is precluded from earning her living by having to look after the appropriate number of young children, to obtain relief. The amount given varies from parish to parish, but is never more than a few shillings. Even so it is not much lower than the average sum granted on a court order under the Maintenance Law and presents none of the difficulties in collection which we have described. More important, accepting relief does not involve any loss of face. The extent to which this procedure is used is shown in the Poor Relief records and in the high proportion of the local relief paid out for which these cases are accountable.

The payment of a weekly dole to a mother, grandmother or guardian is known as Outdoor Relief and has the advantage that the family—even if it lacks a father—is kept together. Indoor Relief consists in sending children to an orphanage or industrial school or boarding them out in private homes. This type of relief is theoretically restricted to orphans or children deserted by both parents and should not be applied in cases where children are living with the mother, unless there is good reason to believe she is unfitted to be their guardian. Nevertheless, the Poor Relief authorities do offer indoor relief in cases where the mother is still of child-bearing age and where the children are by different men. Although this would be very much more costly if it were accepted, it is cheaper in the long run since many mothers are reluctant to part with their children and may refuse the offer of relief in this form. Even so a large proportion of the total expenditure of Poor Relief was spent on maintaining children in institutions many of whom are not orphans.

Underlying this drastic policy is the fear of local authorities lest the Poor Law be made the instrument of providing maintenance for children of 'single' mothers and so encourage irresponsible parenthood and yet further increase the already crippling charge on Parochial funds for poor relief.

FOOTNOTES TO CHAPTER 4

36 See Chapter 5 (iii).
37 See Chapter 2, p. 56 et seq.

CHAPTER 5

The Organization of the Households

———

I

IN view of the complexity of conjugal relationships and the high proportion of irregular types of union which we have shown to occur it is not surprising that there is a corresponding complexity in the structure of the households. (38) The questions we may ask are, to what extent is the household a family group containing a man and woman and their children, what is the pattern of other groupings and what are the differences between the Centres?

We were dealing with a total population of 2,280-1,533 adults and 747 children. There was a considerable difference in the size of the Centres. Sugartown contained 52 per cent of our total population. (39) Of the remainder 29 per cent lived in Orange Grove and 18 per cent in Mocca. (40)

In Orange Grove and Mocca there were more females than males, the proportion being 54 to 46 in each 100 in the former and 51 to 49 in the latter. In Sugartown males outnumber females to the tune of 52 to 48 in each 100. In the Island as a whole in 1943, the Census Reports show that females outnumbered males to the extent of 52 to 48 in the 100.

The percentage distribution of the adult female population shows important differences in the various age-groups between our Centres and in comparison with the All Island figures. (41) Taking the total population in all three centres we have a lower ratio of single women a higher proportion of women in concubinage but almost the same proportion of married women as in Jamaica as a whole in 1943.

In the younger age groups (all Centres) the differences from the Island figures are most pronounced. 35.5 per cent of our 15-19 age group live in marriage as compared with 1.7 per cent for the Island, a difference largely, though by no means wholly, to be explained by the high ratio of marriage in Orange Grove. Our Centres show 24.6 per cent living in concubinage as compared with the 5.3 per cent for the Island. In the 20-24 age group, there are the same considerable differences which however begin to decrease in the 25-29 group. After thirty the differences are mainly in our much higher figures for women in concubinage and our correspondingly lower figure for single women.

The figures for each Centre show, as we have come to expect, important differences.

Thus, for marriage, the nearest approach to the All Island figure of 26.2 per cent is in Mocca (26 per cent) which is, however, lower than the All Island ratio if we assume that to this figure of 26.2 per cent we should have to add a small proportion of widows and divorcees who have remarried. The Sugartown figure of 19.8 per cent and that of 53.6 per cent in Orange Grove both show a very different pattern from that in the Island as a whole.

There is also a great difference between the figures in our Centres and those of the Census in regard to concubinage. Here Orange Grove with 11.7 per cent is the nearest we get to the All Island proportion of 17.4 per cent and in Sugartown and Mocca the figures are more than double.

There is a correspondingly smaller number of single persons in all our Centres but what is particularly marked is the difference in the distribution in the lower and higher age-grades. The figures for Jamaica as a whole start, in the 15-19 age group, with the figure of 93 per cent (a considerably higher proportion than in any of our Centres) decrease steadily in the next three age groups, and from 35 onwards show a consistent 33 per cent. The pattern in our Centres is quite different. In Sugartown 50 per cent of the 15-19 are single, but by 20 the figure has dropped to 39.5 per cent and

47.9 per cent are living in concubinage and 12.5 per cent married. After 40 the number of married women falls from 30.2 per cent to 16.2 per cent, the figures for those living in concubinage remain the same but the number living alone shoots up from 20.9 per cent to 35.1 per cent. In the next age grade there is another striking change. Of all women between 45 and 49, 36.3 per cent are married, while the number living in concubinage is 31.8 per cent as compared with 48.6 per cent in the lower age group. By the time we reach the higher age group (50) a large proportion of the unions based on marriage or concubinage have broken up, and the proportion of women living alone reaches its highest figure in each one of these three Centres, averaging 62.4 per cent. In Sugartown, therefore, there appear to be two periods where marriage tends to occur: between 35 and 39 and between 45 and 49.

In Mocca marriage tends to be entered upon at a much earlier age. The proportion of girls between 15-19 who marry is 31.8 per cent, nearly three times as high as in Sugartown and not much lower than the rate for concubinage in Mocca itself. While concubinage increases rapidly in the next ten years until it reaches the figure of 61 per cent for the 25-29 age group, marriages decrease in the same period, but climb again between 30 and 40 until at 35 the entire population is living in a conjugal union, fairly evenly balanced between marriage and concubinage. But here, as in the other two Centres, after the age of 50 the number of women living alone is over 60 per cent. This, in fact, is the marked pattern in all three Centres.

In Orange Grove the most obvious features are the high proportion of marriage throughout and the absence of concubinage in the 35-44 and 50 age groups, and its low overall figure of 11.7 per cent as compared with 44.1 per cent in Sugartown and 39 per cent in Mocca. It is also noticeable that marriage is not, as in Sugartown and Mocca, entered into generally in middle age; although the proportion of married women is highest between 30 and 44, it is 62.5 per cent in the lowest age group as compared with 11.9 per cent in Sugartown and 31.8 per cent in Mocca. But, not even in Sugartown, is there anything comparable, in this lowest age-group with the All Island figure of 1.7 per cent.

Appendix 11 shows the total and average number of children born by age of mother and also allows comparison to be made between mothers and childless women in the different age-groups. Of a total adult female population of 775, 489 or 68 per cent are mothers and 32 per cent are childless. (In the case of 56 no information was obtained as to fertility.) Comparison between the Centres shows that 73 per cent of women in Mocca and 71 per cent in Orange Grove were mothers as compared with 64 per cent in Sugartown. The average number of children born per mother was 3.5 compared with the All Island average of 4.1 given in Table 40 of the Census Reports. In the Centres the highest number per mother was Orange Grove (4) with 3.7 in Mocca and 3 in Sugartown. The figures for Sugartown, however, are not given with the same degree of confidence as are the others, owing to the difficulty in getting reliable information from some of the women living in casual concubinage when we had to interview them in the presence of their menfolk. (42) Nevertheless, it is still likely to be considerably lower than in Orange Grove where the long unbroken unions have produced markedly large families.

Appendix 12 shows the specified number of children born to all adult women by type of household and basis of the conjugal unions in marriage or concubinage. The distribution of the 230 non-mothers in the three Centres according to their present status shows interesting differences, especially between Sugartown and Orange Grove. In Sugartown 50 per cent live in concubinage as compared with 13 per cent in married homes in simple or extended family households and 37 per cent live without a spouse in one or other of the consanguineous or in a single-person household. In Mocca the highest proportion (40 per cent) live in concubinage, 38 per cent in family homes based on marriage, and 22 per cent in consanguineous and single-person households. The feature of Orange Grove is that only one case, representing 2 per cent, is to be found in family homes based on concubinage, the highest proportion (62 per cent) being in family homes based

on marriage and the remaining 36 per cent in the consanguineous
and single-person households.

The next point of interest was the distribution of the population in the different types of households. We distinguished between six types of residential grouping: (A) simple family type
households consisting of a man and woman with or without their
children and possibly adopted children and non-kin persons; (B)
extended family households, being an extension of simple family
by the addition of other kin; (C) and (D) denuded family households, containing either a mother, or a father, living alone with
his or her children. These might be either of the simple or the
extended type; (E) single person households and (F) sibling
households. These were the main types. They were found, however, to be insufficient for the sort of analysis we required. For
example, in Type A simple family, defined as a man and woman
living together with or without their children, it could not be
assumed that all the children were children of *both* the man and
the woman. Two aspects of the parental relationship with which
we are concerned are, firstly, the extent to which this separation
occurs and the circumstances in which it most commonly occurs,
and secondly, what happens to the children of previous unions
when a new union is contracted. It was, therefore, necessary to
sub-divide this Type into two main groups, (I) a *primary* type
containing children of the couple only and (II) a *secondary* type
showing the presence of outside children. Thus II (a) showed
households containing outside children of both the man and
woman, II (b) those with outside children of the man and II (c)
with outside children of the woman. Since adoption, in all its
meanings in this culture, is the subject of special discussion, it was
also desirable to isolate households in which there were adopted
children. This was done in II (d). In all these sub-types the figures
were shown in relation to the presence or absence of own children
or outside children. A final sub-type (III) distinguished childless
households. The distribution of simple family households on this
basis is shown in Appendix 6 and of extended family households
in Appendix 7. The wide range of kin contained in these latter

households, and the fact that there might be two, three or four generations included, presented us with a complex set of inter-personal relationships and led us to break this group down into four main sub-types: firstly, a kinship discrimination between households consisting of direct descendants of the couple and those including siblings and descendants of siblings; and, secondly, within these sub-types, a distinction between households con-taining two, three or four generations.

In all Centres the highest proportion of the population lived in family households of the simple and extended types (A and B) and it will be useful to deal with these first. The first point is that there is little difference in the proportion between the Centres. Of the adult population 61 per cent in Sugartown and 68 per cent in Orange Grove and Mocca live in these family groups. In both Sugartown and Mocca the largest number live in simple family households the proportions being 47 per cent and 41 per cent respectively. In Orange Grove the position is reversed: 36 per cent of the adult population live in extended family households and 33 per cent in simple family groups. The total population in each of the household types, showing the proportion of total pop-ulation is given in Appendix 2.

Simple and extended families between them contain the bulk of the child population: 71 per cent in Sugartown, 79 per cent in Orange Grove and 78 per cent in Mocca. These children represent, however, only a proportion of the children born to the couples. In Appendix 8 we have shown the children living in the homes according to parentage; column (a) children born to the man and woman living together, (b) outside children of the woman and (c) outside children of the man. It is thus possible to compare the proportion of children living in the homes according to parentage, with the number born and with those not living in the homes, differentiating here, so far as our information allowed, between those under and over 15 years of age.

In all Centres together the highest proportion of children in family homes (Types A and B), whether based on marriage or con-cubinage and also the highest proportion of total children living, are those born to the couple cohabiting. For all Centres together, these represent 89 per cent of the children in the homes and 68 per cent of all their children. 8 per cent are illegitimate children of the woman, representing 28 per cent of her offspring, and only 3 per cent are illegitimate children of the man, representing 14 per cent of his recorded offspring.

In homes based on concubinage the same relative position obtains: 64 per cent are children of the couple and these represent a very much higher proportion of all living offspring. The number of outside children in these unions based on concubinage is, however, three times as high and represents also a higher ratio of total children born, 27 per cent and 36 per cent respectively for outside children of the woman and 9 per cent and 13 per cent of the man. In Sugartown 43 per cent of the children born to the couple live with them as compared with 23 per cent of the woman's outside children and 9 per cent of the man's. In Mocca the households contain 32 per cent of the woman's outside children, and 8 per cent of the man's as compared with 42 per cent of those born to them both. In Orange Grove 42 per cent of the couple's children live with their parents as compared with 23 per cent of the woman's and 21 per cent of the man's. The distinguishing feature in all the Centres is the exclusion of the man's outside children.

It is noticeable that there are no households with outside children of both parents in Sugartown, one only in Mocca (2 per cent) and three in Orange Grove (7 per cent). Families with outside children of the woman are third highest in Sugartown and Mocca and lowest in Orange Grove. Those with outside children of the man are lowest in Mocca, second lowest in Sugartown but second highest in Orange Grove where this phenomenon is associated with the fact that land in most cases belongs to the man.

We have now to consider the relative incidence of marriage and concubinage in family households and the effect if any upon the size of household, and the tendency for the inclusion or exclusion of own or outside children in one or the other.

Appendix 9 gives the number of households in each Centre and indicates those in types A (simple families) and B (extended families) where the couple were married compared with those in which they lived in concubinage. The highest proportion of married families in both types are to be found in Orange Grove: 63 per cent as compared with 19 per cent in Mocca and 14 per cent in Sugartown. In all Centres simple families are more commonly based on marriage than are extended families. Simple families in which outside children are present are based on marriage in 24 per cent of the cases and on concubinage in 76 per cent. In Mocca only 17 per cent are based on marriage as compared with 83 per cent on concubinage; in Sugartown the proportions are 22 per cent and 78 per cent and in Orange Grove 40 per cent and 60 per cent.

In only 14 of 59 households of the simple family type, containing outside children, are children of the current union also present. In general outside children of one or other spouse are more likely to be incorporated in the home when the couple are childless. In 10 of these 14 households the children are the woman's.

Appendix 6 shows that in the 59 households in all Centres containing illegitimate or outside children, representing 22.6 per cent of all households in type A, 14 of the couples are married and 45 live in concubinage. In the 14 married households, nine contain illegitimate children of the woman and four of the husband: in one, illegitimate children of both parents are present. In the 45 households based on concubinage, 12 contain outside children of the man, 30 outside children of the woman and in only three (all in Orange Grove) are outside children of both parents present. There is a greater tendency therefore for the outside children present in the home to be those of the woman whether the couple are married or not.

Orange Grove has the highest proportion of legitimate children in the home (92 per cent as compared with 81 per cent in Sugartown and 90 per cent in Mocca) and the lowest proportion of illegitimate children (7 per cent as compared with 37 per cent in Sugartown and 9 per cent in Mocca). Orange Grove is also the Centre with the highest proportion of children in the home of total children born whether legitimate or not.

Compared with married parents, couples living in concubinage have, for all Centres together, a markedly higher proportion of socially illegitimate children living with them. Outside children of the man living in the household are three times as many in Sugartown and five times as high in Orange Grove. They are, however, lower in Mocca where there is only one representative in married homes and one in concubinage, both adult. In the case of the woman's children the increase is from 15 per cent to 27 per cent in Sugartown, 5 per cent to 12 per cent in Orange Grove, and 7 to 36 per cent in Mocca.

In simple family type households, in all Centres taken together, the largest category is childless couples, which represent 40 per cent of the total; the second largest, the primary type, 32 per cent; the third, households containing outside children of the woman, 15 per cent; those with outside children of the man, 6 per cent; adopted children 4 per cent and those with outside children of both man and woman, only 1 per cent.

Between the Centres, however, there are considerable differences. In Sugartown, the highest group were childless households (50 per cent) with the primary type next (27 per cent). This is to be explained by the large number of casual or housekeeper unions and does not mean that either, or both partners, did not have children elsewhere. In Orange Grove childless couples were only 9 per cent and the largest group was the primary type with 52 per cent. In Mocca the primary type was the highest (36 per cent) with childless couples next (31 per cent) and the only other important group in this Centre were the households containing outside children of the woman, 24 per cent.

Considering the figures for all Centres together, and noting that the figures for Sugartown carry a considerable weight here since there are nearly four times as many households there than in each of the other two Centres, the important points are (1) that there are approximately twice as many of these Type A households that are based on concubinage than there are those based on marriage and (2) that those based on concubinage are equally divided according to the presence or absence of children, whilst those based on marriage are without children in only one-fifth of cases. The figures and proportions for Sugartown show an overwhelming emphasis on concubinage rather than on marriage in these Type A households and the tendency for marriage to involve the presence of children rather than not is less than the average for all Centres, whilst the childlessness of such households based on concubinage is relatively greater than for all Centres together. Orange Grove shows a much greater emphasis on marriage than on concubinage in these Type A households and they almost all have children present, whatever the conjugal basis. Mocca has more of these households based on concubinage than on marriage (69 per cent compared with 31 per cent) and again children tend to be present rather than not, more so in marriage than in concubinage but none the less appreciable in the latter case (66 per cent against 34 per cent). The picture here is one of emphasis on marriage and the presence of children in Orange Grove; of a tendency to concubinage and, again, the presence of children in Mocca; and of concubinage in Sugartown more often than not without children. In all cases, in Type A households based on marriage, children tend to be present: almost always in Orange Grove, less so in Mocca and to a still slightly smaller extent in Sugartown.

The next important point to be considered in our analysis of the roles of marriage and concubinage is whether the family households show a greater tendency to be of the extended rather than the simple type when based on marriage than they do when based on concubinage, and whether this tendency is different in the three Centres. In other words, does marriage tend to lead not merely to the presence of the couple's own children, which we have already shown to be true, but also to the presence of other kin? The relevant comparison here is between the Type A households with children present and the Type B households.

We are dealing with family groups with children or other kin present. Among such family households in Sugartown, two-thirds are of the simple family type containing children and about two-thirds are based on concubinage; among those based on marriage 43 per cent are of the extended type and there is a much smaller proportion (27 per cent) of those based on concubinage that are extended by the inclusion of other kin. In Mocca, the emphasis on concubinage rather than marriage among these family groups is again clear, but there is a greater tendency for them to be of the extended type than is the case in Sugartown, and this is true for those based on concubinage as well as for those based on marriage. This ties in with the greater solidarity of the kin in Orange Grove and Mocca as compared with Sugartown. In both Centres, the extended family households are approximately equally divided between marriage and concubinage. In Orange Grove, the effect of the relatively high level of economic security is seen clearly in the far greater proportion of these family groups based on marriage rather than on concubinage and in the greater tendency for these to be of the extended type, whatever the conjugal basis of the household, than in the other Centres. In Orange Grove, almost as many households are of the extended family type as are of the simple family type with children.

II

Although extended family households account for only 14 per cent of the total number of households in our Centres, they present a number of interesting features and are of the greatest importance in the analysis of the development of kinship roles.

The first point of importance was the wide range of kin which they contained. We finally reduced our original 29 categories based on kinship structure, to four main groups. Our primary group consists of a man and woman living in marriage or concubinage with their direct descendants (children, grandchildren and great-grandchildren) and there are four sub-divisions which enable us to distinguish, if we wish, the presence or absence of own children or those of lower generations, and the addition of adopted children or non-kin persons. The secondary group contains a couple living in marriage or concubinage, but is defined by the presence of siblings and/or the descendants of siblings. The tertiary group consists of couples with or without their direct descendants or siblings' descendants, but defined by the presence of a dependent parent of either spouse, parents' siblings, and/or descendants of a parent's siblings. Again, we may, by reference to the original classification discover the precise kinship structure in each of the eight sub-divisions of this small but sociologically interesting group. The fourth group consists of households where a parent, or a sibling of a parent of either the man or the woman, was included. There were three types of these: for example, two generational, where a grandparent was present; three generational when there were also grandchildren or siblings' grandchildren; and four generational where there were great-grandchildren of a parent of one or other of the couple, but where one of the intermediate generations might be missing.

This analysis allows us to arrive at two interesting conclusions. The largest single group in all Centres is that containing siblings and siblings' descendants with or without direct descendants, and in all three Centres the order in which each group occurs is the same with the primary group always in second place. Secondly, the figures given in Appendix 7 show that in all three Centres there is a higher proportion in the primary group of married families than of couples living in concubinage. In Orange Grove only one household is based on concubinage and in Mocca the ratio is 66 per cent married and 33 per cent in concubinage. In Sugartown the proportions are 56 per cent married and 44 per cent in concubinage.

In the secondary group in Sugartown the proportion is reversed: the number based on concubinage is as high as 75 per cent; in Mocca the proportions are equal and in Orange Grove there is, for this Centre, an unusually high percentage for concubinage of 33 per cent.

All the augmented primary or secondary cases in Sugartown and Orange Grove are based on marriage and all in Mocca on concubinage.

In all Centres the highest proportion of kin in the homes are offspring of the couple living together. These account for 51 per cent in Orange Grove households of this type, 44 per cent in Mocca and 30 per cent in Sugartown. (43) The next highest in all Centres are grandchildren, the proportions being 30 per cent in Mocca and Sugartown (where they are in the same proportions as own children), and 24 per cent in Orange Grove. In Sugartown and Orange Grove siblings' children rank third with 12 per cent and 9 per cent respectively. In Mocca they share third place with outside children of the woman. In Mocca there is an interesting inclusion of parent's siblings' children, grandchildren and great-grandchildren which does not occur in either of the other two Centres and illustrates the emphasis placed on kinship in this community.

Finally in regard to the size of the households. (44) It is to be noted that (a) simple families based on marriage are on the average larger than those based on concubinage. This is true in each Centre. This also applies (except in Mocca) to the extended families. (b) Simple families in Orange Grove are on the whole larger than those in Mocca, where these households are in turn larger than those in Sugartown. (c) Extended family households based on marriage are on the average larger than those based on concubinage in Sugartown and Orange Grove, but the opposite is true in Mocca. The average size of these households based on marriage is as high as 8 in Orange Grove. In order of the average size of all these households in the three Centres, Orange Grove again has the largest household and Sugartown the smallest. The average number of persons in all households in Orange Grove is as high as 5.7 per cent while the figure for Mocca is 3.5 per cent. The average 2.7 per cent persons per household in Sugartown is low because of the large number of single persons and childless households contained in the Centre.

III

We come now to the households with children where there is only one parent present. They may be either of the simple or the extended type and Appendix 9 shows that together they represent 15 per cent of all households in Sugartown, 30 per cent in Orange Grove and 21 per cent in Mocca. These proportions are, however, misleading if we use them to assess their relative importance in the different Centres because the 443 households in Sugartown include no less than 151 single-person households and 88 households of the simple family type where children are absent. Compared with this, the 119 households in Orange Grove include only 2 and 4 respectively of these kinds and the 117 in Mocca 26 and 13. The extent to which family households become denuded by the loss of the principal male or female member can therefore only properly be considered if we set aside these single-person households and the households of Type A without children and consider the denuded types against the background of the remaining households in each Centre. Appendices 13 and 14 have been constructed to make this position clear for the total numbers of households involved in this comparison. 251 of the households in all Centres together are family groups with children present or other kin or both and 129 are of the denuded type (simple and extended). This is a ratio of approximately 2:1. Further, we see that the same ratio holds in each of these Centres, i.e. 131:68 in Sugartown, 71:36 in Orange Grove and 49.25 in Mocca. Hence, if we consider households of the denuded types as arising from the loss from a family of the principal male or the principal female member, the extent of denudation or tendency to broken homes is almost precisely the same in each of the Centres. This is a surprising conclusion if we consider the general economic and sociological backgrounds of the three Centres and the different bases on which conjugal unions are formed. (45)

When we came to examine these households individually however, we found that, particularly in the case of the mother households (which in comparison with father households are in the proportion of 78 per cent in Sugartown of all denuded family households groups, 81 per cent in Orange Grove and 84 per cent in Mocca), there were important internal differences which profoundly affected the character of the institution. For example, there was the extent to which the mother (or grandmother) was the sole breadwinner and wholly dependent on her wage earnings for the maintenance of herself and the children; the ways in which she might earn a living or support the family; and, finally, the extent to which she received male support or was assisted by kin.

From all these points of view Orange Grove and Mocca had a great deal in common, although the standards of living were in no way comparable, whereas Sugartown presented an entirely different picture, with the position of the single mother and her children parlous and depressed in the extreme. In view of the importance of these denuded households in terms of the parental relationship and the position of children living in them we shall have to return to a consideration of the essential differences in these institutions as they are found in the three Centres.

Denuded households are approximately evenly divided between the simple and extended types. (46) In the denuded simple family type there are 19 or 3 per cent 'father' households from which the mother is lacking and 48 or 7 per cent 'mother' households in which no father is present. In the extended father type there are 7 or 1 per cent as against 55 or 8 per cent with a 'mother' basis.

Female denuded households predominate over the male households, overwhelmingly so in the extended family type, this being true for all of the Centres. Also the tendency for denuded households to be of the extended type is greatest in Orange Grove and least in Sugartown with Mocca—as in so many respects—holding an intermediate position.

We have now to consider the proportion of children who live with one parent only in these denuded households. It will be useful to compare these figures with those for children who live in family homes but with only one of their parents.

Returning to the family homes, therefore, we found that there were living in them 557 children representing 51 per cent of the total children born to the parents. Of these 430 were children of the couple representing 75 per cent of the total born to them: 96

(34 per cent of total born) were outside children of the woman and 31 (or 14 per cent) children of the man by other unions.

We can say therefore that 430 or 40 per cent of children in the homes were, at the time our records were made, living with both their parents. Of these 263 or 61 per cent are legitimate and live with married parents and 167 or 39 per cent with parents living in concubinage. 96 or 9 per cent live with a mother and step-father, and of these, 26 per cent live in married homes and 74 per cent with parents in concubinage. 31 or 3 per cent live with a father and step-mother, 26 per cent where the father is married and 74 per cent where he lives in concubinage.

Let us now see whether there are any differences between these Centres in these particulars and for ease of comparison here are the figures extracted from Appendix 8:

		Sugar-town		Orange Grove		Mocca		Total	
Children living with:									
(a)	(M)	70		157		36		263	
Both parents	(C)	90		28		49		167	
	Total	160	50%	185	69%	85	56%	430	58%
(b)	(M)	13		9		3		25	
Mother and	(C)	38		5		28		71	
step-father	Total	51	16%	14	5%	31	21%	96	13%
(c)	(M)	3		4		1		8	
Father and	(C)	13		9		1		23	
step-mother	Total	16	5%	13	5%	2	1%	31	4%
(d)	(M)	15		23		8		44	
Mother only	(C)	60		17		17		96	
	Total	75	23%	40	15%	25	17%	140	19%
(e)	(M)	6		7		–		13	
Father only	(C)	11		8		7		26	
	Total	17	5%	15	5%	7	5%	39	5%
Total in homes:		319		267		150		736	
		100%		100%		100%		100%	

There is thus in Sugartown and Mocca a fairly even distribution of children who live with both parents and the ratio of those living with married parents and with parents living in concubinage is also approximately the same. In Orange Grove, however, 69 per cent of the children have the advantage of living with both parents and 85 per cent of these live with married parents.

Of the illegitimate and outside children Sugartown has 22 per cent who live with the mother and a step-father, as compared with only 7 per cent who live with the father and a step-mother. In Mocca there is an even larger proportion in the first group while in Orange Grove the proportions are almost equal.

We may conclude, therefore, that Orange Grove families contain the highest proportion of children born to the couples, and that the ratio for married couples as compared with those based on concubinage is strikingly high (85 per cent compared with 15 per cent). In Sugartown and Mocca the proportions are more nearly even. In Sugartown the proportion of outside children of the woman is over three times as high as those of the man, in Mocca thirteen times. In Orange Grove the proportions are almost even and the striking difference between the figures in this Centre and the other two is the high number in the homes of illegitimate children of married mothers and (compared with the proportions in Sugartown) of illegitimate children of married men.

The last group of facts to be considered refers to issue of couples in family homes who do *not* live with them.

	Sugartown		Orange Grove		Mocca	
Under 15	127	23%	39	18%	24	22%
15 and over	202	37%	160	73%	98	63%
Not stated	222	40%	19	9%	34	15%
	551		218		156	

In the case of children born to both parents we find that 12 per cent in Sugartown, as compared with 17 per cent in Orange

Grove and 13 per cent in Mocca, were definitely known to be under 15. While however it was known that the remaining Orange Grove and Mocca offspring were all adult this information exists for only 58 per cent of the Sugartown cases.

Both in Orange Grove and Mocca a higher proportion of the children not in the homes with their parents were over age. In the case of Orange Grove this is to be explained by the favourable conditions which exist in the Centre—parents with adequate means able to support their offspring, living in homes large enough to contain the family. When the children leave, it is to marry or go out to work. In Mocca where family sentiment is equally strong, one cannot, however, say that similar conditions exist, either in regard to housing or financial status. The explanation here has to be sought in the close and static organization of the group, and the uniform low level in the standard of living. In Sugartown because of the high rate of concubinage (and be it said of concubinage of a particular category) an even higher figure than 23 per cent might have been expected. We have, of course, very low figures here relating to the absent families of a large number of the male sugar workers, and I do not think it would be extravagant to double or even treble the figure of 317 which we had given us as the total number of children born to men outside the current unions. Even within the figures we were given, however, the proportions of 23 per cent and 37 per cent are so obviously irreconcilable with the high proportion of newly entered into 'housekeeper' unions and promiscuous relationships that it is not unreasonable to presume that the large number of cases where no age is given (40 per cent as compared with 9 per cent in Orange Grove and 15 per cent in Mocca) may very possibly include a considerable number of under fifteens.

In Appendix 5 the whereabouts of children under 15 years of age who are not living in the home are given according to whether they are children of parents living together or outside children of the man or the woman.

The particulars were obtained in regard to 247 children, 173 in Sugartown, 40 in Orange Grove and 34 in Mocca.

The general picture that emerges is that children of parents living together tend, where they are out of the home, to be living with the mother's kin, while outside children of the man remain with their mother. The highest proportion of outside children of the woman are found with the mother's kin in Sugartown and Mocca and with the father's kin in Orange Grove. Although the figures are small the proportions between the Centres are interesting as showing the greater role which is played by the father and the father's kin in Orange Grove than in either of the other Centres.

Children whether with paternal or maternal kin go, in the highest proportions in all Centres, to the grandmother and in Sugartown and Mocca the next most usual relative is the mother's sister. In Orange Grove it is interesting that the father's sister is the adopting mother in two out of six cases.

	Mother's Kin (56 cases)		
	Sugartown	*Orange Grove*	*Mocca*
Mother's Mother	64%	50%	66%
Mother's Father	6%	14%	—
Mother's Mother's Mother	3%	—	—
Mother's Sister	18%	7%	33%
Mother's Brother	9%	14%	—
Mother's Father's Mother	—	14%	—

	Father's Kin (32 cases)		
	Sugartown	*Orange Grove*	*Mocca*
Father's Mother	86%	50%	100%
Father's Father	4%	—	—
Father's Sister	4%	33%	—
Father's Mother's Husband	4%	—	—
Father's Brother	—	16%	—

Although the figures are again too small for any conclusions to be drawn from them by themselves, the proportions are not without interest.

Leaving complete family households (Types A and B) the total number of children (adult and under 15) living with only one parent in the denuded type households (C and D) is 179 (or 24 per cent) of whom 140 (or 78 per cent) live with their mother and 39 (or 22 per cent) with the father. (App. 18.)

These figures represent 48 per cent of the women's given issue, and 44 per cent of the men's but, as we have already explained, the figure of 89 for total children born to the men is certainly too low.

The ratio of adults to under 15 in the homes is slightly higher in mother than in father households, but there is a marked tendency for boys to go with fathers and girls to be found with their mothers.

	Boys	Girls
Mother households	44	52
	(46%)	(54%)
Father households	26	12
	(68%)	(32%)

These figures are for all Centres together.

It will be remembered that we found that there was a fairly even distribution of these denuded households in all three Centres. It remains to see what differences there are between them in the main structural features and whether these particulars go any way towards explaining what at first sight appears to be a somewhat unexpected similarity.

In mother households the ratio of adults to children whether for legitimate or illegitimate offspring is almost identical in Sugartown and Mocca, but there is a higher proportion of adults in Orange Grove.

In father households, for legitimate and illegitimate together, there is a higher proportion of adults in Mocca than in any other Centre and the lowest in Orange Grove. This follows more the pattern for the Centres in family households, where the number of adults to children was also highest in Mocca.

The number of illegitimate compared to legitimate children in mother households is very much higher in Sugartown (80 per cent to 20 per cent) than in either of the other Centres, which is to be expected considering the lower legitimacy rate in Sugartown. In Orange Grove 57 per cent of the children are legitimate and 42 per cent illegitimate compared with 66 per cent and 33 per cent in households in that Centre based on concubinage and 92 per cent and 7 per cent in those where the parents are married. In Mocca the proportion of legitimate children is higher than Sugartown (8 out of 25 as compared with 15 out of 75) and intermediate between Sugartown and Orange Grove.

In father households there are no legitimate children in any of the seven Mocca households in this category. In Orange Grove 53 per cent are illegitimate as compared with 65 per cent in Sugartown. In Sugartown, father households contain therefore a higher proportion of legitimate children than do mother households which might be taken to indicate, if it applied to all Centres, that where a marriage breaks up (for not all these men are widowers) the child goes with the father. In both Orange Grove and Mocca, however, the contrary is the case, the legitimacy rate being higher in mother than in father households.

By definition single-person households contain no children. The sibling households contain 23 adult women of whom 17 are mothers. Of their 48 children 6 were born in wedlock: 43 of these children are still alive; 32 or 74 per cent live in the homes with their mothers. This includes all those definitely known to be under fifteen.

IV

In view of the importance given to the grandmother in all writings on Negro family life whether in America or the West Indies, an attempt has been made to isolate all households containing a grandmother or great-grandmother and subject them to the same type of analysis as was done for the households as a whole, in an attempt to discover the variations in composition of these households and the corresponding differences in the position and role of the grandmother.

A grandmother household is one containing a woman and her

grandchild or great-grandchildren. The parents of the grand-children may also be present in the home, or one or both may be absent for each of possibly several sets of parents. The grand-mother may be living in marriage or concubinage with a man who may or may not be the grandfather of the grandchildren, or she may be single. Also, other persons, kin and non-kin, may be present. All these complicating factors have to be considered in rela-tion to the basic pattern of grandmothers and grandchildren living together in the same household. *Great-grandmother households* are defined as those in which a great-grandmother is present in the home with her great-grandchildren, regardless of the presence or absence of the intermediate links; which may include spouses of the great-grandmother's children.

In the above terms, there were 88 grandmother households and 8 great-grandmother households in our three Centres. Appendix 15 shows how these 96 households were distributed over the three Centres, and the total population contained in them. They repre-sent 14 per cent of the total 679 households in the three Centres and contain 26 per cent of the total population; so that, considered only in a numerical sense, such households are an appreciable social phenomenon. The comparative figures for the three Cen-tres are of great interest. Whereas in Sugartown 9 per cent of all households, involving 17 per cent of the total population in the Centre, contained grandchildren living with their grandmother or great-grandchildren living with their great-grandmother, and in Mocca 18 per cent of the households, containing 29 per cent of the population, the figures for Orange Grove show that no less than 31 per cent of all households, involving 39 per cent of the population in the Centre, were grandmother or great-grand-mother households.

These comparative figures reflect, of course, to some extent the different overall constitutions of households in the three Centres: thus in Sugartown, with its large proportion of single-person households, the average size of household is only 2.7, whereas in Orange Grove with its almost total lack of single-person house-holds the average is 5.7, and in Mocca with its intermediate position the average is 3.5 persons per household. Not unnaturally, grandmother and great-grandmother households are on the whole larger than the average, but in connection with the above remarks it is interesting to notice how the average sizes of grandmother and great-grandmother households differ from the overall averages in the three Centres; the difference being greatest in Sugartown (5.4 against 2.7), least in Orange Grove (7.1 against 5.7) and quite large in Mocca (5.7 against 3.5).

In terms of our classification of household types grandmother and great-grandmother households fall entirely into three types: Type B, extended family households, Type D, denuded extended and Type F with a conjugal-sibling basis. The 96 households of this kind are divided almost equally between the first two types (B and D), only three belonging to Type F, the most interesting one of which has already been discussed in Chapter 2 in relation to family land. In addition to showing the number of these households in relation to the total number of family households our analysis is directed to provide the following information:

(a) the number of cases where the grandchildren traced their descent from one or more children of the grandmother, i.e. *unilineal*, *bilineal* or *trilineal* types;

(b) whether descent was through a daughter or a son of the grandmother;

(c) cases in which one or both parents of the grandchildren formed part of the household;

(d) the conjugal status of the grandmother and the presence of her spouse or concubine in the home whether or not as grandfather of some or all of the grandchildren; and, arising out of interest in the extent to which the grandmother was solely or partially the breadwinner for the family,

(e) the number, and relationship to her, of all adult males in the household.

(a) *Unilineal* households, or those in which the relationship between the grandmother and her grandchildren involves a line of descent through one daughter, or son, only, comprise the majority of households and this is true of each Centre separately (viz 33 out of 35 in Sugartown, 21 out of 32 in Orange Grove and 18 out of 21 in Mocca). In Orange Grove, however, there are also significant proportions of households where there were two (*bilineal*) or three (*trilineal*) lines of descent represented, whereas only odd cases of such households occur in Sugartown and Mocca. The actual figures are:

Bilineal   Sugartown   1, Orange Grove 6, Mocca 2.
Trilineal   „   1   „   5, „   1.

It should be mentioned that where grandchildren have one parent in common who is a daughter of the grandmother they are all treated as her children so far as this classification is concerned, whether or not they have the father in common. For example, one of our Sugartown households contained a grandmother, her daughter and four grandchildren. Three of these children were by the daughter's husband (she was a widow) and the fourth by a subsequent irregular union. Another example consisted of a grandmother, her daughter and three children, all by different fathers. In both these cases there was one line of descent.

(b) Appendix 17 shows the presence or absence of parents where the line of descent is through a son or daughter of the grand or great-grandmother. By far the largest number are offspring of the grandmother's daughters (75 per cent for all Centres, 89 per cent in Mocca, 78 per cent in Orange Grove, 64 per cent in Sugartown). Of the 48 descendants of sons, 21 per cent live with the father, 56 per cent without either parent and the number living with the mother is noticeably low, 6 per cent, none of these cases occurring in Sugartown. Five only live with both parents. Where descent is through the female line 39 per cent are living without either of their parents, 49 per cent with the mother only, 11 per cent with both parents and none with the father only.

(c) We come now to consider the extent to which one or both parents form part of the grandmother household. Appendix 16 gives the figures and also classifies the grandchildren and great-grandchildren according to sex and age-group. Of children under

15 years of age in all Centres living in the grandmother's home, 45 per cent have their mother with them, 12 per cent both parents, 6 per cent their father only and 37 per cent live without either parent. In the case of grandchildren over 15 years, 16 per cent have their mother with them, 10 per cent both parents, 74 per cent live without either mother or father and there were no instances where the father only was present. Between the Centres there were interesting differences. In Orange Grove 51 per cent of the under fifteens live with their mother, 9 per cent with both parents and 5 per cent with their father only, three out of seven of whom were girls. It is noticeable that in the other Centres all were boys. There were no cases where neither parent was present.

In Sugartown the proportions of this group living without either parent present or with the mother only are more nearly equal (37 per cent and 39 per cent). 13 per cent have their father and mother with them and 11 per cent the father only. In Mocca, 40 per cent of this group have their mother with them, 17 per cent their father and mother and 43 per cent live without either parent. There were no households where the father only was present. So far as sex is concerned the numbers are fairly even in this age-group especially for those under fifteen. As has been shown there is a tendency for girls to go with the mother and for boys to go with the father.

(d) Appendix 19 attempts to summarize the complicated *conjugal record* of the grandmothers in relation to their *present status*. The latter term refers to their position at the time of interview when they were found to be either married women living with their husbands, women living in concubinage, or so-called 'single' women living in no current union. In the majority of cases, however, these women had borne children in other unions, regular or irregular. No account was taken, for the purpose of this record, of any history of sexual-relationships (even where they might have involved cohabition) which had not led to the birth of children. It is not to be assumed that the conjugal record for grandmothers and great-grandmothers is any more formidable than for other women for whom similar data was prepared. This Appendix shows that in more than half (55 per cent) of the 96 households, the grandmother or great-grandmother is living in no present conjugal union and the proportions of such households are about the same in each Centre. No great-grandfathers were found living with their great-grandchildren and, in fact, all except two of the great-grandmothers were living without spouses. A relatively small proportion (11 per cent) of the grandmother households were based on the grandmother in concubinage, but here the proportions show interesting differences between the three Centres: only one case in Orange Grove, representing 3 per cent of the grandmother households there, but 15 per cent in Sugartown and 19 per cent in Mocca. Households in which the grandmother was living in marriage are distributed in relative proportions of 33 per cent in Sugartown, 41 per cent in Orange Grove and 24 per cent in Mocca. The basing of a family household extending to three generations on a grandmother living in marriage is therefore an important feature in Orange Grove and is of smaller importance in the other two Centres. In Mocca the role of concubinage is almost as important as marriage in this respect; whilst in Sugartown it is certainly less so than marriage but is none the less appreciable.

Another feature worthy of note is that none of the bilineal and trilineal grandmother households in Sugartown and Orange Grove contain a grandmother living in concubinage, although there is one such bilineal and one such trilineal household in Mocca.

The details given in Appendix 19 show that among women living alone, 4 in Sugartown and 5 in Orange Grove were wives separated from their husbands while 17 were widows. The range of irregular unions is invariably highest in Sugartown with the exception of one 'single' woman in Orange Grove who had borne children by six different men. There was no question, however, of the women being assisted or supported by their previous partners in these broken unions. Although a man might give an occasional present to the woman for the child, this never continued for any length of time, and generally the breach between the couple was complete. The position of the 'single' grandmother was comparable to that of the woman in a denuded home except in so far as she lived on family land and had the assistance of kin or received help from adult members of the household.

(e) The extent of this help has now to be considered. Appendix 18 shows the number of adult males in the households and their relationship to the grandmother or great-grandmother. If we include adult grandsons, there were 108 in the 96 households out of a total population of 588.

The figures for the households are as follows:

	Sugartown	Orange Grove	Mocca
With 1 adult male	10	5	6
With 2 adult males	2	3	2
With 3 adult males	1	3	–
With 4 adult males	1	–	–

In 79 per cent of the households, therefore, there were adult males who contributed to the maintenance of the home. Appendix 16 shows that there were also 13 adult female grandchildren in these households.

It is noteworthy that the highest proportions of males were either husbands or concubines, the proportions in the different Centres being almost equal, viz. 41 per cent in Sugartown and Orange Grove and 39 per cent in Mocca. In Orange Grove, where sons were, as we have seen elsewhere, of value to assist in working the farms, the proportion is 36 per cent as compared with 18 per cent in Sugartown and 17 per cent in Mocca. Another interesting feature is the relatively high proportion of sons-in-law in Sugartown and Mocca as compared with Orange Grove.

A large proportion of the grandmother households are based on family land. This is true to 100 per cent in Orange Grove and the proportions in both the other two Centres, whether for extended or denuded extended family types, is significantly high.

FOOTNOTES TO CHAPTER 5

38 In our first detailed break-down we distinguished not less than 92 categories.

39 The figure for Sugartown does not include 170 persons interviewed when they arrived at the beginning of crop but who were not included in any of the 443 households, nor 315 men and women who were interviewed while working on the estate but who lived in Neighbourhood villages.

40 Appendix 2.

41 Census of Jamaica and its Dependencies (1943) Table 36.

42 Appendix 8. The figures for outside children of the man cannot be taken as accurate, but it can safely be said that the proportion excluded, because not mentioned by the man, was considerably higher than our figures.

43 Appendix 10.

44 Appendix 3 and 4.

45 See Chapter VI p. 149 et seq.

46 Appendix 9.

CHAPTER 6

The Development of Kinship Roles

I

FROM what has gone before it is clear that the primary kinship terms of mother, father and grandmother may bear a variety of different meanings according to the circumstances in which they are first learned—circumstances which correspond largely to the type of residential groupings which we have described.

If we assume that the parental relationship can only develop satisfactorily where the child shares a home with his mother and father during infancy and childhood then there are a large number of children born to men and women, in Sugartown and Mocca especially, for whom this relationship has no opportunity to develop. The figures which we have given in Chapter 5 do not, however, do more than indicate the problem. It is true that 543 or 73 per cent have the advantage of living in family homes. But only 430 (58 per cent) live with both their parents; the remainder live with one parent and a step-parent and the step-relationship is rarely a happy one. Moreover, it cannot be assumed that even those who were, at the time of our investigations, living with both parents had done so from infancy or would continue in this situation throughout their formative years. In Sugartown, especially, many of the unions which we observed were already showing signs of break-down, others were still at the experimental stage when both partners vociferously asserted that they held themselves at liberty to part at any time. The number of conjugal unions in Sugartown where there was from the outset, as the saying goes, 'the intention and will to live together' is relatively small. It is in the slow process of time that some of them achieve stability. We also saw that one of the features of marriage was that it was, in fact, a proven concubinage, occurring normally at a late stage and it is during the earlier experimental period that the children are born. It follows that for the majority even of those who live with their parents, their early and most impressionable years coincided with the period of strain and tension between their parents. There is no privacy in the small overcrowded huts of Sugartown and children overhear and see the quarrels and even fights which occur between their parents. Playing about in the yards they overhear the mother's conversation with neighbours or kin. Inevitably they side with her rather than with the father who is rarely in the home long enough to establish any intimacy.

While in these circumstances the child learns to regard the mother as the person with whom he has the most, if not the only, stable relationship, this relationship develops on different lines not only between the Centres but in the different types of household groupings. The child may learn the meaning of the term where he sees the mother, as in the situation of the first pregnancy, treated as just another child in her mother's home and as a baby may even be taught to call the grandmother 'mother' and the mother by the name, or pet name, by which she is referred to by her parents and other members of the household. He will copy the behaviour pattern towards the mother of her brothers and sisters and be taught to obey and respect the grandmother as the head of the family. Suckling the infant may be the only act which establishes the exclusive maternal relationship: providing for its other needs, fondling and playing with it, may be shared with, or largely taken over by, the grandmother or another relative. When the baby is weaned and the mother goes away (or is sent away) as is usual in these cases, the grandmother assumes all the functions of the real mother who is seen only on rare visits. Where the grandmother is the chief or only support of the family and has to go out to work, an elder sister may become the substitute mother and an intimate relationship established which lasts into adult life. Again the mother-child relationship develops differently in one of the simple family households based on marriage and in what we have called the purposive types of concubinage, compared with its development in the more casual types of housekeeper unions and in the denuded family homes. It becomes necessary therefore at this stage to give an account of home life in the different types of households, with particular reference to the effect this has upon the development of relationships between the members of the family. And since conditions vary considerably betweeen the Centres, to give this account for each Centre.

An example of a married family of the extended type among the relatively well-off farmers of Orange Grove were the Wrights, who lived in a large two-storey house with their six children, the eldest a girl of twenty-four with her baby. The two youngest were still going to school. The three eldest boys helped their father on the farm, where each had his allotted duties. The family rose early. Mr Wright and the sons went out to look after the animals and while the girls polished the floors and tidied the house, Mrs Wright cooked the breakfast. All the family sat at table for this though sometimes the menfolk were late in coming in. Breakfast was generally at seven-thirty and consisted of coffee for the grown-ups and bush tea for the children, eggs, bread and butter or biscuits and corn pone. On another day it might be saltfish and ackee, breadfruit and avocado pear. After breakfast the family dispersed: the younger children went off to school, the older boys went with their father to work on the farm, and the eldest daughter looked after her baby and helped her mother with the washing or other household duties. The Wrights, although well-to-do, kept no servant. Lunch was at noon and all the family assembled for it. There was considerable variety in the menus but there was always a meat course—beef, mutton or chicken, yams, cocos, breadfruit or rice and vegetables. The children cleared the table and helped with the washing up. After this the men went back to the fields and the women took things easy and tidied up for the evening. Supper was between six and six-thirty whenever the men got home. It consisted of home-made cake or biscuits, bread and butter and hot mint tea. On these citrus farms adults and children alike picked and ate oranges at any time during the day when they felt thirsty. In contradistinction to Sugartown, or for that matter Mocca, the family is thus constantly gathered together within the home in a series of joint activities and intimate personal relationships. The father as well as the mother plays with the children, teaches them patterns of behaviour, rebukes or praises. Moreover, the children observe their parents' inter-dependence and co-operation in all the details of daily life. When differences between husband and wife arise, as inevitably they do, there is not the violence or the tacit acceptance that it may mean a final breach.

Another farmer also in the upper class bracket in Orange Grove told us that his wife did not milk the cow or help with the farm work, not even the light work. It was not the custom if they were delicate, only if they were of a rough disposition. She used to have a kitchen garden. He made it but she called it hers but she did not do the work herself. He really did not like the idea of seeing his wife working in the fields. She did all the housework and looked after their six children. She cleaned the floor and scoured the pots and pans. He described their daily routine as follows:

The family rose at 6 a.m. He and a paid labourer cut grass and fed the cows, pigs and the donkey. At seven-thirty they returned for breakfast which the wife had been preparing. This would consist of coffee, with his own cow's milk, bread and sometimes eggs. After breakfast he would go back to the fields while his wife washed the dishes and got the children off to school. She combed their hair, washed their feet and saw them off by eight-thirty. She then did her laundry and mended the clothes—there was always plenty of that. Lunch was at noon and the men and three of the children whose school was near, returned for it. The other child had her lunch at school. She took a bottle of milk with her and twopence or threepence to buy bread and butter. The men remained in the house until three-thirty p.m. when they started looking after their animals. Meanwhile the wife finished up her home duties and at two thirty p.m. began to prepare the dinner which was taken at about

144

four p.m. when the men came in from work. After dinner the husband stayed at home and played his saxophone for the children and amused himself and his family until about eight p.m. when they went to bed. After she has washed the dishes his wife puts the children to bed. On Sunday they rest. They have breakfast and lunch together in one meal at ten o'clock. They do not have a mid-day meal but an early afternoon dinner and supper at night.

Another farmer's wife told us that she and her husband each have their own work to do; his in the field and hers in the home with the children. She does not like field work and she does not interfere with it.

Among the smaller farmers in Orange Grove it was quite proper for the wife to do more of the actual field work. One of these told us that her husband was a stone mason and did not concern himself with the cultivation. The farm of four acres was hers, she had inherited it from her grandmother and had the title and paid the taxes. She and her two sons worked the land. She had an acre and a half of corn which is the staple crop; two hundred hills of yam and two acres in pasture. She had one cow, a pig and kept a few fowls. In the old days the land was better but by stirring and stirring the soil without having a cow to manure it, the yields fell off. The best way to keep the land in form is to cut feeding and feed it to the cows. She planted peas through the corn and has already reaped that crop. She expected to get four bushels of corn and proposed then to grow potatoes in that bit of land. She grew small tomatoes which she thought the most paying thing in the Island. She could sell them on the spot for sixpence for a small basin-full or in Kingston for one shilling and sixpence per pound. By September she would be reaping about twenty lbs a week for six weeks from the two square she had planted.

Her account of their daily routine was as follows: The two sons rose before six a.m. and looked after the cows and weeded the land. She prepared the tea which they had together at eight a.m. unless her husband had to go out early, in which case he had his separately, but it was his wish that she sat with the children for meals. Breakfast consisted of yams, potatoes, coffee or bush tea, bread, cabbage and they each had an egg every day. After breakfast the three children went to school taking the lunch money with them. Threepence was for bread and sugar but she knew they bought sweets with it. The young men went back to the fields. She cleaned and tidied the house and then by 9.30 a.m. was ready to go to the field herself. She did weeding mostly, and the planting of potatoes, cassava and peas. She worked until about eleven-thirty and then went back to the house to rest. By this she meant a rest from field work but actually she prepared the mid-day meal. At noon everybody, except the children who were at school, returned for lunch. This consisted of yam, flour made into dumplings, breadfruit and a meat dish. The meat dish varied according to the butcher's schedule; on Monday they had salt fish; on Tuesday and Thursday cabbage with fat or coconut oil, the oil either from nuts from their own land or bought. On Wednesday and Friday they had herrings. Sunday was rice and peas. After lunch the men returned to the field and after she had put away the dishes she went back by one-thirty to her weeding. At three-thirty she returned to cook the dinner. The children came back from school at four-thirty and her sons and husband at about five o'clock. They all had dinner together. They have soup almost always for dinner followed by the same vegetables as at lunch and occasionally they get pork. After dinner there was nowhere to go. The children played about the yard and she tidied them for bed by eight p.m. She sometimes went to the prayer meeting on Sunday night and to the Salvation Army meetings on Monday evenings. Every second Monday she attended the Credit Union meeting. Her husband did not bother with Prayer meetings. He loved his sport but he slept in his bed at nights. On Sunday, he walked and visited. The boys did not sleep in their beds at night. They went about and 'sported'. Sometimes when they came in she was fast asleep and did not know. Praedial thieves gave them a lot of trouble. They often had to sit up at nights and watch their yams and could not be sure of reaping their crops because of thieves. The poor fellows who worked for wages could not afford to buy food, she said, and had no cultivations so they stole other people's. There was a young man who used to work in her fields. He was the prettiest young man in the whole district. He came one night and dug sixty hills of her yams and went out early to sell them in the market. When her son missed the yams he went down and matched the yams in the market with theirs. The thief had no cultivation of his own and confronted with the proof he confessed. He got two months' imprisonment for it.

In Sugartown home life, in the sense in which we have just described it, centring in the home, and continually renewing itself in a daily routine of co-operative tasks, did not exist. The father, if he was employed, left the home early in the morning and spent much of his leisure in the shops or taverns, returning home late in the evening. It is rare to see a man playing with his children or paying much attention to them. On a Sunday morning we occasionally saw a father carrying the baby, both dressed in their best clothes, along the village street. But it was unusual for him to devote sufficient time to the children to build up any intimate relationship. The house, consisting only too often of one small room or at best two, was little more than a dormitory. The kitchen where the meals were cooked and eaten, was a small wattle hut in the yard containing no furniture. A chair or stool might be brought from the house and put in the doorway for the woman to sit on, but, more often than not, she and her children sat on the ground or on a stone with the dish on their knees and ate. The mid-day meal, which might be eaten any time between noon and five o'clock, consisted of cocos, yams, potatoes or breadfruit cooked in a pot together with a small piece of salt or salt pork. Often there was only one plate and the woman would give the children pieces of food from hers which they ate with their fingers. The man of the household left after an early 'tea' (which in contrast with the Orange Grove family breakfast usually consisted of bread, bush tea and sometimes cornmeal dumplings) and did not return until evening. If he was a sugar-worker he bought his mid-day meal from the food vendors. Supper consisted of bread, bush tea or cocoa. Among the poorest of the population meat was rarely eaten more than twice a week. During the day, life was lived in the yard, where the children played, looked after one another, or ran errands. Washing of clothes was done at the spring or river. It is done unhurriedly because it is an opportunity for meeting friends and exchanging news, but few adults or children have more than two sets of clothes, one for 'drudging' and one for best, so that there are several washing days in a week. While the women were away the children were left in the yard to play, usually in charge of an elder sister who had often to be kept from school for the purpose. There was much freer movement from 'yard' to 'yard' among the children in Sugartown than in Orange Grove for example, where class distinctions were operative, and children tended to collect in groups and play together where they were free from adult interference.

In Mocca, also, the men were absent from the homes for the greater part of the day but their activities rarely took them far afield and they normally returned for the mid-day meal. Although the houses did not allow for these to be taken round a table, it was noted that in several homes the man was served at a small table in the 'hall' or second room of the house, while the woman and children ate in or near the kitchen. In the afternoons the men generally remained at home until it was time to drive up the cattle, which were pastured some distance away. They did odd jobs in the yard in which their women-folk were occupied or sat about gossiping together while the children played around. Coconut-oil boiling was primarily a woman's industry but the men helped in the heavy work of husking the cococuts while the children fetched and carried. There were, in other words, considerably greater opportunities for companionship and shared activities between members of the family at Mocca than in Sugartown. While there is never the degree of familiarity and intimacy in the paternal as in the mother-child relationship, in Mocca unlike Sugartown it was not uncommon to see a father playing with his children, teaching the boys to perform some task, even nursing the baby. Whereas in Orange Grove, however, the child could rely upon his father at adolescence to give him a start in life, there was no way in Mocca where the father could help his grown-up children. As in Sugartown the hope was that he might be taken by some member of the family who had gone away and made good in Kingston or one of the larger towns.

II

We have already discussed the distribution of the denuded family homes and found that in spite of the emphasis on marriage in Orange Grove and the high proportion of lifelong concubinage in Mocca as compared with Sugartown, the ratio in all three Centres was approximately the same. There were, however, important differences in this type of household between the Centres which we shall now describe.

First then, in regard to the home itself. The records show that in Orange Grove all the women lived rent free on family land. The majority were either widows, or wives separated from their husbands, and lived on farms inherited from either a parent or the husband which provided adequate subsistence for them and their children. Moreover, there were few if any cases where the woman could not rely on the help of the men of the family in the cultivation of the farm. In Mocca 6 out of 9 lived on family land but in comparison with Orange Grove the standard of living and housing conditions were low. A little subsistence farming was done; the yards were well stocked with fruit trees and a few vegetables might be induced to grow in the eroded yard around the house. Pigs, goats and chickens were invariably kept but in the main the women relied on coconut oil, the principal cottage industry, for ready money, and our investigations showed that, if the coconuts were purchased, the profits were negligible. They were, however, relieved of the necessity of paying rent, and assured of a roof over their heads. In addition they were not wholly dependent on 'shop food' for which cash had to be found. Above all they could count on the presence of friendly kin in time of trouble.

Now let us compare the picture in Sugartown. Here in 63 per cent of the cases the woman was the sole breadwinner and in another 11 per cent received only spasmodic and always inade-

149

quate help from ex-concubines or adult children in the home. In the remaining 26 per cent of cases she lived on family land and/or received more substantial support from some man. Subsistence farming on Sugartown family land was out of the question. The yards were, however, stocked with the usual fruit trees and particularly breadfruit, the great food stand-by of the peasant. Again she lived rent free. But the only way she could make an income out of the land was by building a shack in her part of the yard and renting it, and this many of them did. The usual rent paid for a room, even in a wattle hut, was 6s. per month. Even this sum was, however, often more than could be afforded so that there were many cases where these tiny rooms housed two or more persons. From the landlord's point of view the sum did not cover the cost of depreciation on the wattle huts. Moreover, credit had frequently to be given and allowance made for absconding tenants.

An examination of the occupations and earnings of the fifty-three women, heads of denuded family households, in Sugartown and a study of their weekly budgets, did more than anything to uncover the poverty and insecurity of their existence. Although coconut oil was manufactured in Sugartown homes it was only to a very small extent. The single mother had to rely on wage labour for the support of herself and her children or 'seek for a partner' to lift the burden from her shoulders.

First in regard to employment. A few worked at home, taking in washing or doing sewing. Two kept a small shop, on their own premises, where they sold home-made patties and cakes. A few were higglers. Seven were domestic servants. Twenty-three, or over 43 per cent were labourers and four had no occupation and no visible means of support. Throughout the Island domestic service is one of the principal female occupations. In Sugartown by far the majority of women, and all in this household type, were employed in middle and working-class homes. It will be recalled that the keeping of a servant confers status and whatever her husband's income, a married women expects to be able to keep one. Wages of domestic servants in working-class homes in our Centres ranged from three shillings to seven shillings a week plus food and a room to sleep in. Drawn from the poorest homes these girls and women had no experience or training in household duties or routine. Few remained in any one situation for any length of time. A few migrated to Kingston or other towns where there was a larger upper-class population and better pay and working conditions. Many got disgusted and took up other forms of labour. One woman told us 'she worked for a black lady for three shillings a week. She was then completely untrained and had to be taught everything. When she had learned, her wage was raised to five shillings. She then went to a white lady who paid her eight shillings and gave her food and uniforms'. (The maximum weekly wage in the handful of upper-class houses in Sugartown, we were told, was at that time 20s.). She had given it up and taken to higglering. Another girl who was paid ten shillings a week said she was required 'to clean floors, wash clothes, cook, wait at table, chop wood for the kitchen fire and go for the milk in the mornings'. She left when, in addition to this, she was told to husk coconuts with an axe. A large number of our life histories record that invariably in these circumstances the girl 'seeks for a man' who, in return for companionship and sexual favours, will give her presents of money, clothes or trinkets. When the inevitable pregnancy occurs the girl had to leave her job but it was rare for the union to be stabilized. The girl would return to her mother's home for the birth of her child, and, if she re-entered domestic service, leave the child with her mother. An overwhelming majority of women in domestic service throughout the Island are supporting or partially supporting, children left in the care of a mother or other relative.

Dressmaking or sewing as an occupation carries a higher status than any other except professional nursing or teaching, and even the village sempstress with the scantiest of skill or training and making the most precarious living, ranks relatively high in the social scale. There were several 'dressmakers' in Sugartown, ranging from a high degree of competence in one case, to little more than the ability to rough-hew a dress or shirt in the others. Work was done at home and paid for by the job, average earnings being about ten shillings a week out of Crop and possibly double in Crop. Girls after leaving school were sometimes apprenticed by their mother to these women to learn sewing but the fees did not amount to much and often the tuition was free as between relatives or friends. Again here, as in domestic service, the earnings were insufficient to maintain the woman alone much less support a family.

Washing clothes for unattached men, especially the newcomers in Crop time, was one of the chief occupations of self-supporting women in Sugartown. The rates of pay varied slightly. One woman said her charges were two shillings for a suit, comprising shirt, merino or vest, underpant and a pair of pants, but the washerwoman had to provide blue, starch, and coal. She told us she was able to do twelve 'suits' a week but seldom got more than three. During the preceding week she earned six shillings for two suits but soap, etc., cost two shillings. Another who charged ninepence for pants and sixpence for a shirt said she could make about three or four shillings and sixpence a week after deducting the cost of materials.

Buying and reselling, or higglering as it is called, is a common form of livelihood for women throughout Jamaica. Higglers buy foodstuffs, yams, vegetables and fresh fruit, from the primary producers in the market at wholesale prices and retail them in the villages nearby. In many country districts they go from house to house, or they may set up their wares on the pavement or the piazza of a shop in the main street of a country village. Their capital is never more than a few shillings, the difference between wholesale and retail prices small, and the turnover correspondingly meagre. Moreover, where they sell in a market they have to pay fees levied by local Government authorities. Few women can support themselves wholly in this way and the occupation is often subsidiary to some other form of work in the home, such as making and selling cakes and patties or laundry work. The higgler ranks socially above the domestic servant or labourer; she is independent as compared with the wage-earner and wears an apron as the badge of her calling. It was noticeable that many of them lived on family land which in itself confers status in the community.

By far the largest number of women in this type of household, as also in single-person households, did some form of manual labour for a living. This is considered the lowest kind of occupation and would be regarded as infra dig. by a married woman or by a woman living in a respectable concubinage. The two principal forms of woman's work on a sugar estate are weeding young cane, which is done with a hoe, and dropping artificial manure at cane roots. Sometimes women also 'head-out' canes cut by their menfolk, which means carrying and heaping them in the intervals where they can be loaded on to the carts or pan-cars. The rates for all classes of field work for women as well as men are fixed annually for the industry and ~ woman regularly employed on the estate might earn as much as 30s. or 40s. a week on task work: but few were regularly employed. In any case women with young children could not leave them for long enough at a time to earn more than a few shillings for two or three days in the week. The other type of work which was sometimes available was hoeing water-tables or breaking stones for the roadways for the Public Works Department. This and other forms of road-work was generally made available in the out-of-crop season and at Christmas to provide against whole-sale unemployment.

In spite of the smallness of her earnings the woman manages to provide for herself and her child or children while they are infants or very small. It will be clear from our description of the meals eaten by adults as well as children that the diet is cheap, inadequate and unbalanced. (47) Clothes are not a problem at this early age. Most children in the homes wear one garment, in the case of many of the toddlers in Sugartown and Mocca this consisted of an abbreviated shirt or blouse reaching to the navel. All go barefoot. In the country children live to a great extent on fruit growing on trees in their own or their neighbours land or on the roadside, and in croptime on a sugar estate vast quantities of sugar-cane are consumed by adults as well as children. There is a saying in Jamaica that 'a child costs nothing'. The problem for the mother begins to become acute when clothes have to be provided for the child to go to school. A uniform in the elementary schools consists of cotton skirt and blouse, or khaki shirt and pants, underclothes for the girls and canvas shoes for both. The child may also have to be given 2*d.* or 3*d.* a day for lunch-money though some elementary schools provide free lunches. From now on the child ceases to be a plaything and becomes instead a source of endless anxiety. Also, going to school means that he or she is no longer available all day to run to the shop, carry messages and perform countless little tasks and duties about the house and yard as heretofore. The result of these two changes in her daily routine —the loss of the child's help and companionship and the burden of providing his new wants, the mother begins as never before to 'discipline' the child. He or she is told he has to perform his household duties in the morning before going to school and he is punished if he does not. He is scolded or punished if he comes back late from school. Finally there is the problem of adolescence: what to do to find him a job after he leaves school so that he can begin to help her in the upkeep of the home. These are not difficulties which only the 'single' mother has to face but they are particularly acute and it is at this stage that she increases her efforts to 'find someone to be responsible for her'.

The last type are the single person households—Type E. They might consist of a single man or woman living alone, or of more than one man and more than one woman sharing a room or house. They are a particular feature of Sugartown where they comprise 34 per cent of all households and contain 14 per cent of the population. In Orange Grove there were only 2—both male —and in Mocca 26, evenly divided as between male and female, and containing 7 per cent of the population. They present a very different pattern in the three Centres. In Mocca 16 of the 26 lived in their own shack on family land or in a room in a family house. The remaining 10 described themselves as 'strangers'. They rented rooms or huts from the old families and supported themselves as best they could. The 5 men included a tinsmith, a fisherman, and an ice-vendor. The other 2 got occasional jobs on the roads or properties. Five of the women described themselves as self-supporting. One got occasional roadwork, breaking stones, another worked on the property, a third was attached to a young man of the village and had obviously come to be near him. These 'foreigners' were not willingly accepted into Mocca society: as one of them said: 'Mocca people do not like strangers'. The women on family holdings were, with one exception, elderly 'widows', living by customary right, for their lifetime, on their 'husband's' land; the exception being a young woman, whose man had recently deserted her and married someone else, keeping their three children. She returned home and, with the help of her brother, erected her own shack on the family land. In this Centre, therefore, the men and women who were acknowledged members of the community had all the advantage of being part of a closely-knit kinship group and of living rent free on family land. So far as the 'strangers' were concerned, they did not belong and were expected to fend for themselves.

In the two cases in Orange Grove, both men were members of Orange Grove families and farming their own inherited holdings.

In Sugartown there were 151 households: 110 male and 41 female. A proportion of the single women were members of the old Sugartown families, lived on family land and supported themselves by renting rooms or the shacks which they erected on their holdings. Of the men, those who also 'belonged', and lived on family land, were a very small proportion of the total. For the most part they did not work on the estates, referring disparagingly to cane-cutters and field labourers. They had no objection to cultivating their own fields and a few rented grounds outside the district. Others were tradesmen, butchers and one was the only beekeeper in the village. Their standard of living was low, and they were often without sufficient food. By far the largest number in this category, however, were men born outside the parish, who had been attracted by the prospect of employment and depended wholly on the sugar industry. They believed that by staying on in the village after Crop they might compete more successfully with the more recent new-comers for the limited number of jobs available. While they might be employed fairly regularly during Crop they suffered long spells of unemployment which their savings were quite inadequate to tide over. While these men lived alone, they by no means eschewed female society even when they already had concubines and children in the homes they left. Many of these casual affairs were fruitful. There is, therefore, a link between many of these households and denuded homes both in Sugartown and out of it.

Of the 44 women in single person households in Sugartown a high proportion were old or middle-aged members of Sugartown families who lived on family land and supported themselves as rentiers. Others were women who were responsible for children left in the care of a relative. The possible means of earning a livelihood available to them have already been described in discussing the denuded (female) households. The remainder were girls or young women who had migrated in the hope of being supported by one or other of the unattached men working on the estate. Some of these, while they remained in their own rooms, did the man's washing and cooked his food; others were frankly promiscuous and were visited by the men.

III

The training of children in the home largely devolves on the mother. The teacher in the private school in Sugartown told us: 'The father is out a lot so most of the discipline is left to the mother. The mother punishes—the father only shouts. The mother has all the burdens'. There was no evidence of any widespead cruelty to children that came to our notice in any of our Centres. Yet, whenever we touched on the subject of upbringing there was hardly a case in which our informant did not expatiate upon what he called the 'floggings' he or she had received in childhood from parent and teacher and our own observations of parental discipline were of the violent manner in which even the youngest of children were often rebuked. (48) Children are shouted at in a way which appears brutalizing to anyone outside the particular culture. The child responds to this by equally noisy and violent outcries. It was not uncommon to see a screaming infant ignored, although apparently in great distress, while the mother was occupied nearby with some trivial task or to hear fearsome yells from a nearby yard. We would, however, be assured that it was nothing to worry about—Johnny had run away and his mother had at last caught him and was beating him. The beatings we actually witnessed were rarely as severe as the outcry appeared to indicate and the child was generally more frightened than hurt. But the constant 'threatening' of children was noticeable as also was the fact that there was very little of quiet, gentle-spoken admonition.

When we consider the things for which children are rebuked and punished, as also the principles which they are explictly taught to be right or wrong, it is clear that there is a serious conflict, in Sugartown and in similar societies elsewhere in Jamaica, between the ideal and the socially accepted pattern of behaviour. I am of the opinion that it is not that there is no intention to establish a pattern of behaviour; or that 'disciplinary efforts seem to be a gesture rather than a real attempt to alter behaviour' but rather that the behaviour pattern is one taken over from a different cultural group, and is unassimilable in the situation in which it is expected to work. (49) For example, children are taught by their mothers (or the grandmother or guardian in her place) that it is wrong to lie or steal but the behaviour of adults or other children around them gives little reality to the admonitions. The woman who punishes a child in the morning for 'stealing' the milk or sugar will herself take him with her later in the day when she goes to 'pick' someone else's coconuts or firewood or send him to tether the cow or goat in someone else's pasture. Within the culture 'stealing' milk or sugar from one's parents is unquestionably and recognizably wrong but the system of values holds good only in given circumstances. There was the case of the man in Sugartown, who, before a crowd of relatives and neighbours, not one of whom protested or tried to interfere, beat his wife into unconsciousness because she had, in mistaken loyalty, gone to the police station to admit complicity in a theft of coconuts for which her companion in the escapade had been caught while she had not. She had disgraced herself and him—not by 'taking' coconuts growing on estate land which was common practice—but by admitting the fact when she need never have been found out. In the same way the emphasis placed, according to so many of our informants, on truthfulness, and the tales of 'floggings' received for 'telling lies' is not to be taken to apply in any realistic way to adult behaviour. 'I can't tell you a lie' frequently prefaces a statement which completely contradicts a great deal of information previously given. The truth, in fact, is something which should only be spoken in favourable circumstances and certainly not if it is likely to create hostility, disapproval or discomfort.

We heard less of 'flogging' or of reprimand for 'stealing' in Orange Grove possibly because there was no necessity for a well-fed child of well-to-do farmers to do any such thing. If he did, he had been 'rude', but it did not, as in the Sugartown family, mean that there was no money to buy more and therefore the rest of the family had to do without. A system of ideals which, among the upper-class farmers in Orange Grove (who formed the majority and set the pattern of behaviour) was realizable within the culture, was found only theoretically operative in Sugartown where it was in conflict with the social pattern of behaviour.

In all aspects of home training the mother is the principal actor. The child's most intimate relationship in the home is with her even in those cases where the father is present and associates himself with the upbringing of the child. We have already given some idea of the extent to which mother and children co-operate in the small daily duties in the home. They are continually together. The woman depends on even very young children to fetch and carry for her. Whatever she may be doing in the yard, the children are never very far away. There is constant companionship, and a constant interdependence. The girl child identifies herself with the mother while the boy has already begun to build up a type of behaviour which might be described as husband substitute.

The relationship between mother and child was not adversely affected by the harshness of the attempts at discipline or the constant demands, even on the youngest child, for exacting services, possibly because these attempts were spasmodic and interspersed with demonstrations of affection and a general pattern of indulgence. The same men and women who regaled us with stories of their mother's floggings would, in the same breath, enlarge upon her devotion to them and theirs to her. One reason for this was to be found in the intimacy and stability of the relationship and the fact that it was often the only stable relationship in the child's life. But principally because the authority of the mother is never questioned any more than the child's duty of obedience to her.

The relationship to the father where he lives in the home is at best ambivalent. He is always more strict, more exacting and infinitely less well-known than the mother. While the mother's violence and threats of dire punishment are one aspect only of a behaviour pattern which includes tenderness and a sense of security, the father's discipline is often tempered by no such conditions and leaves a permanent mark. There were many references to bad fathers but criticism of the mother is rare.

There is nothing worse that can be said of a man or woman than that 'they would curse even their mother'. Fathers are far less tender and their interest in the child more usually centres on his material progress.

Where the man is earning and in a better financial position than the unskilled sugar-worker the plans for the children are often very ambitious. There is always the desire that they should do better than their parents and raise the status of the family. In the conditions outside Orange Grove these ambitions were only too often unrealizable.

One of our most informative fathers was a barber who could make as much as sixteen shillings a day in Crop off the sugar-workers, although during the *tempo moto* he had to live 'on trust'. He had three children by his girl, the eldest five years and the youngest a baby in arms. He assured us she was not like other Sugartown girls but had been respectably brought up and it took about six months for them to get close. He wanted to get married because he loved his children and liked playing with them and he would never like to hear them referred to as illegitimate. Nor could be bear to think of them having a stepfather. He was very ambitious for his son (aged four) and had sent him to private school, as otherwise he would never have time to learn all he has to learn. In the evenings he makes the boy read to him. If he does not do his lessons he 'hits' him. His wife also teaches the children in the home. He is not having them grow up uneducated like himself. But they live in a small rented house and conditions are not satisfactory. He told us, 'You cannot bring up children properly in the crowded housing conditions. You should have a room to sit in and talk or read, then when you go to bed there should be a room for you and your wife and others for the boys and girls separately. People live badly here, which is why girls of twelve and fourteen are having babies. In Jamaica people have too many children.' His three are too many because if he does all he wants for his son what is to happen to the other two? People were talking of a law called Birth Control which he thought should be brought in. 'It should come.' Some said it was contrary to God but he did not see it like that. A man should not run about having children all over the place. He himself had made up his mind not to do that. Another devoted father whose behaviour to his children we were able to observe as they hung about him during our interview, was an East Indian living in barracks with his wife and family. In spite of the crowded conditions the rooms were spotless and tidy and the children well dressed and cared. The little girl sat on his knee and the others ran in from time to time to speak to him. They were obviously on the most intimate and friendly terms. He, also, spoke to us of his 'ambitions' for his children. They are sent to school and in the evenings after work he hears them their lessons: 'teaches them to spell cat and dog and the like'.

In another case a married couple had already decided that their small boy should be a doctor or dispenser and the little girl a nurse and should have all the educational advantages which they had not been able to get. Sugartown we were assured was not a good place in which to bring up children: the people were not 'up to the mark'. As soon as the husband had saved enough money they intended to move to Kingston where the children would have a better opportunity.

In the homes in Sugartown in which there was a full appreciation of parental responsibility, which might as often be where the union between the parents was still based on concubinage as when it was based on marriage, there was still the problem, within the social and economic conditions we have described, of fulfilling the parental conception of duty. Nevertheless, these children had the advantage, despite poverty, of a great deal of tender, if not always completely wise, attention and training from both father and mother and were both better fed and cared for than were children in the unstable or broken homes which we have described.

It has, however, to be said that examples of paternal devotion, and kindness were far outweighed by the cases where he was either no more than the man 'who had only fathered the idea of me [and] left me the sole liability of my mother who really fathered me' (50) or someone remembered for neglect or harsh discipline. Where the mother was indulgent, hasty in her angers but quick to be kind again, the father was remembered for his strictness. As an Orange Grove farmer said, 'You could not fool with your father'. He recalled an incident concerning an elder sister, engaged to be married, who 'did something' on the day before the wedding which was not suitable in their father's sight. He went into the bushes and cut himself a good whip. Then he went back into the house, told her he had been planning for a long time, 'to christen her' before she left home and proceeded to give her a first-class whipping. Sons, especially, often referred to their childhood fear of their father. One boy, in recounting the 'rough beatings' he had received from him, admitted that his mother also flogged him, but that he was never fearful with her. We heard many stories of children running away to an indulgent grandmother or other member of the family because of these beatings. Sometimes they would leave home altogether. The following is an extract from one of our Sugartown records. The account has the violence of expression and is as highly coloured as were most of these stories, but social workers and probation officers in Kingston's west end will recognize the type of 'force-ripe' man.

'One morning we saw a boy running and dancing in the road. When we tried to speak to him he ran like a deer. A man caught him and brought him back telling him that he was foolish to run, we might even be going to give him a short or pant, and that he should at least listen to what we had to say. He stood with great fear and told us his name. Gradually we learned that he was fourteen years of age, and was looking for work as he wanted to earn his own money. When you have money, he said, you feel big. He had never been to school and had run away from home because his father wanted to kill him with beating. From elsewhere we learned that he had recently arrived in Sugartown and was sleeping at nights on the ground underneath Miss X's house, going about the compounds during the day trying to get work and being told he was too young to cut cane. According to Miss X he was a "force-ripe man", and she prophesied that in a few weeks he would "be so fierce around here that you, a big woman, or a little girl would have to watch him or else he would rape you". A neighbour added that "it was little boys like that that make bad for their parents. The best thing would be for a man to hold him and throw kerosene oil on him and then take a match and set him afire." (This is the method of killing mongoose when caught in a trap.) Miss X said she overheard the little boy telling another boy outside her door one night about the quarrel with his father. He stole something from his father and his father tied him to a tree and flogged him and left him tied up. He had a knife on him and started to cut the rope. As he made the last cut his father appeared. He ran and his father made after him but failed to catch him. He escaped and made for the nearest town where, according to his story, he worked until three weeks ago. Then he begged a lift from a truck driver coming to Sugartown.'

The failure to establish the paternal relationship and the excessive reliance upon the mother has its effect upon the young man when he grows up. A mother impresses upon her sons that it is their duty to make up to her for the hardships she endured as the sole or principal support of her children. When the boy begins to earn money he is expected to give her part at least of his earnings and while he is in the home this is the usual practice. In return she continues to cook and wash for him. When he sets up on his own he still feels that he is under an obligation to contribute to her support. Again, this is the ideal mode of behaviour; in reality it may not be possible for him to send anything appreciable or, in fact, to give her anything at all, but once they are working most young men send money back to their mother. While the amounts may be small and the payments irregular, they nonetheless represent a considerable sacrifice in view of the earning capacity of young unskilled workers in their first jobs. A young man who gave his income as between twenty and forty shillings a week said that he had to send four shillings a week to the mother of one of his children and also had to send something for his mother. He could not manage this every week but would send her ten shillings at a time, usually every three months. Another young fellow of twenty-five who earned his living by hiring a hand cart and carrying goods for people, said he used to write his mother regularly and send her between six and twelve shillings at a time. Another told us: 'If I don't send five or seven shillings a month to my mother I feel shame because she is getting old and she works hard'. A son who knew his mother to be in want, and was unable to help her, felt both guilt and failure.

This cycle of reciprocal dependence is part of the social pattern of the mother-child relationship, impressed on the child by the mother herself, and by the society into which he grows. On the other hand, the boy receives no education as to his duty as a father. He accepts from his elders the dictum that children are woman's concern and that there need be no avoidance of procreation until such a time as he is in a position to fulfil the natural obligations of husband and father. Nothing in his own experience has enabled him to learn the meaning of the paternal relationship, nor has the society helped by example or precept. This pattern is true, of course, in its fullest extent, among our Centres only in Sugartown. In Orange Grove, as we have shown, the family is so organized that there is opportunity for the paternal role to develop fully and for the parents to be complementary to one another in the care and education of their children.

One of the features of the exclusive, and often obsessive, mother-son relationship is the persistence of the son's dependence upon her into adolescence and beyond. A result of this is often a failure to develop satisfactory relationships with other people or achieve personal independence. A Sugartown man, aged twenty-five, told us that his mother had two children by his father and when he left her she bore eight more for other men. At the age of seven he was sent to live with his maternal grandparents. After a year with them he rejoined the mother. While with her he got ill and for many years she spent all she had on treatment for him. 'A man had to love his mother when she did all that for him.' After he came out of hospital he went to live with his mother's sister. He did not get on with her and wrote to his mother who came and took him home. He was then seventeen. He lived with her, worked a bit of land and handed over the sale of his produce to her. Then he got a job on a Sugar Estate but did not keep it for long. He went to live with his father's brother for a time. His uncle was very good to him and he worked lands owned by his uncle's wife. But after a while her relatives began to show him a bad face which displeased him so he left.

Where the separation from the mother is complete and permanent, less damage may be done than when the child continually passes from one relative to another, returning for short periods to the mother. One of our Orange Grove mothers felt so strongly about this that she said she refrained from visiting her child she had given away as she thought it better that he should forget her.

Another young fellow, aged twenty-three, said he had given up his job in Kingston after a year and returned home because he longed to see his mother, while yet another grown man told us he could not marry or leave the district to seek work elsewhere because he could not leave his foster-mother (his mother's sister), who had raised him and who was now dependent upon him.

IV

Even if the child has not already been subject to the upheavals that occur in his home life when there is a change of conjugal union, or if he is 'given away' either temporarily or permanently, going to school is a major crisis and confronts the child with a new set of problems. In many cases the school may be two or three miles away from his home and even if his parents could have afforded it, there is no public transport—whatever the distance the child has to walk it. Before leaving he has had to perform the usual household tasks and the only food he has received in many homes is a little bush tea and a bit of bread. The child arrives at school, therefore, after a considerable expenditure of energy and often hungry.

Above all, however, going to school means a break in the continual companionship with the mother. Hitherto she has been 'there'—someone always present, whether hectoring or indulgent, demanding or cajoling, the person who provides every need, whose word is law, the final and undisputed authority in everything. For the first time in the child's life this authority now becomes a source of conflict. The new regime makes it difficult if not impossible for him to perform the home tasks which she requires him to do before leaving for school. If he omits them, or any of them, she will punish him. If he is late for school as a result of doing them, no heed is taken of his excuses—he is 'flogged' by his teacher. His mother, with the conventional respect for propriety, may keep him from school because his one suit is dirty or torn. He may be 'flogged', when he goes back, for having been absent. For the first time in his life his mother's authority is challenged and by someone who has undisputed control over him for the greater part of his day. He suffers not because he disobeys her but if he does what she says. In rural areas, where the parents require the help of the children in the fields on Fridays to reap the produce for the Saturday markets, children are generally kept from school. For this the teacher may scold the mother, sometimes in the child's hearing, and although she may not say much at the time, she will defend her point of view vociferously when he is gone. Of all this the child is aware. He has to choose between obeying the mother and obeying the teacher.

Most of all he has now to submit to a routine which is in violent contrast to anything he has yet experienced. Hitherto his life has been one of almost untrammelled freedom. His world has been the yard surrounding his home. He has played in it all day. He has had the companionship, not only of his mother, but of brothers and sisters and other children from neighbouring yards. Now everything is different and strange. He has to be at a certain place at a certain hour—otherwise he is punished. Once he gets to school there is the new and wholly unpleasant experience of sitting on a crowded bench for hours on end. Gone are the days when he was free to roam about the yard, dawdle over odd jobs, run to the shop or take a message to a neighbour where he could loiter to play with the children for a time. Now he is supposed, at the sound of a bell, to perform a series of actions, stand, sit, recite, copy a pattern, etc., and absorb a series of facts and follow a system of behaviour for which his previous experience has neither prepared nor fitted him.

There is another rude break with accustomed behaviour in the matter of food. In the homes the children are accustomed to eat whenever they are hungry. If there is nothing in the kitchen which they can lay their hands on, there is generally some sort of fruit-bearing tree in their own or a neighbouring yard which can be raided. Now he has to conform to the routine of waiting for the lunch hour. Secondly, there is generally a change in diet. Many schools provide free or cheap lunches which are based on an appropriate diet scale, including meat and green vegetables. There is no question of its superiority to the home diet, consisting as this generally does of a steady ration of carbohydrates seasoned with a small bit of salt fish, but the child does not like the new food. Where there is no school lunch, the children are supposed to bring money to buy from the 'food vendors' but the lure of the 'snow-ball man' or the sweet seller is often too great and the pennies go, not on bread or patties, but on these delights.

The small child has, therefore, a considerable number of adjustments to make quite apart from those involved in the beginnings of his literary education. In some cases the abruptness of the change from the haphazard discipline and freedoms of home life to the rigid routine of the school is bridged by the 'private school'. These private schools are to be found in most country villages particularly where there is no Infant school or Infant centre attached to the Government Elementary school. We came across several in our Centres and admittedly they are by no means ideal. They are run by men and women who have often no educational qualifications. At the same time the women who choose to try and earn their living in this way are usually inspired by a love of children, and a gift for handling them as well as by a sense of social responsibility. Moreover, they are invariably local persons whom the parents can meet and talk with on terms of equality especially since they have to pay for the children. The parents are on a much more familiar footing with them than they can ever be with the head teacher of the Government school who, by virtue of his office is in every village a person of status.

The atmosphere in these little schools is generally homely and the group small enough for each child to receive individual attention. Moreover, through her knowledge of their homes and families, the teacher starts off by knowing a good deal about each child—their background and difficulties outside the school. Taken by and large these little schools fill a need in the community and fulfil their function to bridge the gap between the carefree early home life and prepare the child for the formal work and the stricter discipline of the school.

We have already discussed the degree to which 'flogging' is part of the home discipline. Judging from the accounts by grown men and women of their childhood, corporal punishment for trivial offences was still more the pattern of school-life. Even making allowance for the dramatic over-statement which is a feature of verbal expression, our own observations lead us to conclude that there is over-reliance in the elementary schools on this method of keeping order. Also that the strap is used for trivial offences such as talking in class, and most frequently for being late, although in many instances this was the result of duties which the child has to perform before leaving home (which he will be punished by his parents for neglecting). The worst feature was that corporal punishment was also administered where the child failed to do his work properly. This was so often told us that there seems little reason to doubt its truth.

From our own observation of elementary schools we visited, all teachers made great play with the strap or switch, which most carried in their hands or displayed prominently on their desks. Theoretically only the head teacher in an elementary school may administer corporal punishment, but all were said to do so. In any case it is a constant threat and is often regarded as the only effective means of controlling the children.

On the whole it was less relied upon in the private schools. There were exceptions. In one of the neighbourhood villages the teacher was a morose-looking cripple who carried a strap and banged it down on the desk to call order and continually threatened the children with it. Nevertheless, his pupils did not appear in the least cowed and were cheerful and forthcoming. The teacher in charge of the private school in Sugartown disapproved of flogging. She said parents flogged their children very hard as a result of which after a time they took no notice of it. Some parents lost their temper and beat the children anywhere. When the children ran away they would await their return and then flog them. She believed you should never hit a child in a temper lest you hurt it. In her school she seldom had to hit a child. She tried to teach them to have good manners and not to rough the other children. She often wondered what happened to them when they went to the big school. She was often told that they behaved better than the others but that they lost their zeal.

The teacher in the private school in Orange Grove told us that three of her children who behaved quite normally at home had never spoken at school—they did not even answer their names when the roll was called. From the time they came they remained seated in one position, quite still, till school was over. The boy's father told her to beat him up to make him talk but she would not do it. Even she, however, had her strap on her desk and on one occasion threatened her little grandchild with it. We noticed that this little girl behaved very much like the spoiled grandchild, was always demanding attention and was on this occasion jumping up, asking questions or telling tales of another child. She went up to the table where the teacher was sitting. Before she could say a word her grandmother took down the strap and attempted to hit her, but the child ran back to her seat, while the teacher ignored her and went on with the lesson.

We have already given some account of the problems of adolescence and the omission of any parental instruction or guidance at puberty. The omission is not made up by any other agency. In the elementary schools there was no attempt to face up to the problem of adolescent sex-play between the children themselves or the seduction of school-girls by adult men even within the school. After school closes in the early afternoon there were no organized games or other activities, either sponsored by the educational authorities or any other body, in any of our Centres, to divert the pre-occupation with sex which then occurs. In the case of many boys and girls their first experience of sexual intercourse took place while they were still at school. For the girl this meant, in many cases, that she became pregnant. In the case of the boy he soon ceased to be satisfied with immature experimentation with a girl of his own age and began to go with older women. We had many graphic descriptions by men of their sexual initiation by older women. While they are still at school, therefore, the physical stresses of adolescence create a new set of problems and again there are unresolved social as well as personal conflicts. The school, if it does not tacitly ignore the situation altogether, as is generally the case, is likely to prohibit a type of behaviour for which the child finds no disapprobation in his immediate home and social life. In fact, as we have shown, there is amused, and not always covert, admiration for 'the force ripe little man' no less than for the professional seducer.

This new disturbing element which has come into the child's life may abruptly terminate school-life even before the normal school-leaving age. Even if this does not occur and the child remains, he or she either becomes troublesome and difficult or sullen and resentful, and the only reaction to this appears to be corporal punishment for being 'rude' an expression popularly used to refer to sexual intercourse.

V

The transition to social adolescence presents no less problems, although their gravity and nature differed considerably in the three Centres. But, with the sole exception of Orange Grove, the child was invariably unprepared and inadequately equipped to deal with them. His (or her) sexual maturity is not matched by a correspondingly adult personality. Most children leave school at fourteen or fifteen. From the point of view of formal education only a proportion have attained the highest standard. Their educational equipment may go little beyond the rudiments of the three R's. Once they leave, for the large majority, any form of literary activity ceases. They may never open a book or write a line again. In none of our villages was there a library, or any clubs for boys or girls providing either recreational or educational amenities.

Once he leaves school the boy is now expected to find something to do, and, as soon as possible, earn his living or at least make some contribution to the household expenses. It was at this stage that the mother would loudly declaim that he had no father to help him. In these circumstances he is dependent upon his family or kin. If they can find the money to apprentice him to a tradesman he may become a shoemaker or a carpenter or a mechanic, according to the facilities in his particular district. Or he may in very exceptional circumstances to sent to a technical school. If they have land he may help with the cultivation as an unpaid family help. Only in Orange Grove, however, were the family in this position. In Sugartown the only after-school source of training were the Estate workshops with their apprenticeship system. Boys accepted as apprentices were paid a small weekly wage while learning. There was great competition for the Estate vacancies on this account as private tradesmen (unless they were kin) exacted a fee for training and paid no allowances. But the number of apprentices accepted was limited by the requirements of the factory and was, therefore, insufficient to meet the yearly outflow from the schools. The boy for whom immediate employment was a necessity, and who wished to earn money immediately had to compete with full-grown men for work in the ranks of the unskilled field or factory labourers during Crop. Here the competition was keen and both because of his age and inexperience he was at a disadvantage. As we have already indicated, family land in Sugartown was no longer suitable for growing foodstuffs and was valuable only for house sites. Regular employees of the sugar company had the concession of what were known as *syndicate gardens*. Of the 1,200 acres made available for this purpose, approximately half, in the back lands, was rented at a peppercorn rental per acre of one shilling per year for cane farming. The remainder was distributed in small plots of an acre and less for subsistence farming. A few of the Sugartown men were able to rent small pieces of land on adjoining properties, often ten miles or more from their homes, but on the whole, they and their sons were dependent on the sugar industry or such trades as would serve the community. In Mocca the prospects of the adolescent were still less favourable. Mocca men and women, as we saw, regarded wage-labour with dislike and contempt, and wanted only to follow their traditional way of life—cultivating the land on their own. Although on the periphery of the sugar area, few even attempted to get work on the estates. They professed to look down on the sugar worker and were not to be tempted by the lure of high wages. Of necessity they needed employment and clamoured for work on the adjoining cattle properties, billing and cleaning pastures, running fences or herding stock, but their real ambition was to own, or if this were not possible, at least to rent land to cultivate. While the adolescent in Sugartown had the stimulus of an industry into which he might fight his way, the Mocca boy, with no prospects at home, and all the reluctance of the peasant to leave his village and his kin, fell into a trough of listlessness and frustration.

It is in these circumstances that the family and kinship ties are most fully exploited. When migration was decided upon as inevitable it was invariably in the first place to a member of the family who had moved to another part of the Island where, to the home folk, there appeared to be better prospects of employment. Contact is maintained with kin scattered about the country in many ways. We have already referred to the practice of sending gifts of foodstuffs to relatives, particularly to those working in towns. In both Mocca and Orange Grove the system of marketing the home-grown crops involves regular visits to the markets in the larger towns. These are occasions in which family ties are constantly renewed. Apart from this, members of the family frequently exchange visits. In Sugartown especially, we found that hospitality was often sought and given to newcomers who brought an introduction from a relative or friend in their home town, and who could give news of some member or members of the family. In Sugartown, as in Mocca, the 'stranger' was the man who had no kin in the village, and unless he married 'a woman of the family' he would remain a stranger (or 'bluefoot') however long he lived there. The man who could claim kinship, however distant, with a local relative, was at once accepted into the community. He might be given a spot to build on, or a room to sleep in and would share the family meals.

Again, the widespread practice of sending children back to the grandmother, either on a visit or permanently, meant that the tie between mother and daughter was maintained. The daughter visits periodically or sends as regularly as she can some part of her earnings for the child's maintenance, but in any case she keeps in touch. She is, therefore, the first person to whom the younger brother or sister is sent. All women, even in domestic service where they live in, rent a room of their own which they share with either a friend (male or female) or a relative. However crowded the accommodation, there is no question of refusing shelter to a kinsman or woman. The new housing estates in Kingston, no less than the older slum tenements, reveal the extent to which the younger folk from the country migrate to their relatives in the town.

Our family records show that the relevant kin are invariably on the maternal side—the mother's mother, the mother's sister, and (more rarely) the mother's brother. The next most important relationship is that of the own brother and sister. The pattern of dependence on the older brother or sister, left in charge of the younger ones in the home while the mother goes about her business, extends to adult behaviour. We heard of many cases of older brothers and sisters sending home for their younger siblings to join them, and of boys and girls going to join an older brother or sister. In the case of adolescents it was in the hope of getting a job and being assured of shelter and food until it was found. Unfortunately, the picture sent home had not always been completely truthful and the youngsters arrived to find no job awaiting them and the brother or sister in no position to support them. In many cases they found that precarious conjugal ties had been formed and their introduction into the household increased if it did not create a tension. If the boy or girl failed to get work he might return home but there is great reluctance to do this as it means admitting failure. We were told, you should only go back when you can do so with good clothes on your back, a spare suit or so, and money in your pockets to treat the home folk.

The mother's sister and the own elder sister, provided their circumstances permitted, were the most likely persons (apart, of course, from the grandmother) who would be expected to take a young child, when for some reason the mother was unable to keep it. (51) Favourable circumstances did not necessarily mean an adequate income. There is a general belief that a child costs little to feed. Clothes are considered to be a far more serious problem as the child is not permitted to go to school, or Sunday school or church unless suitably clad. Nor does the absence of adequate accommodation present any serious problem; children can sleep on the floor, under the bed, or for that matter share the bed with an adult couple. They can always be 'squeezed' in if the desire is there, as it invariably is.

The tie between brothers is more apt to weaken after adolescence. The boy who leaves home may keep in touch with the family for a while but unless he makes good he is too proud to return home merely 'to show his nakedness'. In any case he soon enters into some sort of conjugal relationship which does not permit him easily to welcome his younger kinsmen into his home. Nevertheless, there were many instances of help being given and received especially where the brothers had grown up together in the home. The separation of brothers and sisters and half-siblings is, however, as we have already shown, so extensive as to mean that a great proportion of them spend little of their childhood together and lose touch long before they have reached adolescence. Analysis of the extended family type households gave some indication, however, of the extent to which siblings and their descendants tend to remain in or return to the maternal home, for short or long periods. Appendix 10 shows that there are in these households almost as many grand- and great-grandchildren, nieces and nephews and grand-nieces and nephews as there are own children. In the extended denuded female households the number actually exceeds that of own children.

VI

Although there were exceptions, the step-parent relationship was, as we have said, rarely a happy one. There was strong aversion by the woman to having her man's children by another woman brought into her home. This is particularly the case where her union with him is still unsettled and she has the fear in her mind that he may leave her to return to his previous alliance. Where her outside child is an adolescent girl, the woman may be jealous of her husband's interest in her. A married woman who had herself brought her twelve-year-old daughter into the home, said that 'some step-fathers were bad. They would be living with a woman and yet want to put questions to her daughter'. (i.e. ask for sexual favours).

There is also the practical anxiety that there will be so much less money to spend on her own children. The same reasons underlie the man's reluctance to allow his wife or concubine to bring her children into their home but there is in addition the social disapprobation of the man who 'fathers another man's bastards'. It is not surprising therefore, that we found that the number of cases where outside children were included in homes was relatively very small. (52)

An examination of the circumstances in which the household is so constituted brings out a number of interesting facts. In the first place, step-children are most commonly found where the current union is childless. Here the 'shame' felt at barrennesss or sterility taken together with the equally strong desire for children 'to gladden a home' overrides other considerations. The wish to have children is not purely sentimental. They are extremely useful in the home and from a very early age are made to perform a number of small household duties; there is also the belief that children are an insurance against the parents' old age.

The second fact was that step-children, in all Centres, were more often present in homes based on concubinage than marriage. Sugartown and Mocca again show the highest proportion with Orange Grove the lowest. We have, however, to take into account the over-all prevalence of marriage in Orange Grove as compared with the two other Centres.

Thirdly, the figures show that in Sugartown and Mocca the highest proportion of step-children in the home were those of the woman while in Orange Grove of the ten cases, four contain the man's, three the woman's and the remaining three were outside children of both the man and woman. This ties in with the pattern of maternal responsibility which we have seen to be the core of the parental relationship.

Taking into accout the small proportion of conjugal households which contain step-children at all, the number where the relationship is unhappy, or where it threatens the continuation of the union between the consorts, is even more pronounced. Where the step-relationship was a happy one it was usually where the union was childless or where the step-children were young and had been in the home from babyhood.

With strangers, and with us often at first, the fiction was sometimes maintained that the outside child was 'an adopted'. This was most often the case where the couple was married or among the middle or upper middle-classes where it was felt that illegitimacy might adversely affect not only the status of the parents but the child's future in the community. But it occurred also where the step-parent accepted the child as his or her own and wished the true parentage forgotten. Although it was not usual there were a few cases where the step-father gave his name to the child. Even in these circumstances however, it was usual for the child to know the name of his real mother. There was rarely, that is, any entire transference to the step-mother of the attitudes and sentiment felt for the real mother.

Since there may be, and in fact generally is, differential behaviour to the adopted as well as to the step-child it is necessary here to define this term as used in Jamaica and to describe the circumstances in which the institution of fostering occurs.

The first thing to be said is that there is no Adoption Law in Jamaica and no legal recognition of the status. (53) Secondly, the meaning of adoption and the pattern of behaviour associated with it varies considerably. A child may be given away, at any age, to strangers for the reason that the mother is too poor to look after him and hopes that he may have a better chance under the new arrangement. Where the child is an infant, the motive behind the adoption may be the adopted mother's childlessness, and love of children in which case the baby may find a real foster home. But there is another type, where the child is given away to a stranger, usually of a higher social standing or in better circumstances, as a 'schoolgirl' or 'schoolboy'. Here there is no intention to take the child into the family as an equal. The arrangement is primarily a business one: the child is fed, clothed and, theoretically, sent to school or taught to earn his or her living in exchange for services. A woman in Orange Grove who had herself adopted a child explained the difference between 'real adoption' and 'taking a school-child'. 'Some people,' she said, 'adopt children, or rather say they adopt. But they do not treat the child as their own. They take it and treat it as a schoolgirl or a schoolboy. Schooling out is different from adoption; it means to take a child and treat it as a servant. That in itself is not wrong but it is wrong to adopt a child and treat it in that way.'

Another Orange Grove family had three 'adopted girls' in their household only one of whom was described as a 'schoolgirl'. Like the other girls she was expected to help with the housework but unlike the other two she was not sent to school. This farmer's wife told us that in the case of adoption the child is taken as a baby or at an early age, while a schoolgirl (or boy) is usually taken in their teens. She added, however, that even adopted girls would have to leave if they began having illegitimate babies. They could not expect to be kept on *as one's own might be* in such an event.

The most usual form of so-called adoption, however, was between kin, and where this was the case there was little, if any, difference in treatment from the own child. It was said that 'a child of a near relative would be treated more as your own'. This was to some extent due, we were told, to the fact that when they grew up they were more likely to remain with the foster parent and continue to show affection and respect. But underlying this rationalization was the strength of kinship ties and the responsibility accepted in particular for grandchildren, nephews and nieces.

There were many complaints that foster children who were not kin proved 'ungrateful' when they reached adolescence and that all the care lavished on them when they were small was wasted. On the other hand many adults, who had been adopted in their childhood, complained that they had been exploited by their guardian, kept from school to do house-work or run errands, and had not received either affection or kindly treatment. In some of these cases, where the child was old enough to remember his mother, or knew her whereabouts, he would run away to her or to some other member of the family.

This 'running away' of children from one home to another if they are unkindly treated or threatened with punishment, was a common aspect of child-life in Sugartown. It often happened, if the mother and grandmother or the mother's sister lived in the same village, that if the child were chastised by the mother he would run away to the grandmother's home, or vice versa, to be petted and consoled. This involved generally nothing more than an exchange of visits but the child felt that he had a choice of homes. There were, however, cases of step-children or adopted children who at adolescence or even before ran away on their own. The complaint was invariably the harshness or neglect of the foster mother. The former term might mean anything from a 'flogging' to a scolding.

There were 54 cases of so-called adoption in our Centres: 18 in Sugartown, 31 in Orange Grove and 5 in Mocca. The majority in Sugartown and Mocca were kin and they were divided evenly between family homes and denuded type households. In Orange Grove 21 of the 31 adopted children were in married homes and there was a far higher percentage of the 'schoolgirl' or 'schoolboy' type. This is invariably an unhappy relationship and in the long run unprofitable from any point of view. The children were not treated on a par with the children of the family, were often given a great deal of work to do, and grew up with a strong sense of injustice. The foster-parents, on the other hand, accused them of ingratitude and there were many tales of their coming to 'a bad end'. There were a few exceptions: one notable one in Orange Grove where there was no discrimination, and the adopted child was as beloved as the couple's own. This happened most frequently where the child was of the kin.

VII

In view of the importance of the grandmother in the Jamaican family and popular assumptions as to the extent to which she takes the place of the mother we devoted considerable space in the last chapter to an analysis of the structure of these households. The usefulness of this analysis is that it allows us to see the different conditions in which the grandmother-grandchild relationship develops and the consequent differences in the relationship itself.

In an earlier chapter we described what we called the initial situation of pregnancy, where the mother is a young girl, often no more than a child, in her mother's home, and where the father has no place in the household. Here we saw the baby growing up to adopt the same pattern of behaviour to the relatively youthful grandmother as to his own mother and her siblings: often calling her 'mother' and using the same term for his mother as is used by them. When, as often happens, the mother leaves the home, the grandmother more and more assumes the role of mother and the child is absorbed into her family. He is treated in no way differently from the other children; is dressed the same, goes to school with them, performs the same household duties and shares on equal terms all their activities. The strong bond which exists in our society between mother and child colours and shapes the new relationship and the child has the security and satisfactions of being part of a family group,

Where the grandmother's own children are older, her eldest daughter is often given special duties and responsibilities for her sister's child, and so begins a relationship with the maternal aunt which is one of the strongest and most lasting kinship bonds.

Even in these cases, however, the real mother through her own tie with her mother as well as her love for the child she has had to leave, may continue a tenuous relationship. If she is working in the city she sends back what money she can afford and visits the maternal home whenever she can. In rare cases only, however, is she in a position to send for her child. If she is entirely self-supporting she cannot afford to do so, and if she enters into a new conjugal relationship the outside child is not in the majority of cases welcomed. Gradually the tie with her weakens and the grandmother assumes more and more fully the role of substitute mother.

We found no instance where the grandmother showed any reluctance to accept the implications of the relationship or resented the presence of the child in her home. In the first instance, it is the traditional pattern of behaviour, endorsed and approved by the society. Secondly there are the values set upon children; they 'gladden a home', they are a source of companionship, they are useful, they 'cost nothing'. Not least is the belief that the old people may look to them for help when they grow up. It is a cliche that children are believed to be an insurance against old age but it is none the less true. The formidable figures of broken homes, of children separated from their mother, should not be taken to indicate a widespread lack of maternal feeling. On the contrary the woman's desire for children is quite apart from her interest in sexual experience, and overrides any consideration of the practical and economic consequences. The expression that they are 'woman's business' has thus a deeper meaning than merely that she cannot rely upon the father accepting equal parental responsibility. In fact the unequal responsibility which she has to accept induces a high degree of devotion. In view of this mother-child relationship the woman who has to give up her child, has no anxiety if she can send it back to her mother.

Although, as we have shown, the step-father relationship is rarely happy, there were no instances than can be recalled of step-grandfathers resenting the grandchildren. One of the reasons is unquestionably the fact that in so many cases the grandmother households are associated with family land, and, except in Orange Grove, with family land descended in the female line. Although the man may be the main source of income, in such cases 'the home' was said to be the grandmother's, and the right of her daughter's children to participate in the inheritance would be fully recognized.

There is, however, another side to the picture. However much we can assume the grandmother's affection and impartiality in the care of the grandchildren, it cannot also be assumed that her assumption of complete responsibility for him is wholly satisfactory from the child's point of view.

110 out of 194 grandchildren in our three Centres were living with a grandmother in a family home where the grandmother had the support or assistance of a husband or concubine. In Sugartown 57 per cent, in Orange Grove 61 per cent and in Mocca 46 per cent live with 'single' grandmothers and among these the proportion of households based on family land is lower (considerably lower in Sugartown) than is the case of grandmother households of the extended family type.

We have already described at some length the precarious existence of 'single' mothers in homes of the denuded family type and the poverty which they endure. The single grandmother is in the same position, except that she may be older and less able therefore to do the type of labouring work which alone might be available to her. Where it is as hard to earn any sort of a livelihood, it is unrealistic to think of a child 'costing nothing' to keep. Yet, in spite of this, the grandchild is accepted on equal terms with the own children. But it is an equality of privation and, when the child reaches adolescence, of frustration.

Finally there are the cases where the grandmother is an old woman often ailing and living alone and generally in great poverty. Here the child is a mixture of beloved and petted plaything, on whom, nevertheless, the old lady makes continual calls for small services. Unless there is help from kin outside, he may not be sent to school at all, or attend only spasmodically. At adolescence he faces the problem of earning a living and (a fact they both accept) of helping his grandmother, without training of any sort.

VIII

In considering the role of family and kin in the social organization of the three Centres, not only have we to take into account the different socio-economic conditions which obtain in each but the disproportionate size of Sugartown compared with the other two Centres. Nevertheless size alone does not go far in explaining the different role of the family there as compared with Mocca or

Orange Grove. It is possible, given appropriate conditions, to imagine an indefinite extension of Orange Grove without loss either of its essential characteristics or of the part played by family and kin in its organization. It is conceivable that when we consider family organization comparatively, from this point of view, we may find that there are features in its structure which conduce to the limitation or extension of the role it can fulfil in a community. On the other hand it may be that social integration is brought about through other forms of co-operation and social controls. Nevertheless enough has already been said to indicate that Mocca and Orange Grove, in their different ways, are integrated societies in which kinship plays an important role, whereas Sugartown is not so much a social entity as a conglomerate of disparate sections, held together only by a common involvement with the sugar estate. Caste and class, as well as occupation and income, give the upper and middle sections some superficial appearance of coherence without however any homogeneity even within themselves. But in the population of peasants and sugar-workers which were our particular study, the associational ties and the fairly uniform cultural traditions, ideological systems and patterns of behaviour did not in themselves manage to create a society in which there was a consciousness of unity. This in spite of the forms of co-operation (the Trade Union, the Crop Associations, etc.) which we shall presently discuss.

I propose, therefore, to try and show in respect of each Centre, and with reference to the group or groups concerned, firstly the proportion and nature of economic co-operation; secondly the extent of inter-communication in social activities; thirdly, the degree of mutual inter-dependence; fourthly, the similarity, or otherwise, of social norms and patterns of behaviour; and finally, the extent to which public opinion is effective in imposing and maintaining the accepted patterns of behaviour in the society as a whole.

First, then, in regard to economic co-operation. We have already discussed this in regard to the family and seen that in Mocca and Orange Grove the producing unit is the individual family in the home; that men, women and their children have their defined tasks and duties and that in both these villages there is constant, intimate co-operation between the members of the family in their performance.

In Mocca there were no auxiliary organizations and co-operation outside the immediate family occurred only in the matter of house building. It was the custom to erect the frame-work and do the wattling of the sides and the thatching of the roofs with the assistance of friends. The term used in Mocca for this kind of co-operative activity was 'matches' as compared with the term-'partnership' in Sugartown and 'sport' in Orange Grove. But in all the same principle operated: no money changed hands but the owner of the house and his kin provided food and drink for the working-party. Usually the 'match' was only for a morning and the work was slow, so much so that it often took months for the job to be completed. In view of what has already been said about the family structure of Mocca and the attitude to 'strangers' co-operation there, of necessity, was between kin or relatives by marriage or concubinage. Neighbourliness was not as operative in Mocca as in either of the other two Centres—the stranger, in fact, was only accepted into the community if he or she 'married' into a Mocca family.

In Orange Grove while the individual family was the basic unit in working the farms there was an extension of co-operation when additional labour was needed, either at periods of seasonal agricultural activity or because the farmer had insufficient adult males in his household. Where paid labour was used it had to be drawn from outside the district as a rule. The usual procedure of the farmer who needed extra hands was to organize a 'morning sport'. There were three forms of this: the occasional 'sport' for one particular job, such as repairing a tank or building a house; and the regular agreement between a group of small farmers to assist one another as occasion arises in working their respective farms. No money is exchanged in either case, the understanding being that the party benefiting will provide food and drink. Since the services were expected to be reciprocal the members of the team were carefully selected friends who had mutual confidence in one another. At the same time it was not uncommon for men to give a 'morning's sport' for someone whom they knew would never be able to reciprocate, such as a woman living alone or without adult male help. Usually the woman of the house is assisted in preparing the meal by her friends and there is much coming and going between kitchen and field and a great deal of singing, laughing and joking. The third form of co-operation is the system of 'working days' whereby one farmer gives another a day's work on the understanding that it will be 'given back'.

In Orange Grove alone was there co-operation for community services. The only building in the village which was available for public meetings was a church hall and there were certain restrictions on the uses to which it might be put, the chief being a prohibition on the sale or drinking of liquor on the premises. It had been decided, therefore, to build a Community Hall by communal work. One morning a week was set apart for this work and the foundations were laid and the walls begun during our stay and the building completed in a little over a year. There was a building committee which was responsible for organizing the work and for raising the money for the purchase of building materials which were not available locally. The farmers contributed the foodstuffs for the mid-day meal from their farms and the cooking was done on the spot by their wives and daughters.

As members of the Jamaica Agricultural Society they fell in with the Society's project for a Demonstration Plot to exhibit correct techniques of land use and plant-disease control. A bit of land along the roadside had been given by one of the farmers, cleaned and made available. There, however, the matter rested throughout our stay. The farmers were not convinced that the Agricultural Instructor from the Society, who was not himself an experienced farmer, had anything to teach them and were annoyed that when they did apply for specific assistance, offered by the Society to members, it was not given promptly. In their view their own farms were 'demonstration plots' and their interest in the project was lukewarm, and shared the fate of all projects in that community which did not originate from their own felt needs.

The opportunity for formulating these and ensuring full co-operation was the monthly meeting in the Church Hall which was attended by the entire adult community, farmers and their wives, as well as by most of the young people and had a composite function. It combined the regular meeting of all the co-operative organizations in the community: the Savings Union, the Agricultural Society, the Egg Co-operative, the organization for the supply of milk to the Condensary, the Building Committee for the community hall and the Cricket Club. The business part of the meeting was formal: the officers sat before a small table, with the Chairman presiding and minutes were read by the Secretary and confirmed and then matters of general interest discussed. Discussions were always lively and revealed a high degree of technical farming knowledge and experience. On these occasions advice was often given by the more experienced farmers in answer to questions and information passed on in regard to experiments in agricultural and horticultural techniques. All the discussions turned on the functions of the several organizations—to increase the output of the farm by improved techniques by utilizing what national services were available.

The Savings Union had been started for the specific purpose of buying a bull to improve the dairy herd. Each farmer in the 'syndicate', which jointly owned the bull, took his turn in pasturing it. Farmers not in the syndicate paid a fee for servicing. The discussions showed that there was awareness of the value of cattle in mixed farming as well as the need for milk in the diet especially of the children, and also to improve the stock.

Arrangements for the supply of milk to the Condensary had been the result of persistent efforts by the local farmers. A Milk Co-operative Society had been formed and each farmer took his surplus milk every morning to the secretary who kept the individual records, delivered the supply to the truck when it arrived and was responsible for the distribution of payments.

The Egg Co-operative was of fairly recent origin but was developing rapidly. The secretary of this society had a particularly onerous task as she received, stored, graded and packed the eggs which were then sold in bulk to the Marketing Department.

The joint monthly meetings of these Societies was not wholly confined to business. It was also a social occasion. It opened with prayer and either before or after the serious business of the Committees there was community singing and recitations. This might be followed by a formal address (on one occasion the Chairman initiated one on 'The value of machinery to Agriculture' and on another on 'The Benefits of manure in our cultivations'). A popular feature of each meeting was the Roll Call. As each person's name was called they were expected to stand and recite either a text from the Bible or a 'gem'. (54) The evening might close with the children entertaining their elders with songs and recitations which were always vociferously received and applauded.

In Sugartown, by its very nature, any comprehensive forms of co-operation embracing the community as a whole—men, women and their children—had no part. What organizations there were, were sectional. There were local branches of the All Island Cane Farmers Association, and of the Rice Growers' Association. Neither had any large membership in Sugartown itself. The cane farmers, although many were employees of the Company, lived for the most part in the neighbourhood villages or in the backlands where their cane farms were situate. The Rice Growers, predominantly East Indian, lived in the villages near the swamp lands by the coast. Only seventeen out of a total membership of one hundred and seventy-nine were Sugartown residents.

The only organization with a significant membership affecting, directly or indirectly, the community as a whole, was the Bustamante Industrial Trade Union, and although this is not the appropriate place for a detailed account of the history and development of trade unionism in Jamaica, something must be said to allow of an assessment of the role of the BITU within this community.

It had, at that time, a closed shop in the sugar industry with sole bargaining rights. Membership was a necessary qualification for employment whether in field or factory. (This did not apply to specialist and senior staff.) There was a high degree of centralization and local delegates took their orders from the executive in Kingston. These were transmitted, so far as Sugartown was concerned, through a secretary (who lived there but was not a local man) who acted as liaison between the delegates and the head office. His chief function was to enrol all applicants for work and check on the financial standing of all field gangs before they were signed on. There was no relation between the number of new members accepted and the actual number of men required for the work available. Nevertheless, every man who joined did so with the expectation of getting work. This, the secretary achieved in the case of cane-cutters and casual labour by the operation of a rough and ready roster system which ensured the spread of the available work over as many members as possible. It had serious defects: one of which was that, as a result of this, wage-rates ceased to be an index of actual income of individual workers. Moreover, the acceptance of any newcomer was held to put the regular unionist on a par with the newly-joined man and had its effect on the maintenance of payments. The problem of how to keep up membership among seasonal and migrant workers is not, of course, peculiar to the BITU. But there were none of the inducements which unions elsewhere have adopted to hold their members together in periods of unemployment. The preoccupation of the Union—perhaps necessarily so in 1948-9—was with increasing rates of pay and introducing the shift system. To all intents and purposes its functions ceased once Crop was over and the seasonal workers dispersed. It created no responsible local organization which might have continued to function during the annual period of depression with the object of finding the answer to such of the problems which faced the workers as were soluble by co-operative action. The high degree of centralization and the dependence upon the magic of Bustamante's personality and leadership, which characterized the organization. discouraged if it did not actually prohibit the development of any local initiative. In spite, therefore, of the importance of the work of the BITU on a national scale in improving the lot of the worker, and of the high degree of loyalty and devotion to the Leader in Sugartown during that period, the opportunity was lost of organizing this dynamic as a continuing force in the permanent structure of the community.

There was nothing else to take its place. Where Mocca and Orange Grove were integrated by kinship bonds and a common pattern of life, and organized to permit of constant intercommunication, exchange of ideas and the transmission of approved modes of conduct, Sugartown presented itself as a collection of disparate un-assimilated and opposing aggregates. We have already described the water-tight class differentiations: the contrasts between wealth and poverty, both in regard to the composition of the society as a whole and within the working-class itself, in the clear-cut periods of boom and depression marked by crop time and the *tempo moto*. The features of diversity which prevented integration are not, of course, peculiar to Sugartown and are found in other industrial areas in Jamaica. But they were aggravated here by the high proportion of mobility in the population and the violence of the impact upon the relatively small group of permanent residents, of the immigrants and of the different behaviour patterns and systems of values which they brought with them. By and large the histories of these newcomers show that they were habitual migrants, the majority of them attached permanently to no social group elsewhere, and holding only precariously, if at all, to any kindred or conjugal affiliations. Only a proportion, as we have seen, became even temporarily, through the routine and associations of regular employment, an integral part of at least one section of the community. For the majority there was the see-saw of a few weeks with money to spend in the taverns and at the gaming tables followed by weeks of enforced idleness and dependence on the charity of strangers. 'Neighbourliness', the extension of hospitality in free board and lodging, was a much more pronounced feature of social relationships here than in either Mocca or Orange Grove and was evidence of the potential solidarity which might have been generated by a wider interpretation of trade union functions and appropriate organization.

The diversity of Sugartown was further exemplified in the

number of religious sects and cults which were represented. The Jehovah Witnesses attracted a considerable following among the middle and lower middle class of permanent residents. Others were described as Evangelists, Independent Baptists, Balm-yard Healers, and practicers of pocomania. But almost anyone might become 'converted' and set himself or herself up as a preacher and attract a congregation. Apart from the Jehovah Witnesses who had a small mission house, meetings were held in the open, on street corners or in yards, lit by kerosene flares. Many of the leaders were women and wore a distinctive head kerchief when they 'went preaching'. All the cults had this in common that they concentrated on ritual and allowed and encouraged active participation by the congregation. Meetings were the occasions for both the building up and the release of emotional tensions and there was also evidence of the establishment of cult-ties between members. Visiting preachers would be given hospitality for weeks on end and treated with great deference and respect.

Yet if I have been successful in the picture I have tried to draw of Sugartown it should be clear that in its diversity there was potential strength. The impression one got when the village was in full swing after the depression of the *slow-time* was one of intense vitality and opportunity. True there was drunkenness, gambling, prostitution and viciousness; but there was also generosity and kindness. The impact of the strangers brought about a quickening of ideas, whether in opposition or agreement, and a crystallization of views on national as well as local problems— land, housing, labour, education, politics, religion, race, colour, class. They went on—these voluble arguments—on street corners, in shops and taverns, in yards and in the canefields as the men rested in the shade to eat their lunch. Re-reading the accounts of these discussions and recalling the circumstances and the people as we knew them, is to be struck anew with the richness of personality and the reservoir of energy which dissipated itself.

In spite of its charm and the integrity of kinship and conjugal relationships which it presents, the traditional way of life in Mocca is at odds with the modern trends of development and it has not the dynamic to make adaptation probable. On the contrary, it is an example of attempted adjustment by withdrawal rather than face the necessity for migration elsewhere. Orange Grove is, at present, an example of the best that farming life can give and create locally. It cannot, however, remain static. If it is to preserve its present standards it must be through consciousness of the dangers ahead and unremitting vigilance. Its prosperity can be destroyed by over-population and fragmentation as much as by a falling off in the present standards of farming practice and balance. Its future lies, however, in its own hands. But what of Sugartown— and of the other Sugartowns and their prototypes in the industrial areas and slums of the city? There, as we see it, is a serious challenge. The tackling of the problems it presents, some of which we have tried to set out, cannot with either safety or wisdom be postponed.

FOOTNOTES TO CHAPTER 6

47 For an account of Nutrition in the West Indies see *Nutrition in Jamaica*, Agricultural Policy Committee of Jamaica (1945); *Nutrition in the British West Indies*, by B. S. Platt, C.M.G., PhD., M.B., Ch.B., pub. His Majesty's Stationery Office. Colonial No. 195 (1946) and *Your Health in the Carribbean*, by Dr W. E. McCulloch, Pioneer Press (1955).

48 'Flogging' is the term used most commonly to describe any form of corporal punishment given to children where a strap, switch or stick is used. 'Beating' is used for less severe chastisement and would include spanking or slapping.

49 Madeline Kerr, op. cit., p. 45.

50 George Lamming, *In the Castle of My Skin*, p. 11.

51 Appendix 5.

52 Appendix 8 and Chapter V, pp. 118 et seq.

53 An Adoption Law for Jamaica was passed in 1957.

54 M. Kerr, op. cit., pp. 76-7.

APPENDIX I

STANDARD CARD

Sub. District:

Family Record No.

(1) Man's Family (not in home)	(2) Household	(3) Woman's Family (not in home)
MAN'S GENEALOGY No. and basis of other unions	ASCENDANTS Ego M̄ C̄ Spouse	WOMAN'S GENEALOGY No. and basis of other unions
	DESCENDANTS	
DESCENDANTS	1st Generation	DESCENDANTS
	2nd ,,	
	3rd ,,	
	4th ,,	
(4) Period of conjugal unions (a) Present union (b) Previous unions	(5) Whereabouts of children not in home —Place —With whom	(6) House or Room —Inherited and from whom —Bought —Rented —Free
(8) Occupation of adult members of household	(9) Genealogy	(7) Land —Inherited and from whom —Bought —Rented —Free
(11) Adoptions (Principle of)	(10) Birth place Date arrival in Centre	

191

APPENDIX 2

Numbers of Adults and Children (under 15) according to sex for each type of Household

SUGARTOWN

Type of Household	Basis of Household	Adults			Children				TOTAL	Proportion of Total Population
		M	F	Total	M	F	N.S.	Total		
A Simple	Marriage	45	47	92	27	20	1	48	140	12%
	Concubinage	153	146	299	55	50	10	115	414	35%
	Total	198	193	391	82	70	11	163	554	47%
B Extended	Marriage	35	37	72	18	26	—	44	116	10%
	Concubinage	31	40	71	17	8	—	25	96	8%
	Total	66	77	143	35	34	—	69	212	18%
C Denuded Simple	Male	16	3	19	6	2	—	8	27	2%
	Female	7	43	50	15	20	—	35	85	7%
	Total	23	46	69	21	22	—	43	112	9%
D Denuded Extended	Male	6	3	9	3	—	—	3	12	1%
	Female	24	52	76	14	16	—	30	106	9%
	Total	30	55	85	17	16	—	33	118	10%
E Single Person	Male	126	—	126	—	—	—	—	126	11%
	Female	—	44	44	—	—	—	—	44	4%
	Total	126	44	170	—	—	—	—	170	14%
F Sibling		6	9	15	5	5	—	10	25	2%
TOTAL		449	424	873 73%	160	147	11	318 27%	1191 100%	100%

Totals of Types A and B: Marriage and Concubinage

A & B		M	F	Total	M	F	N.S.	Total	TOTAL	
	Marriage	80	84	164	45	46	1	92	256	21%
	Concubinage	184	186	370	72	58	10	140	510	43%
	TOTAL	264	270	534	117	104	11	232	766	62%

192

ORANGE GROVE

Type of Household	Basis of Household	Adults			Children				TOTAL	Proportion of Total Population
		M	F	Total	M	F	N.S.	Total		
A Simple	Marriage	47	49	96	42	31	1	74	170	25%
	Concubinage	13	14	27	10	19	—	29	56	8%
	Total	60	63	123	52	50	1	103	226	33%
B Extended	Marriage	56	61	117	39	52	—	91	208	31%
	Concubinage	11	9	20	9	7	—	16	36	5%
	Total	67	70	137	48	59	—	107	244	36%
C Denuded Simple	Male	9	2	11	7	3	—	10	21	3%
	Female	8	14	22	1	13	—	14	36	5%
	Total	17	16	33	8	16	—	24	57	8%
D Denuded Extended	Male	2	1	3	2	1	—	3	6	1%
	Female	15	45	60	21	20	—	41	101	15%
	Total	17	46	63	23	21	—	44	107	16%
E Single Person	Male	2	—	2	—	—	—	—	2	—
	Female	—	—	—	—	—	—	—	—	—
	Total	2	—	2	—	—	—	—	2	—
F Sibling		13	10	23	6	12	—	18	41	6%
TOTAL		176	205	381	137	158	1	296	677	100%

Totals of Types A and B: Marriage and Concubinage

A and B		M	F	Total	M	F	N.S.	Total		
	Marriage	103	110	213	81	83	1	165	378	56%
	Concubinage	24	23	47	19	26	—	45	92	14%
	Total	127	133	260	100	109	1	210	470	69%

APPENDIX 2 (*continued*)

MOCCA

Type of Household	Basis of Household	Adults			Children				TOTAL	Proportion of Total Population
		M	F	Total	M	F	N.S.	Total		
A Simple	Marriage	20	17	37	9	11	—	20	57	14%
	Concubinage	39	34	73	22	17	—	39	112	27%
	Total	59	51	110	31	28	—	59	169	41%
B Extended	Marriage	15	21	36	7	6	—	13	49	12%
	Concubinage	21	23	44	16	13	—	29	73	18%
	Total	36	44	80	23	19	—	42	122	30%
C Denuded Simple	Male	7	—	7	1	2	—	3	10	2%
	Female	3	14	17	3	4	—	7	24	6%
	Total	10	14	24	4	6	—	10	34	8%
D Denuded Extended	Male	2	1	3	1	1	—	2	5	1%
	Female	9	17	26	10	9	—	19	45	11%
	Total	11	18	29	11	10	—	21	50	12%
E Single Person	Male	13	—	13	—	—	—	—	13	3%
	Female	—	15	15	—	—	—	—	15	4%
	Total	13	15	28	—	—	—	—	28	7%
F Sibling		4	4	8	—	1	—	1	9	2%
TOTAL		133	146	279	69	64	—	133	412	100%

Totals of Types A and B: Marriage and Concubinage

A and B		M	F	Total	M	F			TOTAL	
	Marriage	35	38	73	16	17	—	33	106	26%
	Concubinage	60	57	117	38	30	—	68	185	45%
	Total	95	95	190	54	47	—	101	291	70%

APPENDIX 3

DISTRIBUTION OF THE TOTAL POPULATION IN EACH CENTRE AND FOR ALL
CENTRES IN DIFFERENT TYPES OF HOUSEHOLD

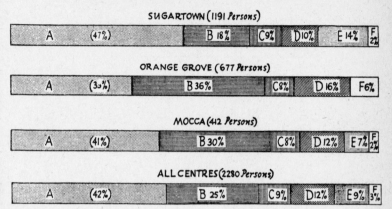

SUGARTOWN (1191 *Persons*)

ORANGE GROVE (677 *Persons*)

MOCCA (412 *Persons*)

ALL CENTRES (2280 *Persons*)

195

APPENDIX 4 (*a*)

DISTRIBUTION OF HOUSEHOLDS BY SIZE IN EACH CENTRE AND FOR ALL CENTRES

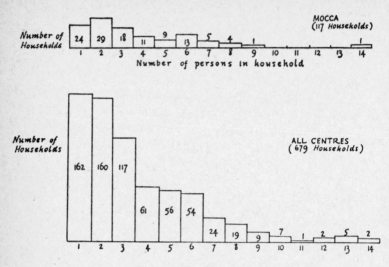

APPENDIX 4 (*b*)

DISTRIBUTION OF HOUSEHOLDS BY SIZE IN EACH CENTRE AND FOR ALL CENTRES

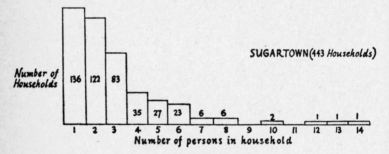

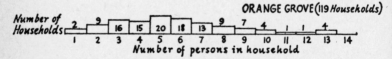

APPENDIX 5

Showing whereabouts of children under 15 years of age not living in home, arranged according to Parentage and Sex.

a) Children of a couple living together (Types A and B) in marriage or concubinage.
b) Outside children of a woman living in a conjugal union (Types A and B) or children of a woman living alone. (Types C, D and E.)
c) Outside children of a man living in a conjugal union (Types A and B) or children of a man living alone. (Types C, D and E.)

M—Male, F—Female, NS—Not specified.

SUGARTOWN

	(a)				(b)				(c)				Totals				
	M	F	NS	T	M	F	NS	T	M	F	NS	T	M	F	NS	T	%
Mother	–	–	–	–	–	–	–	–	30	28	9	67	30	28	9	67	39
Father	–	–	–	–	10	6	–	16	–	–	–	–	10	6	–	16	9
Mother's kin																	
M's mother	–	4	–	4	7	6	1	14	1	2	–	3	8	12	1	21	⎫13
M's father	–	–	–	–	1	1	–	2	–	–	–	–	1	1	–	2	⎬
M's M's mother	–	–	–	–	–	1	–	1	–	–	–	–	–	1	–	1	⎭
M's sister	1	–	–	1	1	3	–	4	–	1	–	1	2	4	–	6	⎱6
M's brother	–	–	–	–	1	2	–	3	–	–	–	–	1	2	–	3	⎰
Father's kin																	
F's mother	–	–	–	–	2	2	–	4	9	2	4	15	11	4	4	19	⎱11
F's father	–	–	–	–	1	–	–	1	–	–	–	–	1	–	–	1	⎰
F's sister	–	–	–	–	–	–	–	–	–	1	–	1	–	1	–	1	1
F's brother	–	–	–	–	–	–	–	–	–	–	–	–	–	–	–	–	
F's M's husband's sister	–	–	–	–	–	–	–	–	1	–	–	1	1	–	–	1	1
Siblings																	
Sister	–	–	–	–	–	1	–	1	–	–	–	–	–	1	–	1	⎱1
Half brother	–	–	–	–	1	–	–	1	–	–	–	–	1	–	–	1	⎰
Lineage unspecified																	
Grandmother	–	–	–	–	–	–	–	–	2	3	–	5	2	3	–	5	⎫
Aunt	–	–	–	–	–	–	–	–	2	–	–	2	2	–	–	2	⎬5
Kin not specified	–	–	–	–	–	1	–	1	–	–	–	–	–	1	–	1	⎭
Non-kin																	
Adopted	–	1	–	1	5	3	–	8	1	2	–	3	6	6	–	12	7
Sch/Orph.	1	1	–	2	2	1	–	3	–	–	–	–	3	2	–	5	⎱7
NS/Working	–	1	–	1	2	1	–	3	2	2	–	4	5	3	–	8	⎰
Totals	3	6	–	9	33	28	1	62	48	41	13	102	84	75	14	173	100

APPENDIX 5 (*continued*)

ORANGE GROVE

	(a)				(b)				(c)				Totals				
	M	F	NS	T	M	F	NS	T	M	F	NS	T	M	F	NS	T	%
Mother	–	–	–	–	–	–	–	–	6	9	–	15	6	9	–	15	37
Father	–	–	–	–	1	2	–	3	–	–	–	–	1	2	–	3	7
Mother's kin																	
M's mother	3	2	–	5	1	–	–	1	2	1	–	3	6	3	–	9	} 27
M's father	–	2	–	2	–	–	–	–	–	–	–	–	–	2	–	2	
M's M's mother	–	–	–	–	–	–	–	–	–	–	–	–	–	–	–	–	
M's sister	–	–	–	–	1	–	–	1	–	–	–	–	1	–	–	1	} 7
M's brother	1	–	–	1	–	–	–	–	–	1	–	1	1	1	–	2	
Father's kin																	
F's mother	1	–	–	1	1	1	–	2	–	–	–	–	2	1	–	3	7
F's father	–	–	–	–	–	–	–	–	–	–	–	–	–	–	–	–	
F's sister	–	1	–	1	1	–	–	1	–	–	–	–	1	1	–	2	} 7
F's brother	–	–	–	–	–	1	–	1	–	–	–	–	–	1	–	1	
F's M's husband's sister	–	–	–	–	–	–	–	–	–	–	–	–	–	–	–	–	
Siblings																	
Sister	–	–	–	–	–	–	–	–	–	–	–	–	–	–	–	–	
Half brother	–	–	–	–	–	–	–	–	–	–	–	–	–	–	–	–	
Lineage unspecified																	
Grandmother	–	–	–	–	–	–	–	–	–	–	–	–	–	–	–	–	
Aunt	–	–	–	–	–	–	–	–	–	–	–	–	–	–	–	–	
Kin not specified	–	–	–	–	–	–	–	–	–	–	–	–	–	–	–	–	
Non-kin																	
Adopted	–	–	–	–	–	–	–	–	–	–	–	–	–	–	–	–	
Sch/Orph.	–	–	–	–	–	–	–	–	–	–	–	–	–	–	–	–	
NS/Working	1	–	–	1	–	1	–	1	–	–	–	–	1	1	–	2	5
Totals	6	5	–	11	5	5	–	10	8	11	–	19	19	21	–	40	100

APPENDIX 5 (continued)

MOCCA

	(a)				(b)				(c)				Totals				
	M	F	NS	T	M	F	NS	T	M	F	NS	T	M	F	NS	T	%
Mother	–	–	–	–	–	–	–	–	1	1	–	2	1	1	–	2	6
Father	–	1	–	1	1	1	3	5	–	–	–	–	1	2	3	6	18
Mother's kin																	
M's mother	1	–	–	1	–	–	5	5	–	–	–	–	1	–	5	6	18
M's father	–	–	–	–	–	–	–	–	–	–	–	–	–	–	–	–	
M's M's mother	–	–	–	–	–	–	–	–	–	–	–	–	–	–	–	–	
M's sister	–	1	–	1	2	–	–	2	–	–	–	–	2	1	–	3	9
M's brother	–	–	–	–	–	–	–	–	–	–	–	–	–	–	–	–	
Father's kin																	
F's mother	1	–	–	1	–	–	–	–	1	2	–	3	2	2	–	4	12
F's father	–	–	–	–	–	–	–	–	–	–	–	–	–	–	–	–	
F's sister	–	–	–	–	–	–	–	–	–	–	–	–	––	–	–	–	
F's brother	–	–	–	–	–	–	–	–	–	–	–	–	–	–	–	–	
F's M's husband's sister	–	–	–	–	–	–	–	–	–	–	–	–	–	–	–	–	
Siblings																	
Sister	–	–	–	–	–	–	–	–	–	–	–	–	–	–	–	–	
Half brother	–	–	–	–	–	–	–	–	–	–	–	–	–	–	–	–	
Lineage unspecified																	
Grandmother	–	–	–	–	–	–	–	–	–	–	–	–	–	–	–	–	
Aunt	–	–	–	–	–	–	–	–	–	–	–	–	–	–	–	–	
Kin not specified	–	1	–	1	–	–	–	–	––	–	–	–	–	1	–	1	3
Non-kin																	
Adopted	1	1	–	2	–	–	–	–	–	–	–	–	1	1	–	2	6
Sch/Orph.	–	–	–	–	–	–	–	–	–	–	–	–	–	–	–	–	
NS/Working	–	–	–	–	6	2	–	8	–	–	2	2	6	2	2	10	29
Totals	3	4	–	7	9	3	8	20	2	3	2	7	14	10	10	34	100

APPENDIX 6

Showing the distribution of own and outside children in simple family homes based on marriage and concubinage

KEY: I Containing children of the couple only

II(*a*) With outside children of both.
  (*b*) With outside children of the man only.
  (*c*) With outside children of the woman only.
  (*d*) With adopted children.

III Childless couples.

	Sugartown		*Orange Grove*		*Mocca*	
	M	C	M	C	M	C
I	18	30	18	4	6	9
II(*a*)	–	–	1	2	–	1
(*b*)	2	9	1	3	1	–
(*c*)	6	20	2	1	1	9
(*d*)	1	2	6	–	2	–
III	11	77	2	2	3	10
Totals	38	138	30	12	13	29

Appendices

Showing the distribution of own and outside children in Extended Family homes
based on marriage and concubinage

SUGARTOWN

		Marriage		Concubinage		Total	
I	Primary	9	56%	7	44%	16	37%
II	Secondary	5	25%	15	75%	20	47%
III	Augmented Primary or Secondary	3	100%	–	–	3	7%
V	Tertiary	3	75%	1	25%	4	9%
	Ratio of Total Households	20	40%	23	5%	43	10%

ORANGE GROVE

		Marriage		Concubinage		Total	
I	Primary	13	92%	1	7%	14	42%
II	Secondary	10	66%	5	33%	15	45%
III	Augmented Primary or Secondary	1	100%	–	–	1	3%
V	Tertiary	2	66%	1	33%	3	9%
	Ratio of Total Households	26	22%	7	6%	33	28%

MOCCA

		Marriage		Concubinage		Total	
I	Primary	4	66%	2	33%	6	30%
II	Secondary	4	50%	4	50%	8	40%
III	Augmented Primary or Secondary	1	50%	1	50%	2	10%
V	Tertiary	–	–	4	100%	4	20%
	Ratio of Total Households	9	8%	11	9%	20	17%

ALL CENTRES

		Marriage		Concubinage		Total	
I	Primary	26	72%	10	28%	36	37%
I	Secondary	19	44%	24	26%	43	45%
I	Augmented Primary or Secondary	5	83%	1	17%	6	6%
V	Tertiary	5	45%	6	54%	11	12%
	Ratio of Total Households	55	8%	41	6%	96	14%

APPENDIX 8

Number of offspring born to heads of households shown according to parentage and type of household compared with those in the home and with those *not* in the home according to age structure

KEY: (a) Children of the Couple (c) Children of the Man Illeg. = Illegitimate
(b) Children of the Woman Leg. = Legitimate (M) = Marriage (C) = Concubinage

SUGARTOWN

Type	Children born a/c parentage (a)/Leg.	(b)/Illeg.	(c)	Total	Children in home a/c parentage (a)/Leg.	(b)/Illeg.	(c)	Total	Children not in home a/c age structure — Under 15	15 & over	N.S.	Total
Type A (M)	89	36	22	147	48 63%	9 30%	3 15%	60 48%	13 20%	14 21%	39 59%	66 52%
Simple family (C)	95	150	124	369	82 96%	27 27%	11 11%	120 42%	60 36%	44 27%	62 37%	166 58%
	184	186	146	516	130	36	14	180 (43%)	73	58	101	232 (57%)
Type B (M)	44	21	18	83	22 58%	4 21%	–	26 40%	–	34 87%	5 13%	39 60%
Extended family (C)	9	26	31	66	8 89%	11 52%	2 7%	21 36%	4 11%	21 55%	13 34%	38 64%
	53	47	49	149	30	15	2	47 (38%)	4	55	18	77 (62%)
Denuded mother households C. Simple	5	75		80	5 100%	43 64%		48 67%	6 25%	2 8%	16 67%	24 33%
D. Extended	25	52		77	10 53%	17 41%		27 45%	–	33 100%	–	33 55%
	30	127		157	15	60		75 (57%)	6	35	16	57 (43%)
Denuded father households C. Simple	13	23		36	5 42%	11 50%		16 47%	5 28%	7 39%	6 33%	18 53%
D. Extended	9	2		11	1 11%	1		1 10%	–	5 56%	4 44%	9 90%
	22	25		47	6	11		17 (39%)	5	12	10	27 (61%)
Single person E. Male	35	100		135	–	–		–	33 29%	20 17%	62 54%	115 100%
Female	13	50		63	–	–		–	6 14%	22 51%	15 35%	43 100%
	48	150		198	–	–		–	39	42	77	158 (100%)
F. Sibling	–	16		16	–	9		9				

APPENDIX 8 (continued)

ORANGE GROVE

Type		Children born a/c parentage (a)	(b)	(c)	Total	Children in home a/c parentage (a)	(b)	(c)	Total	Children not in home a/c age structure Under 15	15 & over	N.S.	Total
Type A	(M)	124	24	12	160	86 / 79%	4 / 29%	2 / 18%	92 / 69%	11 / 26%	25 / 60%	6 / 14%	42 / 31%
Simple family	(C)	19	13	19	51	16 / 84%	5 / 42%	8 / 57%	29 / 60%	13 / 68%	2 / 11%	4 / 21%	19 / 40%
		143	37	31	211	102	9	10	121 (66%)	24	27	10	61 (33%)
Type B	(M)	120	13	8	141	71 / 65%	5 / 42%	2 / 25%	78 / 60%	3 / 6%	48 / 94%	–	51 / 40%
Extended family	(C)	12	10	12	34	12 / 100%	–	1 / 8%	13 / 41%	4 / 21%	15 / 79%	–	19 / 59%
		132	23	20	175	83	5	3	91 (56%)	7	63	–	70 (43%)
		Leg.	*Illeg.*		*Total*	*Leg.*	*Illeg.*		*Total*	*Under 15*	*15 & over*	*N.S.*	*Total*
Denuded mother households C. Simple		11	13		24	4 / 44%	9 / 75%		13 / 62%	2 / 25%	4 / 50%	2 / 25%	8 / 38%
D. Extended		77	24		101	19 / 31%	8 / 36%		27 / 32%	2 / 2%	55 / 98%	–	56 / 68%
		88	37		125	23	17		40 (38%)	3	59	2	64 (61%)
Denuded father households C. Simple		10	25		35	3 / 50%	8 / 36%		11 / 39%	4 / 24%	6 / 35%	7 / 41%	17 / 61%
D. Extended		8	–		8	4 / 57%	–		4 / 57%	–	3 / 43%	–	3 / 43%
		18	25		43	7	8		15 (43%)	4	9	7	20 (57%)
Single person E. Male		–	3		3	–	–		–	1 / 33%	2 / 67%	–	3 / 100%
Female		–	–		–	–	–		–	–	–	–	–
F. Sibling		–	3		3	–	18		18	1	2	–	3 (100%)
		2	10		12	–	18		18	–			
ALL TYPES		383	186		569	215	70		285	39	160	19	218

APPENDIX 8 (*continued*)

MOCCA

Type		Children born a/c parentage				Children in home a/c parentage				Children not in home a/c age structure			
		(a)	(b)	(c)	Total	(a)	(b)	(c)	Total	Under 15	15 & over	N.S.	Total
Type A													
Simple family	(M)	37	23	9	69	25	2	1	28	5	11	2	18
						89%	22%	100%	61%	28%	61%	11%	39%
	(C)	40	59	11	110	29	24		54	11	21	8	40
						81%	51%	9%	57%	28%	52%	20%	43%
		77	82	20	179	54	26	2	82 (58%)	16	32	10	58 (42%)
Type B													
Extended family	(M)	35	2	2	39	11	1		12		17		17
						44%	50%		41%		100%		59%
	(C)	27	12	1	40	20	4		24	3	9		12
						74%	50%		67%	25%	75%		33%
		62	14	3	79	31	5		36 (55%)	3	26		29 (45%)
		Leg.	Illeg.	(c)	Total	Leg.	Illeg.	(c)	Total				
Denuded mother households													
C. Simple		7	19		26	1	11		12	1	3	6	10
						25%	61%		55%	10%	40%	60%	45%
D. Extended		11	33		44	7	6		13	1	15	2	18
						64%	30%		42%	5%	83%	11%	58%
		18	52		70	8	17		25 (47%)	2	18	8	28 (53%)
Denuded father households													
C. Simple			10		10		7		7			3	3
							70%		70%			100%	30%
D. Extended			10		10		7		7				
							70%		70%				
Single person													
E. Male		3	17		20					3	6	10	19
										16%	32%	53%	100%
Female		13	19		32						16	3	19
											84%	16%	100%
		16	36		52					3	22	13	38 (100%)
F. Sibling			1		1		1		1				
ALL TYPES		173	218		391	93	58		151	24	98	24	16

APPENDIX 9

Distribution of Households according to type and conjugal status.

(a) SUGARTOWN

Type	No. of Households	Proportion of Total Households in Centre (443)			Proportion of Total Households in Category in all three Centres	
A. (Marriage)	38	9%			(81)	47%
(Concubinage)	138	31%	50%	M=14%	(179)	77%
B. (Marriage)	20	5%		C=36%	(55)	36%
(Concubinage)	23	5%			(41)	56%
C. Denuded Simple						
Male	10	2%			(19)	53%
Female	29	7%			(48)	60%
D. Denuded Extended			15%			
Male	5	1%			(7)	72%
Female	24	5%			(55)	44%
E. Single Person						
Male	110	25%			(125)	88%
Female	41	9%	35%		(54)	76%
F. Sibling	5	1%			(15)	33%
	443	100%				

(b) ORANGE GROVE

Type	No. of Households	Proportion of Total Households in Centre (119)			Proportion of Total Households in Category in all three Centres
A. (Marriage)	30	25%			37%
(Concubinage)	12	10%	63%	M=47%	7%
B. (Marriage)	26	22%		C=16%	47%
(Concubinage)	7	6%			17%
C. Denuded Simple					
Male	6	5%			32%
Female	10	8%			21%
D. Denuded Extended			30%		
Male	1	1%			14%
Female	19	16%			34%
E. Single Person					
Male	2	2%			2%
Female	–	–	7%		–
F. Sibling	6	5%			40%
	119	100%			

APPENDIX 9 (*continued*)

(*c*) MOCCA

Type	No. of Households	Proportion of Total Households in Centre (117)		Proportion of Total Households in Category in all three Centres
A. (Marriage)	13	11%		16%
(Concubinage)	29	25%	52% M=19%	16%
B. (Marriage)	9	8%	C=34%	16%
(Concubinage)	11	9%		27%
C. Denuded Simple				
Male	3	3%		16%
Female	9	8%		18%
D. Denuded Extended			21%	
Male	1	1%		14%
Female	12	10%		22%
E. Single Person				
Male	13	11%		10%
Female	13	11%	26%	24%
F. Sibling	4	3%		27%
	117	100%		

ALL CENTRES TOGETHER

Type	Basis of Union in				Status of Householder 'Single'		Totals	
	Marriage		Concubinage					
A. Simple family	(81)	12%	(179)	26%	—	—	(260)	38
B. Extended family	(55)	8%	(41)	6%	—	—	(96)	14
C. Denuded Simple								
Male					(19)	3%	(67)	10
Female					(48)	7%		
D. Denuded Extended								
Male					(7)	1%		
Female					(55)	8%	(62)	9
E. Single person								
Male					(125)	18%		
Female					(54)	8%	(179)	26
F. Sibling								
(*a*) Sibling (5)								
(*b*) Conjugal								
Sibling (10)					(15)	2%	(15)	2
	(136)	20%	(220)	32%	(323)	47%	(679)	99

APPENDIX 10

Kin included in Extended Family Type Households

	Sugartown			*Orange Grove*			*Mocca*			*Totals*		
	M.	C.	Total	M.	C.	Total	M.	C.	Total	M.	C.	Total
Children of the couple	22	8	30	71	12	83	11	20	31	104	40	144
Children of the woman	4	11	15	5	–	5	1	4	5	10	15	25
Children of the man	–	2	2	2	1	3	–	–	–	2	3	5
Adopted children	4	–	4	11	–	11	–	–	–	15	–	15
Grandchildren	21	9	30	38	2	40	11	10	21	70	21	91
Great-grandchildren	1	–	1	3	–	3	–	–	–	4	–	4
Sibling's children	4	9	13	14	1	15	3	2	5	21	12	33
Sibling's grandchildren	6	–	6	3	–	3	1	–	1	10	–	10
Parent's sibling's grandchildren	–	–	–	–	–	–	–	2	2	–	2	2
Parent's sibling's children	–	–	–	–	–	–	–	3	3	–	3	3
Parent's sibling's great-grandchildren	–	–	–	–	–	–	–	2	2	–	2	2
TOTALS	62	39	101	147	16	163	27	43	70	236	98	334

207

Showing total and average number of children born to all adult women by age mother

Age Group	No. of Women Childless				Mothers				All Women*	Children born				Average No. per Mother	Comparison with Puerto Rico†
	S	OG	M	Total	S	OG	M	Total		S	OG	M	Total		
15–19	32	23	19	74	10	17	3	30	104	12	24	4	40	1·3	1·2
20–24	19	10	2	31	26	16	15	57	96	43	28	31	102	1·7	1·9
25–29	20	2	5	27	27	17	11	55	86	66	65	28	159	2·8	2·7
30–34	12	1	1	14	35	10	7	52	70	116	42	14	172	3·2	3·5
35–39	7	2	5	14	35	8	5	48	65	100	28	31	159	3·3	3·9
40–44	9	1	1	11	27	3	8	38	50	110	14	32	156	4·1	4·9
45–49	4	4	–	8	18	17	16	51	61	78	119	82	279	5·5	5·2
50–54	1	–	1	2	17	7	10	34	36	50	49	54	153	4·5	5·7
55–59	–	–	–	–	6	7	4	17	17	23	31	14	68	4·0	6·4
60–64	6	1	1	8	11	8	5	24	32	57	48	27	132	5·5	6·1
65+	3	3	1	7	8	12	11	31	40	23	75	42	140	4·5	6·0
N.S.	25	8	1	34	32	14	6	52	118	84	31	18	133	2·6	–
TOTALS	138	55	37	230	252	136	101	489	775*	762	554	377	1693	3·6	4·1

* Including 56 women not specified as either mothers or non-mothers.
† See 'Patterns of Living' by Dr Lydia Roberts, p. 287.

APPENDIX 12

Showing specified number of children born to all adult women according to type household

SUGARTOWN

Type of Household	A (M)	A (C)	B (M)	B (C)	C	D	E	F	Total	Proportion of total women
0	10	52	8	17	15	17	17	2	138	32·5
1	7	35	6	6	8	12	12	3	89	20·9
2	4	15	4	7	6	6	3	1	46	10·8
3	7	13	4	–	4	5	2	1	36	8·4
4	3	13	3	2	2	4	2	–	29	6·8
5	1	1	1	2	4	4	–	–	13	3·0
6	3	6	1	–	1	–	1	–	12	2·8
7	2	5	1	1	2	1	–	–	12	2·8
8	–	2	3	–	–	0	2	–	7	1·6
9	3	–	–	–	–	1	1	–	5	1·1
10	–	–	–	–	–	–	–	–	–	–
11	–	–	–	–	–	1	–	1	2	·4
12	–	–	–	–	–	–	–	–	–	–
13	1	–	–	–	–	–	–	–	1	·2
14	–	–	–	–	–	–	–	–	–	–
15	–	–	–	–	–	–	–	–	–	–
16	–	–	–	–	–	–	–	–	–	–
N.S.	6	4	6	5	4	4	4	1	34	8·0
TOTAL	47	146	37	40	46	55	44	9	424	

APPENDIX 12 (continued)

ORANGE GROVE

Type of Household	A (M)	A (C)	B (M)	B (C)	C	D	E	F	Total	Proportion of total women
0	18	1	16	–	7	11	–	2	55	26·8
1	3	3	14	1	2	8	–	2	33	15·9
2	2	2	3	3	1	6	–	2	19	9·2
3	5	1	5	2	2	3	–	2	20	9·7
4	4	3	3	–	2	7	–	–	19	9·2
5	5	1	–	–	–	2	–	1	9	4·3
6	2	–	4	1	2	2	–	–	11	5·3
7	1	1	1	–	–	1	–	–	4	1·9
8	–	–	1	–	–	3	–	1	5	2·4
9	2	–	3	–	–	–	–	–	5	2·4
10	2	–	4	–	–	–	–	–	6	2·9
11	1	–	1	–	–	1	–	–	3	1·4
12	–	–	–	–	–	1	–	–	1	·4
13	–	–	–	–	–	–	–	–	–	–
14	–	–	–	–	–	–	–	–	–	–
15	–	–	–	–	–	–	–	–	–	–
16	1	–	–	–	–	–	–	–	1	·4
N.S.	3	2	6	2	–	1	–	–	14	6·8
TOTAL	49	14	61	19	16	46	–	10	205	

MOCCA

Type of Household	A (M)	A (C)	B (M)	B (C)	C	D	E	F	Total	Proportion of total women
0	7	9	7	6	5	1	1	1	37	25·3
1	2	5	2	5	4	5	6	1	30	20·5
2	–	5	3	2	2	2	2	1	17	11·6
3	1	4	–	2	–	1	3	–	11	7·5
4	–	1	–	1	1	7	1	–	11	7·5
5	1	2	2	1	–	–	–	–	6	4·1
6	2	2	1	1	–	1	–	–	7	4·7
7	1	1	–	1	2	–	–	–	5	3·4
8	1	2	2	2	–	1	–	–	8	5·4
9	–	–	1	–	–	–	–	–	1	·6
10	–	–	–	–	–	–	1	–	1	·6
11	1	1	–	–	–	–	–	–	2	1·3
12	1	1	–	–	–	–	–	–	2	1·3
13	–	–	–	–	–	–	–	–	–	–
14	–	–	–	–	–	–	–	–	–	–
15	–	–	–	–	–	–	–	–	–	–
16	–	–	–	–	–	–	–	–	–	–
N.S.	–	1	3	2	–	–	1	1	8	5·4
TOTAL	17	34	49	23	14	18	15	4	146	

APPENDIX 13

Distribution of Households in each Centre excluding (1) Households of Type A where children are absent and (2) Single Person Households

Type of Table II	Sugartown	Orange Grove	Mocca	Total
Type A with children	88	38	29	155
Type B	43	33	20	96
Total	131	71	49	251
Type C	39	16	12	67
Type D	29	20	13	62
Total C and D	68	36	25	129
Type F	5	6	4	15
Total	204	113	78	395

APPENDIX 14

Households of the Simple Family Type (Type A) according to the Presence or Absence of Children and the Conjugal Basis of the Households

SUGARTOWN

Simple Family Households	Basis of Union		Total
	Marriage	Concubinage	
With Children (Types A1 and A2)	27 (71%) (31%)	61 (44%) (69%)	88 (50%) (100%)
Without Children (Type A3)	11 (29%) (12%)	77 (56%) (88)%	88 (50%) (100%)
TOTAL	38 (100%) (22%)	138 (100%) (78%)	176 (100%) (100%)

ORANGE GROVE

	Marriage	Concubinage	Total
With Children (Types A1 and A2)	28 (93%) (74%)	10 (83%) (26%)	38 (90%) (100%)
Without Children (Type A3)	2 (7%) (50%)	2 (17%) (50%)	4 (10%) (100%)
TOTAL	30 (100%) (71%)	12 (100%) (29%)	42 (100%) (100%)

APPENDIX 14 (*continued*)

MOCCA

Simple Family Households	Basis of Union		Total
	Marriage	Concubinage	
With Children	10 (77%)	19 (66%)	29 (69%)
(Types A1 and A2)	(34%)	(66%)	(100%)
Without Children	3 (23%)	10 (34%)	13 (31%)
(Type A3)	(23%)	(77%)	(100%)
TOTAL	13 (100%)	29 (100%)	42 (100%)
	(31%)	(69%)	(100%)

ALL CENTRES

	Marriage	Concubinage	Total
With Children	65 (80%)	90 (50%)	155 (60%)
(Types A1 and A2)	(42%)	(58%)	(100%)
Without Children	16 (20%)	89 (50%)	105 (40%)
(Type A3)	(15%)	(85%)	(100%)
TOTAL	81 (100%)	179 (100%)	260 (100%)
	(31%)	(69%)	(100%)

APPENDIX 15

Numbers of Grandmother Households and Great-Grandmother Households in each Centre, and the population contained in them

	Sugartown	Orange Grove	Mocca	All Centres
(*a*) Grandmother Households	35	32	21	88
Number of persons	(183)	(226)	(119)	(528)
(*b*) Great-Grandmother Households	3	5	0	8
Number of persons	(22)	(38)	(–)	(60)
(*c*) Total of (*a*) and (*b*)	38	37	21	96
Number of persons	(205)	(264)	(119)	(588)
Proportion (*c*) of all Households	9%	31%	18%	14%
Proportion of persons	(17%)	(39%)	(29%)	(26%)
Average of Households	5·4	7·1	5·7	6·0

APPENDIX 10

Distribution of 194 Grandchildren living with Grandmothers, and Great-Grandchildren living with Great-Grandmothers, according to sex, age and the presence or absence of their parents in the home.

Grandchild or Great-Grandchild		Sugartown			Orange Grove			Mocca			All Centres		
		M	F	Total	M	F	Total	M	F	Total	M	F	Total
Type W — Without either Parent	Under 15	10	10	20	14	14	28	8	5	13	32	29	61
	15 or over	5	9	14	3	3	6	2	1	3	10	13	23
	Total	15	19	34	17	17	34	10	6	16	42	42	84
Type X — With Mother only	Under 15	8	13	21	18	22	40	5	7	12	31	42	73
	15 or over	–	–	–	1	2	3	1	1	2	2	3	5
	Total	8	13	21	19	24	43	6	8	14	33	45	78
Type Y — With both Parents	Under 15	4	3	7	3	4	7	4	1	5	11	8	19
	15 or over	–	1	1	–	–	–	1	1	2	1	2	3
	Total	4	4	8	3	4	7	5	2	7	12	10	22
Type Z — With Father only	Under 15	6	–	6	1	3	4	–	–	–	7	3	10
	15 or over	–	–	–	–	–	–	–	–	–	–	–	–
	Total	6	–	6	1	3	4	–	–	–	7	3	10
TOTAL	Under 15	28	26	54	36	43	79	17	13	30	81	82	163
	15 or over	5	10	15	4	5	9	4	3	7	13	18	31
	TOTAL	33	36	69	40	48	88	21	16	37	94	100	194

Note. M = Male. F = Female

213

APPENDIX 17

Distribution of Grandchildren living with Grandmothers and Great-grandchildren living with Great-Grandmothers, according to descent through a Son or Daughter of the Grandmother or Great-Grandmother and according to the presence or absence of Parents in the Home

Grandchild or Great-Grandchild	Sugartown			Orange Grove			Mocca			All Centres		
	S	D	Total	S	D	Total	S	D	Total	S	D	Total
Without either Parent	18	16	34	7	27	34	2	14	16	27	57	84
With Mother only	–	21	21	4	39	43	2	12	14	6	72	78
With both Parents	1	7	8	4	3	7	–	7	7	5	17	22
With Father only	6	–	6	4	–	4	–	–	–	10	–	10
TOTAL	25	44	69	19	69	88	4	33	37	48	146	194

APPENDIX 18

Adult Males in Grandmother and Great-Grandmother Households: their Relationship to the Grandmother or Great-Grandmother

	Husband or Concubine	Son	Son-in-Law	Grand-son-in-law	Other Kin	Adopted Son	Adult gd-children (Male)	Total
Sugartown	18	8	5	1	6	1	5	44
Orange Grove	17	15	1	–	4	–	4	41
Mocca	9	4	2	1	3	–	4	23
	44	27	8	2	13	1	13	108

Appendices

Classification of Grandmothers and Great-Grandmothers according to present Sta
and Conjugal Record

Status and record of grandmother and great-grandmother		Sugartown	Orange Grove	Mocca
Living in Marriage				
Number of previous irregular unions	0	4*	11	4
ditto	1	4	3	–
ditto	2	2	2	1
ditto	3	2	–	–
ditto	4	1	–	–
Living in Concubinage				
Number of previous irregular unions	0	–	–	3
ditto	1	2	–	–
ditto	2	1	1	1
ditto	3	1	–	–
Widow		1	–	–
Widow with irregular union	1	1	–	–
Living Alone				
Number of previous irregular unions	1	6*	2*	2
ditto	2	6	2	3
ditto	3	2	3	1
ditto	5	1	–	1
ditto	6	–	1	–
Married woman (separated)		2	3	–
Married woman with irregular union	1	–	2*	–
Married woman with irregular unions	4	1	–	–
Married woman previously widowed		1	–	–
Widow		1	6	4
Widow with irregular union	1	1	3	–
Widow with irregular unions	2	–	–	1
		40	39	21

* Includes one grandmother who is living in a great-grandmother household.

APPENDIX 20

Vital Statistics 1960-1963

(Taken from *Annual Abstract of Statistics 1963*, Vol. 23)

From Table 13

	1960	1961	1962	1963
Population	1,624,647	1,618,676	1,662,079	1,706,318
Live Births	68,413	66,945	66,948	66,806
Deaths:				
Infant Deaths	3,522	3,228	3,218	3,289
Total Deaths	14,331	14,193	14,844	15,288
Still Births	781	819	743	828
Marriages	9,330	8,412	7,854	7,914
Rates:				
Birth Rate per 1000 population	42·1	40·9	40·64	39·65
Infant Death Rate per 1000 live births	50·9	47·15	48·07	49·23
Death rate per 1000 population	8·81	8·66	9·01	9·07
Still Birth rate per 1000 live births	11·29	12·23	11·1	12·39
Marriage rate per 1000 population	5·67	5·13	4·76	4·7

From Table 14

Year	Both Sexes	Analysis of Live Births Male	Female	Births per 1000 population	Male Births per 1000 Female Births	Legitimate	Illegitimate	Illegitimate Births per 100 Births
1938	37,970	19,306	18,664	33·26	1,035	11,013	26,957	70·99
1948	41,742	21,072	20,670	30·92	1,019	13,320	28,422	68·1
1951	48,441	24,378	24,063	33·88	1,013	14,449	33,992	70·2
1952	48,470	24,508	23,962	33·27	1,023	14,476	33,994	70·1
1953	51,131	25,886	25,245	34·41	1,025	14,878	36,253	70·9
1954	53,630	27,076	26,554	35·34	1,020	15,218	38,412	71·6
1955	55,767	28,427	27,340	36·17	1,040	15,823	39,944	71·6
1956	58,177	29,602	28,575	37·21	1,036	16,346	41,831	71·9
1957	60,445	30,561	29,884	39·55	1,023	16,905	43,540	72·03
1958	63,517	32,350	31,167	38·97	1,038	18,033	45,484	71·6
1959	63,874	32,254	31,620	40·85	1,020	17,752	46,122	72·2
1960	68,413	34,529	33,884	41·1	1,019	18,911	49,502	72·3

The Death and Burial of Mrs Malcolm

MRS MALCOLM died in hospital on Monday and the body was brought home early on Tuesday morning.

The first day. Before 5 p.m. the coffin with the body was set on two chairs on the verandah of the house with the family gathered round. There was a glass slot in the lid and people were looking at her face. She was dressed in white satin with her face powdered. In one hand was a fine white handkerchief and another, of inferior material, which was cut through the hem, on her breast. Everyone was singing hymns. The teacher who was to read the service had not yet arrived. The husband was lying, asleep, in a cot under a breadfruit tree in the yard. People said he must be awakened to do the necessaries a husband must do at his wife's funeral. Four men moved him on the cot to another tree and awakened him. Two men supported him round the waist to the verandah. He made loud screeching cries and said he could not bear to see her face. She is my backbone. I never started a thing in my life without telling her. She is mother, sister, father, everything in my life. He was almost falling to the floor. He was told he must take the kerchief in her hand and tear it in half and give her one half and wipe his face with the other half and put it in his pocket. This was a solemn occasion. He wept bitterly and asked to be taken away. He was led back to the cot.

The grave had already been dug by neighbours in the family plot where twelve of the family are already buried. The dead woman's brother, weeping and wiping away his tears, said twelve were already there, this is the thirteenth and I am the last and at any moment I feel I may be called home to be with them.

The coffin was then carried into the yard by four men and everyone gathered round, over 200 in all. The Trade Union delegate led hymn singing until teacher arrived. He read the Anglican burial service and gave a long speech. He did not know the deceased but she had been a member of the church and devoted to the works of God. The coffin was then carried to the grave. As it passed the verandah where the family were gathered everyone began to cry aloud and this was taken up by all present. Some cried Lord have mercy, she is gone to a silent home. Others said Amen, so let it be. Friends encouraged the family to be cheerful because she is gone to be forever with the Lord. The mother of the deceased was supported by her son, the last brother. She could not stand by herself because of sorrow. The husband was held up by his brother. Through his tears he told them he would like to see her put in the grave but it would be very bad for him. It was explained that if he did and got married again, he would bury that wife within a few months. This also applies to a mother if her child should die. If she had 12 children and went to the funeral of the first she would bury the others. The parting of the handkerchief means that the dead will come again and have to do with the one who is alive. The man should not only cut the handkerchief but go to the foot of the coffin and tell the dead how many years they have been living together and that the dead one should not come back to visit him. A woman declared that no powers could tell her not to kiss her husband and go to the grave to see him buried. If she loved him at all she would have to be buried with him. She would not try to give her boy friend a handkerchief because it is a bad sign. If a girl gives her boy friend a handkerchief she must always give a pin with it.

At the grave the rest of the funeral service was read and more hymns sung by the women, all dressed in white or black dresses. Then they all left the grave; the husband was supported by two men including the deceased's brother. He cried out she is gone, Jesus she is gone. Then he went back to the house and was placed in a rocking-chair in the hall. The brother remained by the grave saying that he would be the next, but he would not fret as he had to take care of his mother, if he does not care her he will lose her soon. He was assured by one of the grave diggers that was the best thing he could do.

Teacher, in his robes, was standing by Mr Malcolm, who took us by the hand and called a man to go and buy some rum. Teacher and the other gentlemen must be satisfied even if it cost him £100. Teacher said he must not bother as he wasn't a drinker of rum, but he insisted we must all be satisfied.

The chief grave digger called the others and divided money among them. He took a bottle from his pocket and sent for two glasses. They all had a drink without water.

Seven men in the group began talking about the privileges of women. One said he had been married 25 years and they have lived together as Christ did with His disciples. When in your home with your wife if a man would like to speak to her without your consent take your foot and give him the finest kick in his backside because he is trespassing on your private property. He should ask your permission first and then you should tell him to continue in your presence. Let him know point-blank that you are trusting no shadow after dark. Your wife is a helpmate. God created man after his own image. Woman was not created but made out of a rib of Adam. Women should always be subordinate to their husbands and to all men. Some women today would look in their husband's face and tell him to. . . . If his wife ever did this he would kick her out of his presence because she has no respect for the one who gave his rib for her. Another man said if all men so taught their wives there would be no trouble in the world. Women are only trouble makers in the world today. If it was not for the English women and the French women there would have been no war. English and Frenchmen hate to see their women going into captivity. A man walking with his wife or girl-friend would lose his life to protect her. They all agreed they would fight for their wives or girl-friends. For the rest of the night there was hymn-singing and prayer. Then the Lord's prayer was recited by all and the sit-up was at an end.

The Second Day. By 9 p.m. three groups had already formed in circles with a girl in the centre of each who led the singing of 'Mother Mack'. On the verandah, in the moonlight, men were playing dominoes at two tables. In each of the inner rooms there were again two tables with bibles and hymnals and a girl seated at each. Immediately on seeing us 'Brother' came out and stopped the dominoes and told everyone to start singing hymns. In the bedroom Mr M was lying on his bed with his sister standing beside him. He was in worse condition than the night before. He called to Brother to bring drinks for us. Brother apologized for not offering us food but said there would be a big cooking tomorrow, and everybody must come out. After the hymns one of the family read psalms 31 and 91, Revelations Cap. 17, and Proverbs 2 and 3 interspersed with prayers. She prayed that God would make a telephone link between earth and heaven so that her prayer for Mr M and for mercy on the people gathered here might be heard. Also for letting her see the end of another day. (N.B. A common morning greeting among older people, even when crippled with illness, is 'Thank God for the morning'.) Tonight there were 45 people present, mostly the family.

The Third Day. All day in Sugartown, the only topic of conversation was the Sit-up at Mr M's to which everybody had been invited and what a lot of money Mr M was spending on it. True, the rum came from his own shop and the women helped with the cooking. The feasting will last through the week but Saturday night will be the big night because then guests will be coming from Kingston. Among the gossip was that Mrs M had been the victim of obeah. Our informant (who said all Sugartown called him an 'obeah man') knew this because he had been in the shop with Mr M when he was warned. A little boy came to him and told him his wife was going to die because he saw a woman doing her something which was very bad. Very early one morning after she got sick Mr M was taking her to catch the 4 a.m. bus for Kingston for treatment. He was holding her up on the way to the gate when she told him she was feeling well again and that as it was beautiful moonlight he should take back the lantern to the house. On his return Mrs M was leaning on the gate. She said a woman who had been sitting by the gate had hit her on the head with a mortar stick. She was perspiring profusely and said she was going to die. She asked for water but there was no ice so he fetched a cream-soda. At the first town they stopped because of her feelings and a small boy got on the bus. He told Mr M he was going to lose his wife. Mr M gave his wife some more of the cream-soda but the boy advised him not to or she would die on the bus. He threw the bottle away. All the journey she would not speak but kept pointing to her head telling him the pains had reached to the mole. According to this informant Mr M had already taken his wife to Mother X (a local Healer) but had been told she could do nothing for her—she was too far gone. She gave him a vial with ointment and told him to keep it on her head till they reached the hospital. Mr M said he himself was able to see spirits and any man who can see them can defend himself. He is now certain that the ghost is on him and that he will die very soon. Our informant had been with Mr M from the night of his wife's death and from what he has seen Mr M will be a madman in a few weeks. Not because you see black people fooling around with these things it's they alone—the white people do it too. Yesterday Mr Y (Manager of the Factory) went to see Mr M and the minute he entered Mr M said he saw the shadow of a woman entering the house and knew that they had dug a hole in his wife's grave. Whey they went to the grave there was a deep hole about his height in depth. They planted her deep so that neither Mr M nor anyone else could raise her to put her on someone. Our informant believed the hole was dug by the woman who killed her—he did not believe the family had done it, they were not the type. But if it were done by them then someone in the district will die in the next few days because the deceased will certainly do the job if she is told to do so. All this must happen before the third day because by then she will be raised from the dead and gone about her duties. He would like to help Mr M but it would cost him £5 or £6 and after getting him better Mr M might not want to refund the money. He would like me to see his 'workman'; he works clean. He would charge £5 or £6 but after that no one could discharge you from your job. His mother suffered the same thing as the deceased but he was no fool, he conquered over the enemy. She had got up very early, about 4 a.m. to get his breakfast and on entering the kitchen she saw a woman sitting on the dresser. She had a mortar stick in her hand and as his mother entered she stood up on the dresser and hit his mother on the head with the mortar stick. She fell unconscious and he heard her groaning. He ran out and called for help. They rubbed her with different herbs before she could regain consciousness. He stayed away from work and took her in a taxi to 'his workman' who charged him a small sum, £5, and cured her. He was the luckiest man because if he had waited until evening she would have been a dead woman.

Tonight there were about 75 guests when we arrived. They were singing 'Jerusalem the Golden'. The procedure was that someone chose a song (hymn) and sang the first lines. It was wrong for anyone other than the person who 'gave the preference' to sing the first lines. (During the week we noticed that any breach of this pattern invariably led to quarrelling.) They then sang 'Greenland's Icy Mountains' but all did not know the tune and sang it to do re me fa so la. This was followed by 'Rock of Ages', 'At even when the sun is set', 'Hark my soul it is the Lord', and 'Jesus Lover of my soul'. The groups at each table read alternatively the 31st and 91st Psalms, Revelations Cap. 17 and Proverbs 2 and 3. These seem to be their daily readings. Mr M particularly asked for the 31st Psalm. He was looking cheerful tonight and told us that the breeze of the city had changed his feelings considerably. Tomorrow he will be going on a tour right round the Island. In the yard a group of men were sitting in a circle with two bottles of factory (i.e. proof) rum in the centre. They drank the liquor neat. Someone said 'The place washing with rum', another that it was said there was a duppy in the house. In the house, pandemonium broke out at 2 a.m. when the supper began to be served. This consisted of breadfruit, green bananas with shad, chocolate 'tea' and biscuits. The food had been prepared by the women and was served by one of the family. After everyone had eaten Brother called out 'All right, sing now!' The singing, interspersed with bible readings and prayers, went on till about 5 a.m. One man said they were bringing in the Easter.

The Fourth Day. There were very few people tonight. In the hall only one of the tables was occupied by a boy and a girl. Beside the Bible and the lamp was a pint bottle of rum. A few men were singing but it was half-hearted. Most of the men merely opened their mouths and bawled out the words. They began to drop out one by one and by 1.30 only two old men were left and they were asleep. The young men on the verandah were still going strong with their dominoes. Mr M was in bed in his pyjamas sleeping, with his sister and two other women also asleep beside him. In the other bedroom women and children lay piled on top of one another, also sleeping. Far away we could hear the kumina drums in another village.

The Fifth Day. Yesterday was Good Friday and tonight there is a Scout Camp Fire on the Estate grounds and all the people attending it. Elsewhere in Sugartown there was another sit-up for an old 'bongo man' named Boka, who died a few months ago. Here, in the yard under a large shed, we saw about 200 men and women. They were singing 'Nearer my God To Thee'. In the kitchen 6 or 7 women were preparing the Feast. There were 4 pots on a wood fire made in a hole in the earth. A woman sat on a box peeling green bananas and cocos. We saw many of the people who had been at Mr M's. One of the men told us the big feast was down here tonight and that, as we knew, a man must satisfy his belly so he would not be going to Mr M's tonight.

At Mr M's there were about a dozen men and women, some of the men playing dominoes, others sleeping or talking. Mr M was in a rocking chair. He was very tired having been in the shop all day, leaving his sister to close it. Next Saturday night they would be having the grand Ninth Night with prayer meeting and singing for 25 or 39 friends who could not get away during the week coming from Kingston. People from the villages round here would also be coming. His sister interrupted to complain that he had left one of the windows in the shop open and that it was hard to lose your wife but tough again to lose all the stock in your shop. Everyone was tired and went home.

The Sixth Day. At about 10 p.m. there were 35 people singing but it was half-hearted. Mr M asked for Psalms 31 and 91 which were followed by the doxology and a chapter from the Bible. During the final hymn, 'The sick O Lord, around thee lay' about 14 of the guests went away leaving us with the family. Someone went off to boil 'tea' (chocolate). Someone else said that was a good idea but he would like to hear about the plans for Saturday night; it would not be good to have guests coming with nothing to eat or drink. Someone else said he had a goat valued at 11s.

which he would sell and another man offered to cook it if someone bought it. A man dressed in a black suit and a white shirt with a collar and brown shoes said he had been to a wedding and he was 'well blocked up'. He could not go home until he was sober as this would be teaching his wife and children bad manners. He has not been home since the sit-up began and would have to stay the night as he was very tired. Whereupon he fell asleep. A small boy got a piece of rope and tied him to the chair and someone put a paper cigar in his mouth. The sleeper awoke and tried to puff the cigar and everyone shrieked with laughter. He got up indignantly saying that it was time to go home but found he was still tied to the chair. When he got free he began to talk in great detail about his sexual exploits: he is a very wicked man, there is not a girl of his age in Sugartown he didn't know. After some casual love-making the party dispersed.

The Seventh Day. Tonight there is a dance at one of the neighbouring villages and everyone has gone to it. Mr M was therefore especially grateful to us for coming. Besides the family there were 18 people in the house. They all agreed there would be no singing as they had not enough voices to keep it going full strength. Instead they would tell Jokes and 'Nancy stories. The riddles were all prefaced by the words: Riddle me riddle, John me riddle, guess me this riddle and perhaps not.

First Riddle: Cow a canta paranta Ass-a-limpus to-nus. Bring back me lamp Adina.

Answer: The mother of Adina has a cow and a horse. She could not find them during the night so she went for a lamp. At the entrance she saw the dung of the horse and the cow. Adina took the lamp from her mother and went in search of them. The mother standing at the door saw the animals coming towards her.

Second Riddle: Riddle me riddle etc. Take off me pants you see me hair, take off the hair, you see me seed take off me seed you see me tone.

Answer: A corn cob.

Third Riddle: Riddle me riddle etc. Deep it is, damp it is, fit for any man.

Answer: A grave.

Riddle: Riddle me re etc. As I was going up to St George's Hall, I heard the voice of someone call, his beard was flesh, his mouth was horn and such a man was never born.

Answer: A cock.

Riddle: As I was going up to St George's Hall I met three holy people. They were neither men, women nor children. Who were they?

Answer: Bible, hymn book and prayer book.

Riddle: As I was going to St George's Hall I met a man. He was buttoned from his head to his feet and all round his body. Who was that?

Answer: A pineapple.

Riddle: Me father has a pony in his yard and he wouldn't ride it until it rains.

Answer: House roof that leaks.

The Death and Burial of Mrs Malcolm

Riddle: What is it that if you speak you will break it?
Answer: Silence. If you say silence in the midst of silence you break it.

Riddle: Mr Redman tickles Mr Blackman's bottom.
Answer: A pot on the fire.

Riddle: Why do a policeman and a train resemble?
Answer: The policeman goes from station to station and likewise the train goes from station to station.

Riddle: Why is it a plantain and a tailor resemble?
Answer: Because the plantain is fit to cut and the tailor cut to fit.

This went on for sometime, then the Preacher who had dropped in asked if everybody in the house went to school. The answer being Yes he gave an addition: 1, 2, 3, 4, 5, 6, 7 and 8, but the answer must be in thousands. No one could do it so he gave the answer. 8 plus 1 equals 9; 7 plus 2 equals 9; 6 plus 3 equals 9; 5 plus 4 equals 9. Answer 9999.

The Eighth Day. On our arrival there were about 50 people on the verandah and in the house singing. There were many strange faces in addition to the family and the regular guests. The hymn they sang was 'Low in the grave, Jesus my Saviour' which completely shattered Mr M and the people were told to stop after the second verse. He was then sent to bed to rest. When he returned after about 15 minutes he took us into the shop and fed us with sardines, bread and rum. He said he needed to eat as he had been in Kingston all day and had not had time for food. He had bought some stock for his shop: shoes and handbags. He said his enemies had made a plan that he should go out of business as bankrupt. He took me to the breadfruit tree in the yard and when we were seated told me that his wife's own blood-cousin (Jettina) had killed her. They had been having some contention because she had married a bluefoot (see p. 172 supra) who was helping her to a high stand in life. Jettina did not come openly and threaten his wife but the woman in Kingston whom he had consulted had described her accurately and it could be no one else. This woman in Kingston also told him that his wife would be buried on Tuesday and that when taking the body home he would meet Jettina on the road coming to dress his wife's body. All this happened but he refused to let Jettina dress the body. The woman in Kingston also told him that Jettina would try to get his pyjamas to do away with him and that he must hide all his clothes. During the burial his sister saw Jettina taking his pyjamas and they had a struggle in which the pyjamas were torn and Jettina got away with one leg. He went back to the woman in Kingston and she advised him not to have Jettina arrested because she herself had everything under control: her science was greater than Jettina's. Mr M said he knew some brains were better than others. No ordinary man could compare his brain with the scientists who have made the Atom Bomb. God has made differences in man and beast alike. A mother cow can have two heifer calves and one will give 14 or 15 quarts a day and the other 4 to 6, yet both are from the same mother. The woman in Kingston whom he now identified as 'Mother Williams' also told him that Jettina had taken his wife's drawers and set the ghost to hit her on the head, after getting his wife to send him back to the house with the lantern as she could not have hit her in his presence. He said that on reaching Kingston he had not really taken his wife immediately to the hospital but straight to Mother Williams who had told him to prepare for a funeral on Tuesday. She also told him that Jettina gave him nine days to live from the death of his wife. Being no fool he has guarded himself against that. He has given Mother Williams the job of taking off the ghost. It was spread abroad he was going off his head. He was really going off but he is now better. She instructed him to stock up the shop, even to buy shoes and handbags first thing, and put his sister in charge. His wife's brother met a similar death. A fellow worker in the factory who coveted his job set a ghost on him. One day he fell into the robin where the cane is dumped and broke his head. He is buried in the family ground.

All this time the singing and Bible reading in the house had continued. A quarrel broke out between two men as to whose hymn was to be read first and one of them started to leave but was called back and had his song taken first.

From his bedroom, to which he had retired, Mr M called for Psalm 35. A thermos of coffee was taken to him and after drinking two cups he fell asleep again. Aunt Phibby (mother of the deceased) and the other women brought a bucket of chocolate and trays of bread to us on the verandah. The people ate as fast as the bread was served, some passing to their friends outside; some stored the bread away. One of the serving women told them not to do this but to eat it now. One guest drank two mugs of chocolate and asked for more. The servers coaxed them to eat and not let anything go back to the kitchen. Jollification continued for sometime and then someone called out 'Start something else now!' and they began singing hymns and continued until 4 a.m. when we left.

The Ninth Day. Only a dozen people attended the sit-up tonight. Aunt Phibby said they were taking a rest after every night sit-up. The men were playing dominoes. They were gambling and a squabble arose over the stakes. One of the teamsters called for a machete which he gave to the men on the opposing team telling them to kill one another and not grumble at their losses. Amid loud laughter a man on the losing side threw down a ten shilling note but the stake was refused and he reduced it to a shilling. The stakes were then taken to buy drinks. The games ended with more hymn singing but they were tired and soon resorted to telling stories. One man asked if anyone knew how to extract the milk poured in coffee leaving the black coffee in the cup. No one could tell so he gave the answer: pour the juice of a lime in the cup; the milk will curdle and can be skimmed off. Story telling was carried on till about 1.30 when the party dispersed.

The Tenth and Eleventh Day. Brother apologized that there were no visitors. The family were sleepy and resting.

The Twelfth Day. The Nine Night. Tonight is the Nine Night which will end the Burial rites. In the afternoon Mr M was in his shop as usual, very fussed because his sister was absent, the bread he had ordered had not been delivered and the goat for supper had not been killed. Also Roland was going about boasting that he is doing this and that and not really helping. It was after 5 p.m. before Roland arrived with the bread and a boy was called to kill the goat. He threw the goat on the ground and called for a machete to chop off the head. Mr M demanded if he thought it was a fowl he was killing and sent for a man to do it properly. It took an hour and 20 minutes to skin the goat. Uriah came to get the curry and other ingredients but was told by Mr M that he had arranged for women to do the cooking. Uriah was indignant; he had been in his shop selling ice and had put that aside to come up only to find that the fire had not been started. He took a machete and began cutting up the goat. Twenty minutes later the women arrived and Mr M told him to hand over to them. Aunt Phibby and a helper had been scouring nine large pots which were set out in the yard together with plates, cups, saucers, and pudding pans. In the booth there were two long tables covered with white cloths on which were lamps, Bibles and hymn books. A lantern hung from the roof and long wooden benches were ranged along the sides. The cooking in the yard was now in full swing. A little before 7 p.m. a woman brought in a bunch of bananas on her head, a gift to help with the feeding of the bereaved family and their guests. These now began to arrive.

A small boy ran in to tell Mr M that Mother Williams was at the gate and he went to meet her. She is very short and fat and has one long canine tooth which we were told she had been born with and never had any others. She is a very good scientist, keeps a Mission House in Kingston and has come to help at the Nine Night and to stay over the week-end and hold services in Sugartown. She is light skinned and was said to have been born in Spain. With her at the gate were her followers: about 30 including children and a small baby, said to be hers. She called upon a short man with a staff to 'Carry on Brother' to which he responded by holding up his hand and reciting the 23rd Psalm, in which the group joined. He then prayed that God would bless Mr M and come in right away and drive the enemy from his threshold. He led the visitors through the gate, spinning in circles. Inside they continued to spin and sway. A tall man, whom we learned was Captain Williams, Mother's husband, dressed in a tweed suit and a helmet, asked 'Children, will you all have a drink?' and led his followers into the house. Mother W took off her shoes before entering and went into the bedroom calling for her baby. The tall man took bottles from a suit case and drinks were passed round: rum for the men and beer mixed with aerated water for the ladies. He then went outside and said he would like to start singing but they all had cigarettes in their mouths and it could not start that way. The cigarettes were put out and everyone went into the booth. Captain then called for 'Peace, perfect peace', led by a man whom we were told was Mother's eldest son, followed by 'Hear me pleading evermore, May I come in?' The short man said a prayer, again demanding that the evil spirits depart from the home. 'Depart, I say, depart and seek after righteousness' after which he staggered back to his seat. The hymn 'All hail the power of Jesus' name' was then raised, the short man marking the time with his hand in the air and ejaculating 'Yes, Amen, Allelujah!' Captain Williams demanded to know why the people were not helping the visitors to sing. He went into the shop and returned with a paper bag of peppermint sticks which he handed out and then said 'You have all had peppermint sticks to clear your throats, now please sing and keep the company of dear Brother M'. A man in the party called out that they had not all had peppermint sticks—only the people who had come with him. Another man rebuked him for going on like that: he should know that these people had come from Kingston and would think they were hooligans. He himself was a Sugartown man but he had travelled the Island and lived in Kingston many years: the people there can appreciate good behaviour and are better trained than people elsewhere. After raising 'Abide with me' Captain W took one of the Sisters by the hand and told her to read to her hearers. She went to the table and recited the 23rd Psalm in which all joined. They then sang 'Jerusalem the golden' after which the short man prayed again. By this time the company in the booth had increased to over 300 and some fifty or more stood outside the gate. Some of these had set up tables and were gambling at Crown and Anchor. Among them women vendors moved selling mangoes, naseberries, oranges and mint sticks, fried fish and cakes.

Meanwhile in the yard some 7 women and two men were preparing the curry goat and rice. Maud, the chief cook, insisted that she did not mind if the dinner was late but everything had to be clean. She could not cook without water, clean plates and towels. She boasted that she had cooked 2 goats and 50 lbs of rice for a feast for the Scout party and the Scouts themselves had roasted 100 breadfruit. Although there were sandwiches provided by the Management, only the Scouts ate them: the people were crazy for the curry goat and rice. Mr M's younger brother asked for the seed of the goat. When given it he said 'This is not for women. It will cause you to call for plenty men.' When cattle and goats are slaughtered on the properties, it costs a man pounds in rum to get the seed. Once he had asked for the seed and the headman had had his dog castrated and gave him the seed. Not knowing, he took it, roasted it in the fire, ate it and said now he would be able to fix up those girls who were playing strong. The people laughed at him when the headman told him it was the seed of the dog but he did not take it to heart, because he played cricket for the team and the seed caused him to see very far and aim at the wicket.

We were invited into the house, seated and served with large helpings of curry goat and rice, beer and cream-soda with ice, the men being given rum. Everything was spotlessly clean. Someone remarked how wonderful it was to see so many people joined together; that's what we want, more of this brotherly love, it's the only answer to the world's troubles. Aunt Phibby was called to join us and receive our condolences. She said what she found hardest to bear was that her daughter had told her never a word. She only heard that she had put back her head and gone quietly to sleep and then her hands dropped to her side and she was dead.

In the booth Mother Williams was leading the singing, holding the short man's hand above her head and turning the roll with him, her eyes shut.

She passed on to another man, doing the same thing. By this time all the company was singing and swaying.

Outside in the yard a group of men were discussing America and Russia. One said there were 64 Powers ranged against Russia: another that if America plunges into war she would have the small nations on her side. Another interposed that in that case America must win because the little nations would be afraid of being tried as war criminals if she lost. Another, who was very drunk, declaimed 'We are the Anti-Communists' and that all the world was against Russia. Babu Jacques joined the group to say 'Yes, yes, yes, we are the Anti-Communist League!' Some of the young men went round hunting girls. One of them asked us to 'change a cheque' for him. In the half-light it looked something like a $5 bill. We took it to the light and the man followed us to say he needed the money for a worthless girl he had gone to bed with and he had to leave in a hurry as he was giving her the slip. The 'cheque' turned out to be a Guarantee Note for foreign baking powder which read: 'Your money back plus 10 per cent if you have any complaint.' We gave it back to him and he disappeared in the crowd. Later the girl asked us for the money which she said her friend had told her to collect from us. She was very displeased when she heard that we had returned the 'cheque'.

In the booth we found the Sugartown crowd now in control. There was confusion when people tried simultaneously to raise different hymns. From time to time the singers went to the table and took a pinch of salt from a saucer. Two very drunk men took charge of the table and tried vainly to get their song raised. Someone tried to bring order but pandemonium reigned. When we left, soon after midnight, the party was beginning to break up.

INDEX

Abortion, 96
Adolescence, 170 *et seq.*
Adoption, 176 *et seq.*; law, 176, 190
Adultery, 77, 90–1
Appendices, (1) 14; (2) 11, 22, 113, 117–19, 123; (3) 125; (4) 125; (5) 130; (6) 117, 120–3; (7) 117, 121, 124; (8) 118 *et seq.*, 126 *et seq.*, 131–3; (9) 119, 126–7; (10) 124, 130–1; (11) 116; (12) 116; (13) 126; (14) 126–7; (15) 134; (16) 136–7; (17) 136; (18) 139; (19) 137–9
Apprenticeship, 170–1
Back Lands, 20, 34
Bastardy and maintenance: law, 91, 108, 163; orders under, 106, 109–10
Beckwith, Martha Warren, 45
Birth: control, 160; registration, 108; in mother's home, 98–9
Board of Supervision, 111
Burn, W. L., 70
Bustamante, Sir Alexander, 187–8; Industrial Trade Union (BITU), 25, 186–7
Carberry, Dossie, 11, 71
Census of Jamaica (1943), Reports of, 12, 29, 113, 114, 116
Centres (Sugartown, Orange Grove, Mocca): described, 22–8, 181 *et seq.*
Children: birth, 116, 118, 124, 186; attitude to, 95, 98–9; legitimacy, 95–6; mother, 74–5; 108, 176; father, 142–3, 162–4, 165, 177–9; separation from parent(s), 84, 99, 107, 133, 159–62, 170; training in home, 91–2, 100–2, 104, 107–8, 117–23, 125–33, 141–2; school q.v., 97–8, 143 *et seq.*, 153–4, 156–7
Clark, John, 37
Class, 21, 37, 148, 182
Clothes, 153, 173–4
Colour: bar, 33
Conception, 96
Concubinage: defined, 30, 108; white, 21; variety of meanings, 101–2, 104–5; comparison between Centres, 26–8, 92–3; dissolution, 106–7; legal aspect, 108–10; children, 141–2
Concubine: status, 80, 91, 105–6
Contraceptives, 96
Co-operation, 182 *et seq.*
Courtship, 81, 104–5
Crown Lands, 20, 34, 38
Daily routine, 143–9
Denuded: family households, 100, 107–8, 125 *et seq.*, 131, 149 *et seq.*
Divorce, 74, 77
Domestic service, 150–1
East Indians, 160, 186
Eating habits, 143–8, 166
Emancipation, 19–20, 34, 35, 37

Firth, Raymond, 11
Flogging, 156–7, 165, 167–9
Frazier, Franklin, 11, 34–5
Grandfather, 134, 137–9
Grandmother, 178 *et seq.*
Graves: ancestors, 45
Henriques, F. M., 29–30
Higglers, 23, 150, 152–3
Households: definition of types, 30–1; population, 117 *et seq.*; kin contained, 123–4; children, 127 *et seq.*
Houses: inheritance of, 55 *et seq.*; housing, 23, 55, 90, 94, 103, 147, 160, 173–4, 183
Illegitimacy: legal and social, 17–18, 30, 39, 116 *et seq.*, 191; surname, 91
Incest, 75
Jamaica Welfare Ltd (Social Welfare Commission), 17
Kerr, M., 14, 190
Kin, 19, 64, 92, 107, 131, 148–9, 164, 172–4, 177, 182–3
Labour, 13–14, 24–5, 93–4, 171–2; women, 153
Lamming, George, 50
Land: family land and principles of inheritance, 20, 33–69; settlement, 20, 37; fragmentation, 46, 190; effect of reforms, 68
Little, Kenneth, 11
Maintenance, *see above* Bastardy and Maintenance Law
Manley, N. W., 17
Marier, Roger, 32
Marriage, 29, 73–88, 90–2, 105, 107, 114–15, 129; matrilocal, 103–4
McCulloch, W. E., 190
Mead, Margaret, 22
Menstruation, 98
Olivier, Lord, 7, 21, 35–6
Platt, B. S., 190
Polygamy, 30
Poor Relief, 111–12
Pregnancy, 97–100, 179
Promiscuity, 30, 99
Religious: sects, 188–9; sanction for marriage, 80–1
Richards, Audrey, 11
Schapera, I., 11
School, 165–71
Sex, 90–1, 93, 94–8
Simey, T. S., 32
Slavery, 18–19
Smith, M. G., 11, 70
Step-parent, 174 *et seq.*
Tempo-Moto, 14, 24, 27, 93, 105, 188, 189
Wedding: ritual, etc., 78, 85–8
Wife: status, 78 *et seq.*